Black Women in   1st ed.
Texas History

Black Women in Texas History

edited by

BRUCE A. GLASRUD

and

MERLINE PITRE

with

Angela Boswell, James M. Smallwood,
Barry A. Crouch, Rebecca Sharpless,
Stefanie Decker, Kenneth W. Howell,
Jewel L. Prestage and Franklin D. Jones

TEXAS A&M UNIVERSITY PRESS
College Station, Texas

This paper meets the requirements of ANSI/NISO z39.48–1992 (Permanence of
Paper).
Binding materials have been chosen for durability.

Library of Congress Cataloging-in-Publication Data

Black women in Texas history / edited by Bruce A. Glasrud and Merline
Pitre ; with Angela Boswell . . . [et al.]. — 1st ed.
    p. cm.
Includes bibliographical references and index.
    ISBN-13: 978-1-60344-007-3 (cloth : alk. paper)
    ISBN-10: 1-60344-007-0 (cloth : alk. paper)
    ISBN-13: 978-1-60344-031-8 (pbk. : alk. paper)
    ISBN-10: 1-60344-031-3 (pbk. : alk. paper)
    1. African American women—Texas—History. 2. African American
women—Texas—Social conditions. 3. African Americans—Texas—
History. 4. Texas—Race relations. I. Glasrud, Bruce A. II. Pitre,
Merline, 1943–   III. Boswell, Angela, 1965–
E185.93.T4B55 2008
976.40089'96073—dc22
                                                              2007026474

CONTENTS

PREFACE

Within the past three and one-half decades, scholars have amassed a rich body of literature dealing with black women's history, struggles, survival, and progress. Yet, the literature on black women in Texas leaves a lot to be desired. Ruthe Winegarten, *Black Texas Women: 150 Years of Trials and Triumphs,* is the only topical anthology, and there is still no comprehensive history on the subject. *Black Women in Texas History* is an attempt to fill this void. The study heeds the advice of Elsa Barkley Brown, who argued "that being a woman is in fact not extractable from the context in which one is a woman—that is race, class, time, and place." The contributors of this volume have pursued the theme "race, class, time, and place" by providing specialized studies on African American women from slavery through the civil rights movement to the present. They have shown that black women of the Lone Star State have been shaped not only by the historical specifics of race and gender, but also by politics and culture. Additionally, this study explores the myriad ways in which black women influenced and were influenced by the experiences of diverse people in the state.

Informed by recent scholarship, this volume demonstrates black females' critical role in the development of Texas; therefore, we present our narrative in a straightforward chronological manner. The chronological organization accords with our belief that it is important for one to see the interconnections among a variety of historical experiences; for example, slavery and freedom, Reconstruction and post-Reconstruction, the dawn of the nineteenth century and beginning of the twentieth century, politics and culture, as well as public events and private experiences. Our chronological synthesis allows the reader to appreciate the relationships while capturing the spirit of each age. An element of importance in this volume is the emphasis placed on recent Texas, the vastly overlooked years from 1974 to 2000. For this period two sets of authors, one set of historians and one set of political scientists, have focused their skills toward providing readers with information about black Texas women during this critical period.

Putting this collection together has been a labor of love despite the distance between the two editors. Academicians, as well as the general public, will benefit from this work. It is a collection from a diverse group of scholars (some black, some white, some men, and some women) who share a common interest in African American women's history. To be sure, this is not the only work on black women in Texas. *Black Women in Texas History* reminds us also that there remains an enormous amount of work to be done for an even more comprehensive examination of the black female tradition in Texas. The work of all the contributors here certainly points us in the right direction.

As noted, this volume would not have been successful without our conscientious authors; thanks go to Angela Boswell, James Smallwood, Barry Crouch (unfortunately deceased), Rebecca Sharpless, Stefanie Decker, Kenneth Howell, Jewel Prestage, and Franklin Jones. Two readers for Texas A&M University Press provided us with encouragement and solid suggestions/comments. And, without whose support this work would not have been born nor completed, we effusively thank the editor-in-chief at Texas A&M University Press, Mary Lenn Dixon.

Merline Pitre
HOUSTON, TEXAS

Bruce A. Glasrud
SEGUIN, TEXAS

BRUCE A. GLASRUD
and MERLINE PITRE

Black Texas Women

MAKING COMMUNITY

Resisting, Creating, Struggling, Overcoming,
Migrating, Learning, Uniting, Leading

In Darlene Clark Hine's first-rate collection of essays, with its aptly named title, *Hine Sight: Black Women and the Re-Construction of American History,* Hine argued that black women sought to "make community." "Making community," she wrote,

> means the processes of creating religious, educational, health-care, philanthropic, political, and familial institutions and professional organizations that enabled our people to survive. . . . Black women created essential new communities and erected vast female networks during the transitions from slavery to freedom, and from farm to city. It was through "making community" that Black women were able to redefine themselves, project sexual respectability, reshape morality, and define a new aesthetic.[1]

Community making describes the approach pursued by African American women in Texas, and provides a measure of their accomplishments over the years from their first entrance into Texas until the present. As the chapters in *Black Women in Texas History* illustrate, black women had no easy task. Hine asserts that "Black women's history by its very nature seeks to empower and make visible the lives and deeds of ordinary folk."[2] The scholarly chapters in our book, as well as any additional reading of black Texas women's history, we think, are a confirmation of Hine's conclusions. The women's efforts in Texas were arduous; black women resisted, created, struggled, overcame, migrated, learned, united, and led in this feat of making community in the Lone Star State. These efforts have been largely unexamined by historians.

As yet there is only one general survey history of African American women in the United States, and, outside of Texas, none of any other state. While black women have been a prominent part of the life and prospects of U.S. history since its beginnings, the study of African American women's history is a relatively "new field" of investigation. The most complete state history is undoubtedly that of Hine on Indiana, even though it begins after the Civil War. At the moment, the only other statewide work is on Texas, Ruthe Winegarten's topical anthology *Black Texas Women: 150 Years of Trial and Triumph.* Together with her *Black Texas Women: A Sourcebook,* these constitute significant resources. Quintard Taylor and Shirley Ann Wilson Moore edited a collection of essays about black women in the West titled *African American Women Confront the West, 1600–2000.* There are two collections of source materials, mostly covering the nineteenth century, Dorothy Sterling's *We Are Your Sisters: Black Women in the Nineteenth Century,* and Gerda Lerner's *Black Women in White America: A Documentary History;* the latter also includes twentieth-century sources.[3]

The single historical survey of black women in the United States, Darlene Clark Hine and Kathleen Thompson, *A Shining Thread of Hope: The History of Black Women in America,* points out that black women's history "is more than a story of oppression and struggle. It is a story of hope." Paula Giddings, though more thematic, also covers black women's history in *When and Where I Enter: The Impact of Black Women on Race and Sex in America.*[4] Darlene Hine, with Wilma King and Linda Reed, edited the principal anthology of black women's history, *"We Specialize in the Wholly Impossible": A Reader in Black Women's History.* Hine, additionally, is responsible for at least three valuable resources that aid the study of African American women's history. In 1993, Hine, with Elsa Barkley Brown and Rosalyn Terborg-Penn, published a two-volume set titled *Black Women in America: An Historical Encyclopedia;* twelve years later she expanded, updated, and revised the set into a three-volume edition. Hine, with Elsa Barkley Brown, Tiffany R. L. Patterson, and Lillian S. Williams, also produced *Black Women in United States History,* a sixteen-volume compendium of scholarly articles.[5]

The previous paragraph did not begin as a paean for Darlene Clark Hine, though it rightfully became one. Hine, moreover, has connections to Afro-Texas history. Her first book was *Black Victory: The Rise and Fall of the White Primary in Texas.* As she reflected on the fact that she overlooked some of the contributions of women in *Black Victory,* she revised the book to include a chapter by Texas Southern University scholar Merline Pitre, which discussed the role of Lulu B. White and other black women's efforts to eliminate the white primary.[6] Linda Reed, one of Hine's coeditors for *"We Specialize in the Wholly Impossible"* is a professor of history at the University of Houston. Jewel L. Prestage,[7] one of the contributors to our work, *Black Women in Texas History*, is among a number of African American Texas women included in Hine's historical encyclopedia, *Black Women in America*.

Texas is a microcosm of the United States, and in many ways this "first" analytical and chronological survey of black women in the state may serve as a measuring rod for other states and as a means of understanding black women's lives and efforts in regions beyond Texas. The survey also is a way of acknowledging what other authors have remarked about particular aspects of African American women's history in different states. It is important to understand that although black Texans were in the forefront of political and civil resistance, as well as efforts for "making community" over many years, they too often are ignored in regional and national publications.

One of the purposes of this book is to provide a history of African American women in Texas that reflects an open-ended narrative. We seek to tell the story of African American females in the Lone Star State without its ending in utter tragedy (as if nothing ever changes for the good) or taking a flight into fantasy (as if progress is automatic). Rather, this book is an attempt to provide a human side to the theoretical notion that black females, so long on the margins of history and the periphery of power, shaped history and power in profound ways in the Lone Star State.

The book, *Black Women in Texas History*, began as an idea in the minds of Bruce Glasrud, Merline Pitre, and Mary Lenn Dixon, the latter the editor-in-chief at Texas A&M University Press. They determined that such a work was needed, and that it could provide a vital contribution to the study and knowledge of black women in Texas, the South and Southwest, and the nation. Upon discussion and consideration, Pitre and Glasrud realized that they could not research, write, and publish the work alone. Since they could not complete the book without help, they considered asking prominent scholars who knew the fields—black women's history, black history, women's history, Texas history, as well as particular time periods—to join them. Arriving at a list of possible contributors, the editors asked the requisite individuals to become a part of the project, and were rewarded with supportive affirmatives. They were extremely fortunate in inducing top scholars to join the undertaking as well as acquiring a couple of blossoming younger writers.

Pitre, Glasrud, and Dixon also discussed the basic approach to the book. Since Ruthe Winegarten previously had put together two works that topically considered black Texas women, they determined upon an approach that was analytical and chronological; that is, one that surveyed black Texas womanist history. Chronologically the book would be divided into seven time periods, generally reflecting standard U.S. historical epochs. With the general approach determined, Dixon agreed to provide an advance contract for the project and Glasrud and Pitre presented the approach and the concept of the book to each chapter author. They stipulated to the contributing authors that each should present a complete overview of the lives of African American women in Texas for their particular chronological period, economically, socially, politically, and culturally. They established a page limit of approximately thirty pages. The rest was left to the authors; they were the scholars and the authorities.

The contributors did not read one another's essays, yet the resulting chapters indicate a close awareness of themes of African American women's history, Texas history, U.S. history, and women's history. The outcome is a cohesive whole, an analytical and chronological history of black Texas women from the Spanish period to the present, and especially the years from 1820 to 2000. Always, as Darlene Clark Hine put it, "within the context of racism, sexism, and economic deprivation."[8]

The authors accomplished their goals, and in the process it is interesting to note that eight themes emerged, though not to the same extent in each chapter. As a whole these themes supported the context of "making community" in Texas: resisting, creating, struggling, overcoming, migrating, learning, uniting, and leading. The themes are listed below with a few comments:

1. Creating—institutions (churches, schools)—artistically;
2. Learning—vital role of education, influence on teaching, leadership, cultural attributes, and contributions;
3. Migrating—to Texas, north and west, within the state; rural to urban—mobility a key;
4. Overcoming—race and class and gender barriers; slavery, share-

cropping, domestic service; last hired, first fired; challenge the system;

5. Resisting—discrimination, lack of vote, lack of civil protections, rape, sexual exploitation, segregation—a means of resisting was protest;
6. Struggling—survival, against the glass ceiling, to hold family together, and community aloft, against racism and sexism;
7. Uniting—working together; clubs, neighbors, family, politically—support one another, organize, "communal womanism";
8. Leading—Lulu White, Barbara Jordan, prohibition, women's suffrage, antilynching, "bridges," education, CEOs.

Readers will find that these themes become apparent as they review the individual chapters as well as complete the entire book.

Black Women in Texas History consists of eight chapters written by scholars of their respective eras. The work covers the span of Texas history, and may be viewed either as a group of separate parts, or as a comprehensive work. It is the progression, sometimes incremental, sometimes vaulting, of African American women's experiences, which adds to our understanding of this too-little-examined part of our history. This introductory essay will review the major points, the themes and issues, of the individual chapters.

The first chapter, "Black Women during Slavery to 1865," by Henderson State University professor Angela Boswell, focuses on the dominant institution affecting black women at the time, slavery. Texas slavery varied little from the full-grown institution of the Deep South. Although it was a harsh, debilitating system, slavery did not destroy the lives of black Texas women or their friends and family. Instead, the women created within slavery a community that protected the family, supported networks, resisted pernicious aspects of the institution, and enabled survival.

In the second chapter, "Texas Freedwomen during Reconstruction, 1865–1874," James M. Smallwood, professor emeritus of history at Oklahoma State University, and Gallaudet University historian, the late Barry A. Crouch, examine the problems and prospects for the former Afro-Texas slave women. They pursued the benefits of freedom with hope and dignity while resisting white pressures designed essentially to reenslave them. For many black women, even locating family members was difficult. Black women endured white violence and intimidation but created a sense of community. Overall, education, family, homes, civil rights, and economic survival occupied their efforts.

The third chapter covers the years of the latter nineteenth century. In "'Us Has Ever Lived De Useful Life': African American Women in Texas, 1874–1900," former Baylor and current Texas Christian University author and scholar Rebecca Sharpless determined that by 1874 more than 250,000 African Americans lived in Texas, comprising almost a third of the state's population. By 1900, the African American population of Texas more than doubled. While an increasing number lived in the state's cities, many continued their traditional agricultural roles. Women formed unions with men and had children. Some relationships were happy and some were not. African American women worked outside the home in large numbers, usually as domestics but sometimes as teachers. Women played active roles in accumulating wealth, but despite these gains they also suffered from racism and racial violence. They contested racism through lawsuits, religion, and social organizations.

Bruce A. Glasrud, in the fourth chapter, "Time of Transition: Black Women in Early Twentieth-Century Texas, 1900–1930," discovered that these years were pivotal for black Texas women. They joined clubs, campaigns, and churches, sought community improvements and opposed such racist white behavior as lynching and Jim Crow. The middle class expanded, creating time for cultural contributions, education, and interactions. Increased mobility fed migration, both within and without the state. For a large number of women who moved to the urban areas, economic work meant exchanging farming for domestic service. Families, and extended families within the community, remained the focus of their lives.

As Texas Southern University professor and dean, Merline Pitre, explains in chapter 5, "At the Crossroads: Black Texas Women, 1930–1954," the years from the Great Depression to 1954 were indeed trying ones for the black female in the state of Texas. The Great Depression of the 1930s was the most catastrophic period of American history to date. Almost every American suffered economic hardship. But the African American female was hardest hit. The majority of black women held the lowest paid jobs in the depressed economy. By 1931, most of the black wage-earning women lost their jobs; as the Depression worsened, that number increased. At the same time, black women faced continued racial discrimination and segregation. President Franklin D.

Roosevelt's New Deal program offered some relief for economic hardship, but his program was discriminating in its assistance and had a mixed impact on black women. Black women received smaller monetary assistance than whites, were restricted to "women's work," and were paid lower wages than men or white women. Nonetheless, black women devised a variety of strategies to cope with hardships and to reconstruct their lives. Embroiled in a fierce struggle for jobs, housing, education, and first-class citizenship, they migrated from rural to urban areas, sought the right to vote, created community churches and schools, protested against lynching, and struggled to hold their families together. In the process, they turned to political activism and became bridge leaders in their community and state.

Amarillo College instructor and Oklahoma State University graduate student Stefanie Decker constructed chapter 6, "African American Women in the Civil Rights Era, 1954–1974," to present the role of black women during the civil rights era as well as in the struggle for civil rights. African American women were able to take advantage of the opportunities that they helped to create, in politics, in education, in the arts, in athletics, and in a host of economic endeavors. The gains were sometimes limited but they constituted an important step for advancing the black community.

For the post–civil rights era, 1974 to 2000, we called on the talents of two groups of authors, one of historians (Kenneth Howell and James Smallwood), and the other of political scientists (Jewel Prestage and Franklin Jones). Kenneth Howell, on the faculty at Prairie View A&M University, and James Smallwood in chapter 7, "Expanded Opportunities: Black Women in the Modern Era, 1974–2000," discovered the overarching theme to be the continuing struggle of black Texas women to overcome adversity, as well as the effort by African American women to establish their presence not solely in the black community but well beyond. Black women in the modern era experienced triumph, often at personal and social cost. As the twenty-first century approached, Afro-Texas women could look back at their accomplishments and take pride in the fact that they ushered in a new era of progress for their race and their gender. The black women's determination and desire to create a better world for their children established a lasting legacy, a legacy that will undoubtedly guide future generations of black women as they push toward greater heights in the twenty-first century.

Former Southern University and Prairie View teacher/leader, Jewel Prestage, and Franklin Jones, professor and department chair at Texas Southern University, in chapter 8, "Contemporary Black Texas Women, Political and Educational Leadership, 1974–2000," emphasized the increasing options available for African American women in educational and political leadership. The glass ceiling cracked, and in some instances, broke in contemporary Texas. A century earlier, black women could not vote or hold political office, even though some held offices in organizations such as the Thurman Woman's Christian Temperance Union. Few held college degrees; the ensuing century, and particularly the last quarter century, witnessed the entry of black women into universities and in pursuit of leadership opportunities in the professions, in education, and in politics.

Black Women in Texas History could not have been written without the foundation of earlier historical writings. We have included a Selected Bibliography at the end of the book. That bibliography comprises studies that have black Texas women as their focal point. The works in the bibliography, though excellent scholarly studies, do not generally cover larger eras or topics, and consist principally of articles, theses, and dissertations, though an increasing number of monographs are also being published. General studies that contain information about black families and black women, such as James M. Smallwood's *Time of Hope, Time of Despair: Black Texans during Reconstruction* (Port Washington, N.Y.: National University Publications, 1981), are not included. However, the notes at the end of each chapter in *Black Women in Texas History* direct readers and students to the numerous additional sources that contain material on black Texas women, but that otherwise might not be considered as a viable source. Each of the authors in *Black Women in Texas History* includes such citations, in addition to those discussed in this introduction or included in the selected bibliography.

Some principal works deserve mention in addition to those already described. Certainly each of us used the works of Ruthe Winegarten and Darlene Clark Hine. Winegarten's prodigious research and her two previously mentioned studies are packed with data; they helped us immeasurably. Understanding black Texas history also meant perusing Alwyn Barr, *Black Texans: A History of African Americans in Texas*, 2nd ed. (Norman: University of Oklahoma Press, 1996) as well as his, with Robert A. Calvert, *Black Leaders: Texans for Their Times* (Austin: Texas State Historical Association, 1981). Bruce A. Glasrud and Laurie

Champion's *Exploring the Afro-Texas Experience: A Bibliography of Secondary Sources about Black Texans* (Alpine, Tex.: Sul Ross State University Center for Big Bend Studies, 2000) provided numerous useful citations. Material on African American women in *The New Handbook of Texas,* in hardcopy or the online version, proved very useful.

In monographs by scholars, friends/colleagues, and in their own words, the recognition of African American women in Texas proceeds. The finest scholarly monograph on a black Texas woman is Merline Pitre, *In Struggle against Jim Crow: Lulu B. White and the NAACP, 1900–1957* (College Station: Texas A&M University Press, 1999). Another leader of the Texas civil rights movement can be discovered in Juanita Craft, *A Child, the Earth, and a Tree of Many Seasons: The Voice of Juanita Craft* (Dallas: Halifax Publishing, 1982). Filled with photographs, drawings, and commentary, a poignant and delightful work covering the early years of the twentieth century by Rick Hyman and Ronda Hyman, *My Texas Family: An Uncommon Journey to Prosperity (Featuring Photographs from 1912–1927)* (Charleston, S.C.: Arcadia Publishing, 2000), is must reading. Sunny Nash, *Bigmama Didn't Shop at Woolworth's* (College Station: Texas A&M University Press, 1996), chronicles a black family in white-dominated, segregated Texas.

Although a number of biographers have covered the life and career of Barbara Jordan, her autobiography, Barbara Jordan and Shelby Hearon, *Barbara Jordan: A Self-Portrait* (Garden City, N.Y.: Doubleday, 1979), is an insightful introduction to this imposing figure that is explored in depth by Mary Beth Rogers, *Barbara Jordan: American Hero* (New York: Bantam Books, 1998). Bessie Coleman, the first black female aviator, is the subject of several studies. The two principal investigations are Doris L. Rich, *Queen Bess: Daredevil Aviator* (Washington, D.C.: Smithsonian Institution Press, 1993) and Elizabeth Hadley Freydberg, *Bessie Coleman: The Brownskin Lady Bird* (New York: Garland Publishing, 1994). Two works by and about influential members of the urban black community are Julia K. Gibson Jordan and Charlie Mae Brown Smith, *Beauty and the Best: Frederica Chase Dodd, the Story of a Life of Love and Dedication* (Dallas: Delta Sigma Theta Sorority, 1985), and Naomi Lede, *Precious Memories of a Black Socialite* (Houston: D. Armstrong, 1991).

Three additional monographs covering the lives of African American women in Texas are Carroll Parrott Blue, *The Dawn at My Back: Memoir of a Black Texas Upbringing* (Austin: University of Texas Press,

2003), Dorothy Redus Robinson, *The Bell Rings at Four: A Black Teacher's Chronicle of Change* (Austin: Madrona Press, 1978), and Ruthe Winegarten, ed., *I am Annie Mae; An Extraordinary Woman in Her Own Words: The Personal Story of a Black Texas Woman* (Austin: Rosegarden Press, 1983). Finally, for a valuable and informative book, look at Maceo C. Dailey Jr. and Kristine Navarro, eds., *Wheresoever My People Chance to Dwell: Oral Interviews with African American Women of El Paso* (Baltimore: Inprint Editions, 2000).

Many Texas historians have included African American women in their studies, not always directly. Michael R. Heintze, *Private Black Colleges in Texas, 1865–1954* (College Station: Texas A&M University Press, 1985) acknowledged numerous black women who played prominent roles in the establishment of colleges for black students. Francis E. Abernethy, Patrick B. Mullen, and Alan B. Govenar edited a splendid work, *Juneteenth Texas: Essays in African-American Folklore* (Denton: University of North Texas Press, 1996) that includes material that is much broader than the title indicates. Howard Beeth and Cary D. Wintz edited *Black Dixie: Afro-Texas History and Culture in Houston* (College Station: Texas A&M University Press, 1992), an anthology that contains essays of significance to black Texas women. Bruce A. Glasrud and James M. Smallwood contributed the *African American Experience in Texas History* (Lubbock: Texas Tech University Press, 2007), an anthology that offers works about and by black Texas women. *Bricks without Straw: A Comprehensive History of African Americans in Texas* (Austin: Eakin Press, 1997), is an anthology edited by David A. Williams that includes African American women in the Lone Star State.

Among historians whose books helped measurably toward understanding the status of African American women in Texas were authors who covered broader subjects in their research. Julia Kirk Blackwelder, *Women of the Depression: Caste and Culture in San Antonio, 1929–1939* (College Station: Texas A&M University Press, 1984), and *Styling Jim Crow: African American Beauty Training during Segregation* (College Station: Texas A&M University Press, 2003) examined the underpinnings of black women's social interaction. Angela Boswell, in *Her Act and Deed: Women's Lives in a Rural Southern County, 1837–1873* (College Station: Texas A&M University Press, 2001), and Rebecca Sharpless, in *Fertile Ground, Narrow Choices: Women on Texas Cotton Farms, 1900–1940* (Chapel Hill: University of North Carolina Press, 1999), focus on women who resided in the rural economy that dominated the nineteenth and much of the twentieth centuries.

As valuable as were the secondary studies, neither they nor our chapters could have been completed without careful scrutiny of primary sources. The primary sources quite obviously provided crucial documentation. Important materials for investigating the lives and roles of black Texas women include the WPA slave interviews, publications of the U.S. Census Bureau, and public documents and records from cities and counties as well as state and national governments; Labor Department publications are a good example of the latter. Newspapers, and some magazines, provide a wealth of information. For the Reconstruction period, the Freedmen's Bureau records are a must. The Federal Writers' Project of the 1930s produced volumes of information about African Americans in the cities of Texas that provide worthwhile information about women in the first thirty-plus years of the twentieth century.

V. O. Key argued that local friends and neighborhood networks formed nuclei of the white establishment in South Carolina in the 1930s and 1940s.[9] *Black Women in Texas History* finds a counterpart in the black female networks that created an enduring institutional framework for community advances in the Lone Star State. Concerned with race, space, place, class, and gender, this work moves black females into the center of Texas history. Enslaved, "Jim Crowed," disfranchised, and relegated to the periphery of the social, political, and economic life of Texas, black females actively pursued ways to make their voices and concerns heard. Individually and collectively they helped shape the course of Texas history and in this endeavor they "made community."

Notes

1. Darlene Clark Hine, *Hine Sight: Black Women and the Re-Construction of American History* (Bloomington: Indiana University Press, 1994), xxii.

2. Ibid., xxiii.

3. Darlene Clark Hine, *When the Truth Is Told: Black Women's Culture and Community in Indiana, 1875–1950* (Bloomington: Indiana University Press, 1981); Ruthe Winegarten, *Black Texas Women: 150 Years of Trial and Triumph* (Austin: University of Texas Press, 1995); Ruthe Winegarten, *Black Texas Women: A Sourcebook* (Austin: University of Texas Press, 1996); Quintard Taylor and Shirley Ann Wilson Moore, eds., *African American Women Confront the West, 1600–2000* (Norman: University of Oklahoma Press, 2003); Gerda

Lerner, ed., *Black Women in White America: A Documentary History* (New York: Pantheon, 1972); Dorothy Sterling, ed., *We Are Your Sisters: Black Women in the Nineteenth Century* (New York: W. W. Norton, 1984).

4. Darlene Clark Hine and Kathleen Thompson, *A Shining Thread of Hope: The History of Black Women in America* (New York: Broadway Books, 1998), 6; Paula Giddings, *When and Where I Enter: The Impact of Black Women on Race and Sex in America* (New York: William Morrow, 1984).

5. Darlene Clark Hine, Wilma King, and Linda Reed, eds., *"We Specialize in the Wholly Impossible": A Reader in Black Women's History* (Brooklyn, N.Y.: Carlson Publishing, 1995); see also Sharon Harley and Rosalyn Terborg-Penn, *The Afro-American Woman: Struggles and Images* (Port Washington, N.Y.: Kennikat Press, 1978). Darlene Clark Hine, Elsa Barkley Brown, and Rosalyn Terborg-Penn, eds., *Black Women in America: An Historical Encyclopedia*, 2 vols. (Brooklyn, N.Y.: Carlson Publishing, 1993, and Bloomington: Indiana University Press, 1994); Darlene Clark Hine, ed., *Black Women in America, 2nd ed.*, 3 vols. (New York: Oxford University Press, 2005); Darlene Clark Hine, Elsa Barkley Brown, Tiffany R. L. Patterson, and Lillian S. Williams, eds., *Black Women in United States History*, 16 vols. (Brooklyn, N.Y.: Carlson Publishing, 1990).

6. Darlene Clark Hine, *Black Victory: The Rise and Fall of the White Primary in Texas* (Millwood, N.Y.: KTO Press, 1979); Hine, *Hine Sight*, xvii–xviii; Merline Pitre, "In Retrospect: Darlene Hine's *Black Victory*," in Darlene Clark Hine, *Black Victory: The Rise and Fall of the White Primary in Texas*, 25–40; rev. ed., (Columbia: University of Missouri Press, 2003).

7. Jewel Prestage initiated an agenda of engaged scholarship with her work on *Black Women Officeholders* in the early 1970s. Several generations of black women scholars have followed Prestage's lead. Together, this handful of black women forms an elite core within the field of political science. This small number is reflective of the field at large and is aggravated when the focus in narrowed to Texas.

8. Hine, *Hine Sight*, xxxiii.

9. V. O. Key Jr., *Southern Politics in State and Nation*, 1949; new ed., (Knoxville: University of Tennessee Press, 1984).

ANGELA BOSWELL

1. Black Women during Slavery to 1865

Africans and their descendants have been a part of Texas history for as long as Europeans and their descendants have. An African slave named Esteban accompanied the first Spanish expedition and exploration of land that eventually became part of Texas. Like the Spanish and later French explorers, the first Africans in Texas were male. Although the explorers were males, true efforts to populate and control any American colony, including Texas, obviously required women. It is not clear when African women or their descendants first arrived in Texas, but they were present in the eighteenth-century Spanish settlements and almost certainly even earlier—the 1792 Spanish census of Texas listed 167 mulattas and nineteen black women, both free and slave.[1]

The Spanish settlements of Mexico, including Texas, allowed considerable latitude socially, economically, and legally for persons of color. Full-blooded Spaniards were at the top of the social system, but intermarriage and interracial procreation produced many mixed-blooded children of Spanish, Indian, and African descent. Any white blood elevated a person's social status, whereas in the American South, any black blood consigned a person to the lowest caste in society. Because of the more fluid social structure, and because Spanish and Mexican law gave free persons of color legal, and even political, rights, Texas became a haven for runaway slaves from the southern United States. Even enslaved women in Spanish Texas understood their worth, humanity, and legal rights. In one San Antonio de Bexar case in 1791, a slave woman sued for a change in ownership due to mistreatment.[2]

By 1821, when Mexico gained its independence from Spain, many African American women, both slave and free, lived in Spanish Texas settlements. Thereafter, Mexican laws remained inconsistent but tended to favor freedom over slavery. African American women intermarried with other African Americans as well as mulattoes, Native Americans, and whites. They formed families and supported themselves through domestic labors that were in high demand on the Texas frontier: nursing, cooking, sewing, spinning, taking in laundry, and serving. Some women were able to accumulate property or build healthy and thriving businesses, such as boardinghouses, interacting both economically and socially with their Spanish neighbors.[3]

Although under Mexican sovereignty the social fluidity and legal freedom offered by Texas encouraged many free blacks and runaway slaves to emigrate, it was also under Mexican rule that the seeds were sown that would eventually condemn thousands of African Americans to a state of slavery in Texas. The vast majority of African American women to inhabit Texas before 1865 arrived with the Anglo colonists. Stephen F. Austin received permission from the new Mexican government in 1823 to settle families from the United States. Lured by cheap land on which they could grow cotton, many Anglo settlers brought with them slaves, both male and female. Although the independent Mexican government passed contradictory laws regarding the status of slaves and the legality of the institution, even Austin's colony granted acreage to slaveholders based upon the number of slaves. As a result, large numbers of enslaved blacks were imported into Texas from the U.S. South, as well as directly from Africa.[4]

By the time Texans struck their blow for independence in 1836, one of the valued ideals for which they fought was the right to own slaves. Texans moved quickly in 1836 to solidify their social ideals into law. They believed that all persons having any African parentage within the last three generations should make up the lowest rung of society—and that lowest rung should be consigned to perpetual slavery. Free blacks, especially successful ones, within the population belied whites' basic ideals and undermined the institution the Anglo Texans hoped to fasten upon Texas as they had in the rest of the South. Because of Texas' proximity to Mexico and its frontierlike conditions, it was even more necessary to control the black population and limit the number of blacks who were not enslaved. The Texas war for independence had provided an opportunity for a few slaves to earn freedom by fighting for the Texans or by taking advantage of the turmoil of war and running away. For the most part, however, Texas' independence decreased the opportunities for Texas blacks to ever receive their freedom. The new Texas constitution and laws allowed only those African Americans who were free and living in Texas at the time of Texas' independence to stay in Texas as free persons. All other blacks, whether freed by migrating to Texas or by manumission, had to either leave Texas or "choose his or her master, and become a slave." As a result, only a very few free African American women left any evidence of their presence at all. Some petitioned (mostly unsuccessfully) to remain in the state freely. That these petitions included the endorsements of free whites speaks to how valuable these women's skills were, especially in frontier or city settings. Nevertheless, the population of free blacks remained small, reaching only 355 in all of Texas in 1860—174 of whom were women.[5]

Although the predominantly white southern settlers brought with them their ideals and concepts regarding slavery, and by 1860 the institution very closely resembled slavery in other southern states, the Texas frontier changed the circumstances of slaves' lives considerably. Between 1823 and at least 1850, settlements in Texas were sparsely populated. Although slaves made up a significant portion of that population (13 percent in 1837, 27 percent in 1850), many slaves experienced isolation. A greater number of households owned fewer numbers of slaves in 1850 than in 1860. Even though settlers concentrated in the eastern two-thirds of Texas, slave owners and their slaves also lived far away from other families.[6]

The first challenge that enslaved women faced was the trip to Texas. A large segment of the Texas slave population migrated there with their owners and owners' families—and most of those migrated overland. Such a journey overland to Texas was a difficult one. The white family often traveled in covered carriages, while both male and female slaves walked alongside, tied or chained together, closely watched to prevent escape. In addition, slaves worked hard to help the traveling family at crucial times. Male and female slaves alike helped push wagons out of mud, move obstacles like fallen trees, and load and unload wagons. Certain tasks fell exclusively to the female slaves. When the family stopped to "rest," enslaved women made fires, cooked, cleaned, and washed clothing along the way.[7]

In addition to the physcial difficulty of making the journey, some slaves were mourning the loss of family members. When all of a master's slaves made the trip together, fewer families were separated. But even those slaves often had families on other plantations, as marrying abroad was a common practice throughout the South, especially in the frontier states like Kentucky and Tennessee from where many southern families migrated to Texas. Ann Hawthorne never heard of her master, Norseworthy, "breaking up a family. But when they were living in Georgia, my ma marry a man named Hawthorne in Georgia. [Hawthorne's master] wouldn't sell him to Master Norseworthy when he came to Texas." Ann Hawthorne's mother and father were not reunited until many years after the Civil War. But many slaves migrating to Texas faced the very real probability of never seeing or hearing from those family members again. Texas never passed laws forbidding teaching slaves to read and write, but because other southern states had made this illegal, written communication with family and friends left behind was nearly impossible. And, of course, they were not free to return home to visit. Nor did all settlers bring all of their slaves at first. Just as many men planned to clear land and make a home before sending for their wives, some men took only part of their slaves, intending to send for the rest once they were settled. These slaves had hopes at least of seeing family and friends again.[8]

The slaves who traveled with their masters to Texas, however, were luckier than the ones sold from other southern states and bought for slaveholders in Texas. This type of slave migration was common; farmers and planters needed more and more slaves in Texas as cotton production increased and brought a much higher price. Houston had a healthy slave market for this purpose. Under Mexican rule, the African slave trade flourished in Texas, and continued to some degree, although illegally, after Texas' independence. Rarely were slaves sold in slave markets elsewhere and transported to Texas in complete families. As Mary Armstrong remembered, when she was a young girl her master had sneaked her family to the Texas market to avoid creditors and clearly put profit above slave family structure. "He's so mean he never would sell the man and woman and children to the same one. He'd sell the man here and the woman there and [their] children, he'd sell them some place else."[9]

After the trip to Texas, slave women faced circumstances both similar to and different from their former states of residence. Unlike the white population, the slave population had an almost even gender ratio. By 1850, 50.6 percent of the slaves were female, similar to other southern states. In making the decision of which slaves and which type of slaves to take to the frontier of Texas, slave men would seem the most useful in the labor intensive work of clearing new land, planting the first crops, and building houses and other structures. According to several historians, males were preferred on frontier farms for precisely these reasons. However, there were several reasons slave women were just as valuable as slave men and likely to be well represented in the slave population.[10]

First, many slaveholders moved to Texas with slaves they already owned in other states. Therefore, men, women, and children were well represented in that slave population. Second, many southerners (and even northerners) moved to Texas in hopes of investing in land and slaves and making a profit. This dream appealed to those of all classes, even those who did not already own slaves. As a result, those with minimum amounts of capital chose slaves who could work the land and represent future income and wealth by producing slave children. In addition, female slaves were cheaper than male slaves, making the purchase of one female slave within the reach of more entrepreneurs, or allowing for the possibility of purchasing more female slaves than male slaves.[11]

Ironically, the very scarcity of white women made black women more valuable in frontier Texas. The opportunities in Texas enticed a great proportion of single white men and married white men who wished to be single. Even married men often left wives behind temporarily until setting up a home for their families. As a result, men greatly outnumbered women in Texas' white population. Because of the nineteenth-century gendered division of labor, the unbalanced gender ratio in Texas created a deficiency of laborers in those tasks typically assigned to women. Cooking, sewing, weaving, canning, washing, and cleaning were necessary even on the Texas frontier.[12]

A gendered division of labor existed within the slave labor system as well. When slaves learned skills or performed other work than in the field, the men served as carpenters, builders, blacksmiths, wagon drivers, brickmasons, coopers, cobblers, and tanners. Women were the laundresses and cooks and the seamstresses responsible for sewing, spinning, weaving, and quilting. When slaves served as ranch hands, they were invariably male. However, females were preferred for domestic work. Those who ran hotels or boarded paying customers (such as teachers) relied heavily on female slaves.[13]

While female slaves could perform the traditional female duties, white slaveholders showed no hesitancy in putting slave women to work in the fields just as they did slave men. Slave women generally were prohibited from holding only a few positions in the fields: only slave men held positions of authority over other slave men and almost exclusively served as drivers. Yet a female slave was just as likely to be put to almost all other tasks as a male slave. Large slaveholders-undoubtedly divided work according to gender more easily, with certain slaves dedicated to the "house" except under special circumstances (like picking season). But the majority of slaveholding Texans claimed few slaves and were more likely to own female slaves, whether for cost or flexibility. According to the 1850 and 1860 census of one rural county, of those who owned five or fewer slaves, they were almost four times more likely to own adult females only than they were to own adult males only.[14]

While slave women could be assigned to heavy labor, especially in the fields, male slaves almost never performed the female duties of cooking, cleaning, sewing, and weaving. Slave women, therefore, could perform both the typical female occupations that were in scarce supply on the frontier as well as the heavy labor associated with clearing land and planting crops. As Phoebe Henderson remembered, "I worked in the field many a day, plowing and hoeing. . . . I worked in the house, too. I spinned seven curts a day and every night we run two looms, making large curts for plow lines. We made all our clothes." Because of their strength and flexibility, those men who were wealthy enough to own slaves probably preferred taking at least one female to perform domestic duties as well as fieldwork.[15]

Another reason that some slaveholders preferred female slaves also related to the absence of white women. The presence of more white men than women and more black women than men encouraged miscegenation, especially in areas with a heavy black concentration. Although Texas passed some of the harshest laws in the South punishing miscegenous relationships (2 to 5 years in prison), such illegal intercourse apparently occurred at least occasionally. How often it actually took place is impossible to determine. The long-term nature of some of these relationships might suggest more than merely a master taking advantage of a slave. Ann Patton Malone maintains that "black female concubinage, often an arrangement based on affection as well as convenience, was common on the early Texas frontier." There may have indeed been true emotion and love between white master and black slave; but even if there had been none, a slave woman could not legally make a substantially different decision. According to the former slave Jim Green, "the masters and the drivers takes all the nigger girls they want. One slave had four children right after the other with a white master. Their children was brown, but one of them was white as you is." Whether or not the slave woman loved or wanted the white man who had power over her, he could "take" her. There was no such thing in law as rape of a slave. Even so, some slave women successfully resisted unwanted advances.[16]

Slave women might consent or even seek out relationships with their white masters out of love or to get better treatment. Southerners often assumed that this was the case as the general belief was that African American women were naturally promiscuous. These southerners believed that slave women willingly had sex with white men or even seduced them. White men and women alike preferred to blame slave women for being lusty rather than truthfully to evaluate the power relationships that allowed white men to use slave women.[17]

The unbalanced ratio of white males to white females during the frontier era made it especially tempting for white men to have relationships with black female slaves. But within the slave population, black women just slightly exceeded the number of black men, theoretically creating equal opportunities for men and women to find spouses. Absolute numbers, however, were not necessarily the deciding factors in finding marriage partners or forming families. In addition to the geography of the frontier, because no law recognized the validity of black families, the laws or rules of the master could exert much influence upon the decisions slaves could make.[18]

Slave owners usually encouraged the formation of families (even if they did not always recognize them) because the children born of their female slaves symbolized an increase in the worth of their personal property holdings. Southern slave owners calculated that at least 5 to 6 percent of their wealth would accrue from natural increase among their slaves, and there is no evidence that Texas slaveholders believed differently. This attitude can be seen particularly in the case of a Smith County woman whose will dictated that the executors of her estate hold in trust a slave named Caroline and "that she was constantly kept with child" until all of the heirs "shall receive one child of the increase."[19]

To insure that their female slaves reproduced quickly, some slaveholders gave their slaves little choice in their sexual or marriage partner. Particularly callous slaveholders would pair slave men and women in a so-called marriage in order to produce stronger, healthier slave children. According to one slave, James Green, "no one had no say as to who he was going to get for a wife." Although extremely rare, there is evidence of at least one Texas slaveholder who "bred" slaves by keeping mostly female slaves and bringing in a strong male from another plantation to impregnate several women.[20]

Most Texas slaveholders, however, left the decisions of partners to the slaves themselves. Even then, however, masters used rewards and threats (such as the threat of sale and separation) to prompt enslaved women to begin bearing children at a young age. Added to that were longstanding traditions, perhaps originating in Africa, that permitted and even encouraged women to have their first child before marriage. As a result, slave women in Texas, as in the rest of the South, were likely to have their first child before they had married. During the frontier times, slaves' marriage choices on their own plantation were rather limited because most slaveholdings were small. Thirty-eight percent of the Texas slaves lived in households with fewer than ten slaves. Marrying abroad, or marrying someone from a different plantation, required the permission of the master. Some masters would not allow slaves to marry abroad, but others would give such permission. Lizzie Jones remembered that her master "allowed the boys and girls to court but they couldn't marry before they were 20 years old, and they couldn't marry off the plantation."[21]

In frontier Texas, marrying abroad was extremely risky. Small farmers took enormous risks to move to Texas, and often those financial risks did not pay off. They would be forced to sell their slaves, or pick up and move yet again. The high frontier death rate also meant that frequently slaves were divided among the owner's heirs. Not all these heirs lived in the same vicinity as the deceased slaveholder, and some would immediately sell those slaves they inherited. When slaves were sold, given as inheritance, or the slave owners moved, husbands and wives, as well as children, on different plantations were separated often by such long distances as to never see each other again.[22]

Despite the obstacles and the high possibility of past and future heartbreaks due to separation, slaves continued to form families. The security of the slave family depended greatly upon the security of the master and the degree to which the slaveholder recognized and valued slave families. Some masters recognized slave families and felt it a moral obligation to keep them together. In his will, William R. Turner asked that his personal property be divided among his heirs, "and my slaves to remain in families as I am opposed to separating man and wife or families of Negroes." Other slave owners also at least recognized families of slaves, whether or not they insisted they be kept together. By far, the most acknowledged slave relationship in letters and legal documents was that of the slave mother and her children.[23]

Even when whites recognized slave families, most slaveholders still put legal and financial interests ahead of the sanctity of slave family ties. Slave owners who needed cash could sell, mortgage, or "hire" out their slaves. In these transactions, masters might take the slave family into consideration before sale or separation by hiring out, but if necessary they would break up enslaved families to protect their white family first and foremost. Executors of wills and administrators of estates might try to keep enslaved families together, but their primary goal was to insure that the white heirs received equal portions of the estate.[24]

While husbands and wives were less recognized and more frequently separated, the most heart-wrenching separation was probably that of a mother from her children. No Texas law prohibited the sale of children away from their mothers (no matter how young), much less the separation of spouses. The Texas Supreme Court upheld the ideals of white slaveholders who wished to protect their property rights in slaves above the sanctity of slave relationships. That court found that even enslaved mothers and children were "distinct" pieces of property and must be assessed separately from one another in the division of estates. While the separation or sale of young children did not occur every day, it did occur with sometimes devastating effects on families. Even very small children, as young as age three, were sold to other households. Some of these sales or transfers might have occurred after or because the mother had died. But many parents of young children separated can be ascertained to have still been living.[25]

No matter how considerate the master or how much he might recognize the family relationships in the slave community, hard financial times and especially death could suddenly split slave families apart. Slave mothers and fathers lived with the possibility of never seeing their children again and even facing the possibility that the children would not even remember them. After emancipation, when former slaves desperately tried to reunite families torn apart during slavery, fathers and mothers relied on the Freedmen's Bureau to help them find and retrieve their children. On a rare occasion, the Freedmen's Bureau passed along the sad information that the children had no interest in returning to their parents. These children had grown up not knowing their parents and were happier to stay where they had called home.[26]

Despite all the impediments to forming lasting marriages and families on the Texas frontier, slaves continued to do so. Slaves drew great strength from these family relationships. Although not recognized by white Texas law, slave communities formed and enforced their own sets of beliefs regarding the sanctity of marriages. The ideal family among slaves remained the two-parent nuclear unit. As immigration to Texas increased in the 1850s, this nuclear unit became somewhat easier to achieve. The number of slaves on plantations increased (as a smaller percentage of whites in Texas owned slaves and owned more of them). In 1850, 38 percent of the slaves lived in households with fewer than ten slaves each. However, by 1860, this had decreased to 29 percent. In addition, a greater population in the rural areas of Texas offered slaves more opportunities to find marriage partners on other plantations. By 1860, these marriages were still subject to separation by sales, at the death of owners, and by the relocation of slaveholders. However, as more of Texas became settled, "the frontier" receded in many places. The relative economic stability of the 1850s, the claiming and settling of the fertile land of eastern Texas, and the lessening of dangers from wars with Indians (or Mexicans, such as in the Texas Revolution or the Mexican War), led to increased stability within white families by 1860. As the white families became more stable, the slaves had more opportunities to form lasting communities and lasting marriages and families.[27]

While not recognized by law, marriages were important events within the slave community and for the married couple. Some slaves had elaborate wedding ceremonies provided by their masters. Others were allowed no ceremony at all. Most, however, celebrated marriage in simple ceremonies recognized by the slave community. Preachers might officiate at the ceremony, but more likely the master or a respected member of the slave community would preside. While the master had to approve of any slave "marriage," the man and the woman who wanted to marry might also have to seek out the permission of the slave community in which they lived, usually by approaching the "Granny," an older and respected slave woman.[28]

Marriages were celebrated within the community and fidelity to marriage enforced by the codes of the slave community, even in the absence of legal sanctions. Yet although slave marriages were similar to white marriages in many ways, there were differences. When separation ended a marriage, both partners were likely to remarry. Slaves also recognized "divorce" for reasons other than separation. Quarrelsome spouses, abusive spouses, or spouses who just fell out of love could "quit" their husbands and wives and take new ones. When mutual splits occurred, the slave community usually accepted new marriages made by one or both of the partners. And as long as a slave could find another spouse, most masters did not object either.[29]

Even with the availability of divorce or "quitting," and even with the interference of masters in marriage choices, evidence shows that most Texas slave marriages were long-term affairs that produced many children. The majority (60 percent) of the former Texas slaves interviewed by the Works Progress Administration (WPA) remembered living in a household with both parents, while another 9 percent remembered living with their mothers while their fathers lived nearby. Because the WPA slave narratives interviewed former slaves so many years after slavery had ended, the majority had been young children at the time the Civil War began. Thus, they were recalling the times after the Texas population had swelled and the economy had stabilized. There is no evidence, but the earlier years of Texas settlement probably did not enjoy nearly as stable nuclear family units.[30]

When able to maintain their families, the family provided a source of comfort and identity to slaves, including women. However, the function and role of wife and mother in the slave family differed substantially from that of the white family ideal. Because the true authority over both male and female slaves was the master, the slave husband's role was not the same as in a white family where the husband maintained authority over his family, including his wife. Slave women could not even necessarily guarantee their husbands' exclusive sexual rights. In addition, slave men did not fulfill the "ideal white husband" role of provider and protector. Masters dictated where and in what slave families were to live and portioned out food and clothing rations. Slave husbands could not "protect" their wives from physical or verbal punishment by their masters. Masters even arbitrated marital and family disputes, diminishing the power slave husbands and fathers might try to exercise over their families. Although paternal authority was weaker among slave families than in white families, the slave families were not matriarchal. The same circumstances that denied black men authority in the household denied black women from exercising that role as well.[31]

The small minority of slaves who lived in the urban areas such as Dallas and Houston were predominantly female, both in the 1850 and 1860 census. These small townships supported milliners, doctors, lawyers, wagonmakers, merchants, innkeepers, and, especially in Houston, commercial houses to store, sell, and ship cotton from the surrounding environs. The vast majority of slaveholders in these areas owned only one or two slaves. Most of these slaves were females and worked as household servants, performing the arduous domestic tasks of washing, ironing, sewing and spinning, cooking, cleaning, gardening and preserving, and above all, being on call twenty-four hours a day. While some of these tasks were performed exclusively for the white families with whom they lived, the domestic skills were also often employed to increase the income of the masters. For example, innkeepers and others who took in boarders relied upon slave labor to keep their businesses profitable.[32]

The vast majority of female slaves (94 percent), however, lived in rural and agricultural areas. On large plantations, female slaves might be assigned full-time to household duties similar to those in towns. Most likely, however, those few who performed domestic duties split their labor between the white household and field labor. Corn and cotton were Texas' main crops, although some others included sugar, rice, and even some tobacco. Although they did not consider working in the fields appropriate for white females, planters and farmers assigned most female slaves to work in the fields. Women hoed, picked, weeded, thinned, ginned, pressed cotton into bales, grew food, tended livestock, and formed all-female gangs that performed all manner of tasks from trash gangs to fence repairs. Some women gained renown for the amount of cotton they could pick or the amount of rows they could hoe.[33]

Some women took pride in their work and their abilities to do their work well. However, slaves, male or female, performed the work assigned to them because they were forced to do so. The whip was a common form of punishment for disobeying the master or overseer, but other forms of physical chastisement were used as well. Even one of the most even-handed of the plantation owners, Charles Tait, urged his overseers to "never punish a Negro when in passion," but he certainly endorsed physical punishment. Texas law guaranteed masters the right to punish their slaves, and the courts did not strictly enforce the few laws against cruel treatment of slaves. Masters also had other punishments at their disposal, such as reduced food rations, sale and separation, or refusing passes to visit family on other plantations.[34]

Masters had the primary claim over slave women's productive and reproductive labor. Yet after working for the master all day, five and a half to six days a week, there were chores that slave men and women had to do for their own families. Slave men hunted and fished and repaired slave quarters in their free hours. Enslaved women, however, had the more daily chores. When slave households received rations from the masters, women had to cook for their families. Women rose well before daylight to build a fire, prepare breakfast for their families, and meals that would be easily eaten at the midday break. After returning from the fields late in the evening, they sometimes had to build a fire for supper, but oftentimes they relied upon light leftovers for the evening meal.[35]

On some plantations, a central kitchen might prepare the breakfast and dinner meals for all hands, but usually supper was still prepared in the slave cabins. Whether prepared communally or by individual families, the main fare for Texas slaves consisted of cornmeal, molasses, and small amounts of meat, usually pork. If food was distributed to individual families, women added to their chores the necessity of rationing that food to last the entire week. The cornmeal given to slaves had to be processed into consumable foods, the most common dishes being corn breads, corn mush, or "hoecakes." When fresh corn was available, the process of making it into hominy could consume hours of a day.[36]

After preparing supper, a slave mother then had to clean up after the meals and begin spinning, weaving, or sewing either as extra assigned work by the master or for her own family. On days off, women added to the family's rations by tending to a garden and preserving and canning the produce. They also skinned, prepared, and cooked the small game, like opossums, raccoons, rabbits, and squirrels, that their husbands and sons hunted. Men might perform the more strenuous work in the fields, but women worked more hours.[37]

Living conditions for slaves also contributed to women's labors. During the frontier and settling era of Texas, slaves probably slept on kitchen floors of the white household, in the attic, or in lean-tos. Masters who owned only a few slaves probably continued this practice well into the 1850s and 1860s. Larger plantations, once established, built small cabins for individual slave families, or larger cabins for many slaves. Most cabins measured only about 20 to 25 square feet and, according to one county study, averaging four to five people in each. The small, dingy cabins were extremely difficult to keep clean, with dirt floors, large chinks or cracks in the walls, and few or no windows. The cabins that housed just one family each were small and cramped, serving both as places to sleep and places to prepare and eat meals. The fires required to keep the cabin warm, as well as to prepare meals, no doubt kept the bedding, clothes, furniture, and cooking utensils constantly filthy.[38]

Some slave women took great pride in cleaning and caring for their homes and children, even after working long hours in the field. Yet, even care of the family's slave cabin was not the core of a slave woman's life and identity. In many cases, the decisions of when and how to clean the cabins were not left to them—some masters oversaw even the whitewashing and cleaning of bedding in their homes.[39]

Husbands and children indeed gave slave women love, comfort, and nurturing. Yet separations both permanent and temporary that occurred because of sales or hiring out caused women to learn to rely on more than their families for support. The slave community played a tremendous role in the lives of all slaves. Because of the white predilection for recognizing mothers and children as families rather than parents and children, enslaved women often found themselves as primarily responsible for raising children. Throughout their lives, African American women in Texas, therefore, relied upon the slave community to help them in their lives and in their motherhood. The strong female networks that formed within the slave community particularly helped with this burden.[40]

As children, girls were incorporated into segregated female work gangs as soon as they were old enough to do even light duties. The "trash gang" was often where slave girls began, working alongside older women who had been given lighter workloads due either to their age or physical condition, usually pregnancy. In this female world of work, the young slave girl was introduced not only to the world of labor that would shape her life, but also was instructed by the older women on how to survive the system of slavery with her own self-worth intact. The oldest women could impart valuable advice. And although the secrets of sexuality were kept from children as long as possible, working with pregnant women inculcated into girls the meanings of bearing children from the slave women's point of view, not just from the masters.'[41]

Pregnancy and childbirth indicated an important passage into adulthood for girls. Although it varied, slave women usually had their first child around the age of nineteen, younger than white women generally had their first child. Masters expected slave women to have children early, offering rewards for pregnancy such as reduced workloads and rewards for children such as extra rations or other material benefits. In addition, slave women who did not demonstrate fecundity risked sale and separation from their family and friends. Any special consideration given to pregnant slave women depended upon the needs and priorities of the master at the time of pregnancy. The master balanced the future new slave "wealth" suggested by an unborn child against the labor needs of the present. During cotton-picking season, a small farmer could not afford to lose a laborer because she was pregnant and thus was likely to drive her to work as hard as usual. If possible, masters would reduce loads, allow pregnant women to join older women and children on the trash gangs, or assign them to jobs considered less strenuous than fieldwork, such as child care. Although women might be expected to work less while pregnant, they were still expected to frequently bear children and work.[42]

Because women still worked, sometimes strenuously, during pregnancy and because slave diets were often poor, miscarriage and infant mortality was high. Slave women depended heavily upon other female slaves and the slave community during this period of her life. Family members and other slaves might take up the slack by a woman who could not work as hard due to pregnancy, or in some cases protest because she was being expected to work too hard. When it came time for childbirth, slave women especially called upon one another. Masters might be able to and willing to pay for doctors to assist with the deliveries, yet slaves and masters both seemed to prefer that it be African American midwives, either on the plantation or from another plantation, that attended to slave women during the birth. From the master's point of view a midwife was less expensive than a doctor; from the slave woman's point of view, the midwife was more likely to observe African American customs and accede to wishes of the new mother during delivery and after.[43]

Once the children were born, female networks continued to serve an important role in women's lives. On many farms and plantations, child care was shared, by the choice of their masters, not by slave mothers. Masters required women to return to work within weeks or even days of giving birth. A nursing mother sometimes took her baby to the fields with her so that she could nurse it. Or she might be permitted lighter loads or work close by the quarters that would allow her to visit her newborn to nurse. Although Sarah Ford remembered her overseer as "so mean" that the devil must have appointed him, still "the women that had little children don't have to work so hard. They work around the sugar house and come 11 o'clock they quit and care for the babies till 1 o'clock, and then work till 3 o'clock and quit." When nursing ceased, and sometimes before, the bulk of the baby's time was spent with another caretaker for the day. Those in charge of feeding and caring for the children were usually older women who could not work as hard in the fields as other younger women. Sometimes very young children were put in charge of caring for the even younger children.[44]

While slave girls learned many of the coping skills from the women with whom they worked, they also often learned other valuable skills as well. Slave mothers who were cooks, seamstresses, weavers, and especially midwives, taught their occupations to their daughters, but women would also teach and share this information with other female members of the community. Because of the instability of the slave families due to sales, separations, and early deaths, the slave community formed complex kinship networks to help its members and act as surrogate families to those left without any. When children were left without parents for any period of time, the community took over the functions of the parents, providing for and teaching young children.[45]

Besides taking care of orphaned children, the slave community played other very important roles in the lives of slave girls and women. The community extended beyond any one plantation. The practice of marrying abroad reinforced traditions brought over from Africa by extending kinship networks beyond the immediate area. This extended kin helped preserve other African traditions adapted to the environment of slavery in the South. African heritage could be seen in Texas slaves' music, healing practices, dances, folk tales, and even in slave women's distinctive approach to domestic handicrafts such as basket making and quilting. Over generations, mothers passed down to daughters the strip patterns of quilts similar to West African designs.[46]

Even though most slaves adopted Christianity, they approached their religion through the framework of their African heritage in which there was no division between sacred and secular. Most Texas masters encouraged their slaves to attend church, where they sat and worshiped in the back or in special sections. Slaves joined almost all the denominations of Christianity found in Texas, but most became members of the Methodist and Baptist churches whose more energetic approach to worship corresponded more closely to African religious practices. Some slaves even became preachers and were allowed to hold services on plantations, and in some Texas cities (such as Galveston) separate black congregations formed. However, slave owners preferred to oversee the slaves' practice of religion, because while Christianity could reinforce slavery, it could also be subversive. Slaves especially responded to the tenets of Christianity that held all men and women were created equally and that promised freedom in this life or in the hereafter for God's children.[47]

The distinctive slave culture that developed apart from the white culture nurtured slaves, allowing them to retain their humanity within the legal and social institution of slavery that regarded them primarily as property. Slave women drew strength from this culture and played a prominent role in nourishing it as well. The most prominent persons in the slave community were preachers, slave conjurers or magician/curers, musicians, midwives, and "grannies." While almost all preachers were males, and many of the slave conjurers were males, women were midwives and grannies and sometimes conjurers as well. These women held high esteem within the slave community. Their expertise and treatment for physical ailments and assistance in childbirth was sought after. Their advice on other matters was valued highly, and sometimes they could make decisions affecting the lives of other slaves (for instance, in some communities grannies gave permission to slaves to marry).[48]

The strength of the slave culture, the formation and prominence of slave families, and the white attitudes toward slavery prove that by the coming of the Civil War, Texas was not just a slave frontier but an integral part of the institution of slavery in the South. Western portions of Texas still experienced frontier conditions that affected slaves' lives and opportunities. But given the history of the development of slavery in the eastern two-thirds of Texas, it is possible that even these areas would have developed slave communities and the familiar southern approach to slavery had the Civil War and emancipation not ended the institution. While even eastern Texas remained a frontier until the mid-1850s in some areas, slaves faced some difficulties reforming their communities and founding lasting marriages and families. Yet the rapid immigration of slaves and slaveholders, the increasing economic and geographic stability of Texas slaveholders, and the consolidation of slave owning into fewer hands, had by 1861 allowed the creation of a slave culture in Texas. While the Civil War created some disturbances of the slave system in Texas when men left for war, Texas was spared the wholesale desertions of slaves and destruction of property that other southern states experienced. Therefore, the lives, roles, and experiences of most African American women, mostly unaffected during the Civil War, would face the most dramatic changes at emancipation, announced in Texas on June 19, 1865.[49]

Notes

1. Ruthe Winegarten, *Black Texas Women: 150 Years of Trial and Triumph* (Austin: University of Texas Press, 1995), 2; Randolph B. Campbell, *An Empire for Slavery: The Peculiar Institution in Texas, 1821–1865* (Baton Rouge: Lousiana State University Press, 1989), 10–11; David A. Williams, *Bricks without Straw: A Comprehensive History of African Americans in Texas* (Austin: Eakin Press, 1997), 1–2.

There are very few published chapter-length works that concentrate primarily on the African American woman's experience in Texas before emancipation. The most comprehensive of these are the first two chapters of Winegarten, *Black Texas Women*. There is a very good chapter dealing specifically with African American women's lives on the frontier in Ann Patton Malone, *Women on the Texas Frontier: A Cross-Cultural Perspective* (El Paso: Texas Western Press, 1983). For research based on public records for one Texas county, see the chapter "The Law of the Master: Slave Women," in Angela Boswell, *Her Act and Deed: Women's Lives in a Rural Southern County, 1837–73* (College Station: Texas A&M University Press, 2001). Other scholarly works on slavery in Texas also include discussions of slave women throughout (see note 4).

2. Victor H. Treat, "William Goyens: Free Negro Entrepreneur," in *Black Leaders: Texans for Their Times*, ed. Alwyn Barr and Robert A. Calvert (Austin: Texas State Historical Association, 1981), 22–24; Dedra S. McDonald, "To Be Black and Female in the Spanish Southwest: Toward a History of African Women on New Spain's Far Northern Frontier," in *African American Women Confront the West, 1600–2000*, ed. Quintard Taylor and Shirley Ann Wilson Moore (Norman: University of Oklahoma Press, 2003), 46–47; Winegarten, *Black Texas Women*, 2.

3. Winegarten, *Black Texas Women*, 2–5; Campbell, *Empire for Slavery*, 10–34.

4. Winegarten, *Black Texas Women*, 3–4; Campbell, *Empire for Slavery*, 3–22; Williams, *Bricks without Straw*, 1–2. Slavery in Texas has been the subject of many good scholarly works. One of the first articles, Abigail Curlee Holbrook, "A Glimpse of Life on Antebellum Slave Plantations in Texas," *Southwestern Historical Quarterly* 76 (April 1973): 361–83, argued that the lives of Texas slaves were "usually somewhat easier than that" of slaves in other southern states. Holbrook's argument, however, has been pretty thoroughly refuted by more recent works. Randolph B. Campbell, alone and in coauthorship with other scholars, has since published a profusion of articles on slave life and the institution of slavery in Texas. The most comprehensive of these works is his book-length *Empire for Slavery*. Campbell's work remains the cornerstone of understanding about Texas slavery, although some other scholarly endeavors add to this study by concentrating on particular regions, periods, or aspects of slavery. See for instance, Kenneth L. Brown, "Material Culture and Community Structure: The Slave and Tenant Community at Levi Jordan's Plantation, 1848–1892," in *Working toward Freedom: Slave Society and Domestic Economy in the American South*, ed. Larry E. Hudson Jr. (Rochester, N.Y.: University of Rochester Press, 1994); Tamara Miner Haygood, "Use and Distribution of Slave Labor in Harris County, Texas, 1836–1860," in *Black Dixie: Afro-Texan History and Culture in Houston*, ed. Howard Beeth and Cary D. Wintz (College Station: Texas A&M University Press, 1992); Thomas H. Smith, "African Americans in Dallas: From Slavery to Freedom," in *Dallas Reconsidered: Essays in Local History*, ed. Michael V. Hazel (Dallas: Three Forks Press, 1995); Treat, "William Goyens: Free Negro Entrepreneur"; Janis Hutchinson, "The Age-Sex Structure of the Slave Population in Harris County, Texas: 1850 and 1860," *American Journal of Physical Anthropology* 74 (October 1987): 231–38; T. Lindsay Baker, "More Than Just 'Possum 'n Taters: Texas African-American Foodways in the WPA Slave Narratives," in *Juneteenth Texas: Essays in African-American Folklore*, ed. Francis Edward Abernethy et al. (Denton: University of North Texas Press, 1996); and the chapter on blacks in Paul D. Lack, *The Texas Revolutionary Experience: A Political and Social History, 1835–1836* (College Station: Texas A&M University Press, 1992). William Dean Carrigan's, "Slavery on the Frontier: The Peculiar Institution in Central Texas," *Slavery and Abolition* 20 (August 1999): 63–86, is the only work to attempt to directly challenge Campbell's arguments by exploring the frontier edges of Texas in the 1850s and 1860s, arguing that access to Mexico and Indians in the West allowed slaves more of an escape route than in other southern states, thus somewhat altering the institution of slavery in Texas.

5. Williamson S. Oldham and George W. White, *A Digest of the General Statute Laws of the State of Texas . . .* (Austin: John Marshal, 1859), 26, 120, 225, and 504; Campbell, *Empire for Slavery*, 35–49, 112, 113; Haygood, "Use and Distribution of Slave Labor," 37; Peter W. Bardaglio, *Reconstructing the*

Household: Families, Sex, and the Law in the Nineteenth-Century South (Chapel Hill: University of North Carolina Press, 1995), 59, 64; Winegarten, *Black Texas Women*, 1–13; Elizabeth Fox-Genovese, *Within the Plantation Household: Black and White Women of the Old South* (Chapel Hill: University of North Carolina Press, 1988), 307.

6. Campbell, *Empire for Slavery*, 56; Boswell, *Her Act and Deed.*

7. Campbell, *Empire for Slavery*, 51; Winegarten, *Black Texas Women*, 16; Boswell, *Her Act and Deed*, 79–91; Malone, *Women on the Texas Frontier*, 47; Ellen Eslinger, "The Shape of Slavery on the Kentucky Frontier, 1775–1800," *Register of the Kentucky Historical Society* 92 (Winter 1994): 4–13; Joan E. Cashin, *A Family Venture: Men and Women on the Southern Frontier* (Baltimore: Johns Hopkins University Press, 1991), 59; Smith, "African Americans in Dallas," 124.

8. Eslinger, "The Shape of Slavery," 2–5; Campbell, *Empire for Slavery*, 51–56, 162; Cashin, *A Family Venture*, 32–70; Federal Writers' Project, *Slave Narratives: A Folk History of Slavery in the United States, from Interviews with Former Slaves—Texas Narratives*, vol. 3, part 2 (St. Clair Shores, Mich.: Scholarly Press, 1976), 124–25. Although Texas never passed a law making it illegal to teach a slave to read and write, the majority of southern states from which slaves moved had done so. Winegarten, *Black Texas Women*, 22. Some slaves had messages passed along by their masters (Cashin, *A Family Venture*, 70). Campbell and Pickens have published a letter from a wife to her husband separated during the Civil War. Even in this letter, however, it is unclear who actually wrote it and whether or not the husband would need to have someone read it to him. Randolph Campbell and Donald K. Pickens, "'My Dearest Husband': A Texas Slave's Love Letter, 1862," *Journal of Negro History* 65 (Fall 1980): 361–64.

9. Winegarten, *Black Texas Women*, 16–17; Malone, *Women on the Texas Frontier*, 47; Eslinger, "The Shape of Slavery," 4–13; Campbell, *Empire for Slavery*, 39, 46–48, 54; Brenda E. Stevenson, *Life in Black and White: Family and Community in the Slave South* (New York: Oxford University Press, 1996), 179–222; Federal Writers' Project, *Slave Narratives*, vol. 3, part 1, 27.

10. The interstate slave trade and possible "slave-breeding" is very controversial among historians. Most scholars still argue that male slaves were preferred in the interstate slave trade because of the heavier physical labor they could perform, thus leading to a slight male majority. For instance, see Stevenson, *Life in Black and White*, 175–84; and Cashin, *A Family Venture*, 50, 67. Ellen Eslinger's study of the Kentucky frontier found that there was a preference for younger slaves, but no preference for males over females. Eslinger, "The Shape of Slavery," 1–23. See also Boswell, *Her Act and Deed*. Frankel found similar patterns in Mississippi (Noralee Frankel, *Freedom's Women: Black Women and Families in Civil War Era Mississippi* [Bloomington: Indiana University Press, 1999], 2–3). Richard Lowe and Randolph Campbell have looked at slave population as a whole in Texas, and because the proportion of males and females and representation of ages is approximately the

same as in older southern states, they assume that the majority of slaves came with their owners to Texas and did not participate in a "slave-breeding" trade (Richard G. Lowe and Randolph B. Campbell, "The Slave-Breeding Hypothesis: A Demographic Comment on the 'Buying' and 'Selling' States," *Journal of Southern History* 42 [August 1976]: 401–12); Campbell, *Empire for Slavery*, 51.

11. Stephanie McCurry, *Masters of Small Worlds: Yeoman Households, Gender Relations, and the Political Culture of the Antebellum South Carolina Low Country* (New York: Oxford University Press, 1995), 50; Malone, *Women on the Texas Frontier*, 26–30, 42; Campbell, *Empire for Slavery*, 51. Women's lives, roles, and expectations within the system of slavery in the American South has generated much very good scholarship. Most of the general works on slave women also include Texas in the data, even scholarship on different areas of the South illuminate the ideals and realities that slave women took to Texas. For general works, see Deborah Gray White, *Ar'n't I a Woman? Female Slaves in the Plantation South* (New York: W. W. Norton, 1985); Jacqueline Jones, *Labor of Love, Labor of Sorrow: Black Women, Work, and the Family, from Slavery to the Present* (New York: Basic Books, 1985); Darlene Clark Hine and Kathleen Thompson, *A Shining Thread of Hope: The History of Black Women in America* (New York: Broadway Books, 1988). For general works incorporating a major discussion of African American women, see Fox-Genovese, *Within the Plantation Household*; and Sally G. McMillen, *Southern Women: Black and White in the Old South* (Arlington Heights, Ill.: Harlan Davidson, 1992). For works on slave women in specific southern places other than Texas that still shed light on slave women's lives, see Stevenson, *Life in Black and White*; Frankel, *Freedom's Women*; Victoria Bynum, *Unruly Women: The Politics of Social and Sexual Control in the Old South* (Chapel Hill: University of North Carolina Press, 1992); Patricia Morton, ed., *Discovering the Women in Slavery: Emancipating Perspectives on the American Past* (Athens: University of Georgia Press, 1996); and for frontier conditions, see especially Eslinger, "The Shape of Slavery."

12. Boswell, *Her Act and Deed*; Eslinger, "The Shape of Slavery," 1–23; Haygood, "Use and Distribution of Slave Labor," 39–49.

13. Jones, *Labor of Love, Labor of Sorrow*, 29–30; Stevenson, *Life in Black and White*, 192–97; White, *Ar'n't I a Woman?* 29; Malone, *Women on the Texas Frontier*, 31, 37; Frankel, *Freedom's Women*, 6; Hine and Thompson, *A Shining Thread of Hope*, 77; Winegarten, *Black Texas Women*, 17; McMillen, *Southern Women*, 12–47; Campbell, *Empire for Slavery*, 123–26; Fox-Genovese, *Within the Plantation Household*, 157–67; John B. Boles, *Black Southerners, 1619–1869* (Lexington: University Press of Kentucky, 1984); John Michael Vlach, *By the Work of Their Hands: Studies in Afro-American Folklife* (Charlottesville: University of Virginia Press, 1991), 76–81.

14. White, *Ar'n't I a Woman?* 142–60; Frankel, *Freedom's Women*, 6; Hine and Thompson, *Shining Thread of Hope*, 75–92; Cashin, *A Family Venture*, 68; Fox-Genovese, *Within the Plantation Household*, 167; Slave Schedules, Sev-

enth and Eighth Census of the United States (1850 and 1860), Texas, Colorado County.

15. Jones, *Labor of Love, Labor of Sorrow*, 17, 28, 38; Hine and Thompson, *Shining Thread of Hope*, 75; Stevenson, *Life in Black and White*, 187–93; Fox-Genovese, *Within the Plantation Household*, 177, 293; Federal Writers' Project, *Slave Narratives*, vol. 3, part 2, 135.

16. Narrative of James Green, February 8, 1938, in George P. Rawick, ed., *The American Slave: A Composite Autobiography* (Westport, Conn.: Greenwood Press, 1977). Reprinted in Bill Stein, ed., "The Slave Narratives of Colorado County," *Nesbitt Memorial Library Journal* 3 (January 1993): 12; Malone, *Women on the Texas Frontier*, 28, 42; Winegarten, *Black Texas Women*, 27–30; White, *Ar'n't I a Woman*, 28–46; Bardaglio, *Reconstructing the Household*, 49–59; Hine and Thompson, *Shining Thread of Hope*, 94–99; Darlene Clark Hine, "Female Slave Resistance: The Economics of Sex," *Western Journal of Black Studies* 3 (Summer 1979): 123–27; Stevenson, *Life in Black and White*, 239–46; Boles, *Black Southerners*, 132; McMillen, *Southern Women*, 22–25. "Whether or not slave women desired relationships with white men was immaterial, the conventional wisdom was that black women were naturally promiscuous, and thus desired such connections" (White, *Ar'n't I a Woman*, 38).

17. "Narrative of James Green," 12. Malone, *Women on the Texas Frontier*, 28–43; Campbell, *Empire for Slavery*, 201; White, *Ar'n't I a Woman*, 28–46; Bardaglio, *Reconstructing the Household*, 49–59; Hine and Thompson, *Shining Thread of Hope*, 94–99; Stevenson, *Life in Black and White*, 239–46; Boles, *Black Southerners*, 132; McMillen, *Southern Women*, 22–25; George C. Rable, *Civil Wars: Women and the Crisis of Southern Nationalism* (Urbana: University of Illinois Press, 1989), 36.

18. Malone, *Women on the Texas Frontier*, 47; Hine and Thompson, *Shining Thread of Hope*, 79; Stevenson, *Life in Black and White*, 209, 226; Boles, *Black Southerners*, 90.

19. White, *Ar'n't I a Woman?* 98; Malone, *Women on the Texas Frontier*, 41; Winegarten, *Black Texas Women*, 22–24.

20. "Narrative of James Green," 12; White, *Ar'n't I a Woman?* 68–69, 98–105, 156–57; Winegarten, *Black Texas Women*, 27–28; Malone, *Women on the Texas Frontier*, 38–41; Catherine Clinton, *Tara Revisited: Women, War, and the Plantation Legend* (New York: Abbeville Press, 1995), 31–34; Frankel, *Freedom's Women*, 13; Hine and Thompson, *Shining Thread of Hope*, 79–81; Brown, "Material Culture and Community Structure, 97.

21. Campbell, *Empire for Slavery*, 118; White, *Ar'n't I a Woman?* 97–101, 149–55; Winegarten, *Black Texas Women*; Eslinger, "The Shape of Slavery," 19; Jones, *Labor of Love, Labor of Sorrow*, 31–36; Stevenson, *Life in Black and White*, 160; Federal Writers' Project, *Slave Narratives*, vol. 3, part 2, 246.

22. Death of the master was the most dangerous time in a slave community. Marriage was another. At these times, slaves were split up on the basis of fairness to "heirs" and not always on the basis of slave families. Malone, *Women on the Texas Frontier*, 41–48; Winegarten, *Black Texas Women*, 16–17; Stevenson, *Life in Black and White*, 209–24; Jane Turner Censer, *North Car-*

olina Planters and Their Children, 1800–1860 (Baton Rouge: Louisiana State University Press, 1984), 140; Rable, *Civil Wars*, 39. In addition to being separated by sale, there was the likelihood of being separated by being "hired out" while the estate was settled. Campbell, *Empire for Slavery*, 83, 161; Randolph Campbell, "The Slave Hire System in Texas," *American Historical Review* 93 (1988): 107–14.

23. The mother/child relationship was the most recognized throughout the South. White, *Ar'n't I a Woman?* 132–34, 159; Stevenson, *Life in Black and White*, 213–22; Ann Patton Malone, "Searching for the Family and Household Structure of Rural Louisiana, 1810–1864," *Louisiana History* 28 (Fall 1987): 357–79; McMillen, *Southern Women*, 12–47; Campbell, *Empire for Slavery*, 161; Malone, *Women on the Texas Frontier*, 41; Boswell, *Her Act and Deed*; Fox-Genovese, *Within the Plantation Household*, 322.

24. Campbell, *Empire for Slavery*, 92–93, 164; Censer, *North Carolina Planters and Their Children;* Randolph Campbell, "The Slave Hire System in Texas," *American Historical Review* 93 (1988): 107–14; Haygood, "Use and Distribution of Slave Labor," 44; Malone, *Women on the Texas Frontier*, 38–50; Fox-Genovese, *Within the Plantation Household*, 322; Stevenson, *Life in Black and White*, 213–24.

25. Winegarten, *Black Texas Women*, 16–17; Boswell, *Her Act and Deed*, 79–91. Campbell shows that slaves were hired out, sold, and mortgaged for extra cash. He has documented one case of a six-week-old female being "mortgaged" (Campbell, *Empire for Slavery*, 164). There was no legal provision in Texas prohibiting separating slave mother and child (Malone, *Women on the Texas Frontier*, 50).

26. Regarding separation of families and the desire to reunite them after emancipation, see Winegarten, *Black Texas Women*, 42–45; Barry A. Crouch, "The Freedmen's Bureau in Colorado County, Texas, 1865–1868, Part 3," *Nesbitt Memorial Library Journal* 8 (January 1998): 3–5; James Smallwood, "Black Freedwomen after Emancipation: The Texas Experience," *Prologue* 27 (1995): 303–17; Peter Bardaglio, "The Children of Jubilee: African American Childhood in Wartime," in *Divided Houses: Gender and the Civil War*, ed. Catherine Clinton and Nina Silber (New York: Oxford University Press, 1992), 226; Laura F. Edwards, *Gendered Strife and Confusion: The Political Culture of Reconstruction* (Urbana: University of Illinois Press, 1997), 46; Hine and Thompson, *Shining Thread of Hope*, 148–51; Tera W. Hunter, *To 'Joy My Freedom: Southern Black Women's Lives and Labors after the Civil War* (Cambridge, Mass.: Harvard University Press, 1997), 40; Jones, *Labor of Love, Labor of Sorrow*, 55, 78; Leslie A. Schwalm, *A Hard Fight for We: Women's Transition from Slavery to Freedom in South Carolina* (Urbana: University of Illinois Press, 1997), 151–55, 209, 267; Cheryll Ann Cody, "Sale and Separation: Four Crises for Enslaved Women on the Ball Plantations, 1764–1854," in *Working toward Freedom*, ed. Hudson, 119–42.

27. Campbell, *Empire for Slavery*, 118; Winegarten, *Black Texas Women*, 22–23; Boswell, *Her Act and Deed*.

28. Winegarten, *Black Texas Women*, 22–24; Malone, *Women on the Texas*

Frontier, 30, 52; Stevenson, *Life in Black and White,* 228; Frankel, *Freedom's Women,* 11–13; White, *Ar'n't I a Woman?* 133.

29. Stevenson, *Life in Black and White,* 160, 221–28; White, *Ar'n't I a Woman?* 151–57; Malone, *Women on the Texas Frontier,* 47.

30. Campbell, *Empire for Slavery,* 156; Malone, *Women on the Texas Frontier,* 48; White, *Ar'n't I a Woman?* 133; Jones, *Labor of Love, Labor of Sorrow,* 32; Hine and Thompson, *Shining Thread of Hope,* 83. Stevenson has challenged some of the arguments that slave families were mostly nuclear units, but clearly argues that families were stable no matter what the structure (Stevenson, *Life in Black and White,* 160–62, 223).

31. Malone, *Women on the Texas Frontier,* 33, 47–50; Winegarten, *Black Texas Women,* 23–24; Campbell, *Empire for Slavery,* 153–76; Fox-Genovese, *Within the Plantation Household,* 35–49, 299; Stevenson, *Life in Black and White,* 209; Clinton, *Tara Revisited,* 31–34; Jones, *Labor of Love, Labor of Sorrow,* 14.

32. Winegarten, *Black Texas Women,* 18; Haygood, "Use and Distribution of Slave Labor"; Smith, "African Americans in Dallas."

33. Winegarten, *Black Texas Women,* 18; Malone, *Women on the Texas Frontier,* 37; Campbell, *Empire for Slavery,* 118–19, 131; Hine and Thompson, *Shining Thread of Hope,* 75; Frankel, *Freedom's Women,* 6–29; Cashin, *A Family Venture,* 68; Fox-Genovese, *Within the Plantation Household,* 172; Jones, *Labor of Love, Labor of Sorrow,* 13–19; White, *Ar'n't I a Woman?* 129.

34. Winegarten, *Black Texas Women,* 24–25, 30–31; Boswell, *Her Act and Deed;* Charles William Tait Papers, Center for American History, University of Texas.

35. Baker, "More Than Just 'Possum 'n Taters," 96–104; Winegarten, *Black Texas Women,* 17–18; Campbell, *Empire for Slavery,* 160; Malone, *Women on the Texas Frontier,* 33; Clinton, *Tara Revisited,* 31–35; Frankel, *Freedom's Women,* 1–7; Hine and Thompson, *Shining Thread of Hope,* 78; Fox-Genovese, *Within the Plantation Household,* 161–77; Jones, *Labor of Love, Labor of Sorrow,* 28, 36; Stevenson, *Life in Black and White,* 161.

36. Baker, "More Than Just 'Possum 'n Taters," 108; Campbell, *Empire for Slavery,* 134–36; Jones, *Labor of Love, Labor of Sorrow,* 36; Fox-Genovese, *Within the Plantation Household,* 161.

37. Campbell, *Empire for Slavery,* 136, 151, 160; Stevenson, *Life in Black and White,* 192; Baker, "More Than Just 'Possum 'n Taters," 96–104; Vlach, *Black Craft Traditions in Texas,* 76–81.

38. Winegarten, *Black Texas Women,* 19; Cashin, *A Family Venture,* 72; Fox-Genovese, *Within the Plantation Household,* 150; Rhonda Ragsdale, "Chains to Change: African American Women in Cooke County, Texas, 1860–1880," presented at the Texas State Historical Association Annual Meeting, March 4, 2006, Austin, Texas, 3 (paper in possession of author).

39. Campbell, *Empire for Slavery,* 151.

40. Winegarten, *Black Texas Women,* 22–25; Campbell, *Empire for Slavery,* 153–76; White, *Ar'n't I a Woman?* 119–40, 159; Stevenson, *Life in Black and White,* 222.

41. Winegarten, *Black Texas Women,* 24–25; Malone, *Women on the Texas Frontier,* 37; White, *Ar'n't I a Woman?* 96; Frankel, *Freedom's Women,* 161.

42. White, *Ar'n't I a Woman?* 97–98; Winegarten, *Black Texas Women,* 26–27; Fox-Genovese, *Within the Plantation Household,* 322; Stevenson, *Life in Black and White,* 192–93.

43. Winegarten, *Black Texas Women,* 24–25; Malone, *Women on the Texas Frontier,* 30; Marie Jenkins Schwartz, *Born in Bondage: Growing Up Enslaved in the Antebellum South* (Cambridge, Mass.: Harvard University Press, 2000), 19–47.

44. Winegarten, *Black Texas Women,* 24–25; Stevenson, *Life in Black and White,* 250; Schwartz, *Born in Bondage,* 48–74; Bardaglio, *Reconstructing the Household,* 216; Federal Writers' Project, *Slave Narratives,* vol. 3, part 2, 44–45.

45. Winegarten, *Black Texas Women,* 17–18, 24–25; Malone, *Women on the Texas Frontier,* 52; Frankel, *Freedom's Women,* 161; White, *Ar'n't I a Woman?* 129–133; Stevenson, *Life in Black and White,* 160, 221–28; Clinton, *Tara Revisited,* 34; Jones, *Labor of Love, Labor of Sorrow,* 31–32; Hine and Thompson, *Shining Thread of Hope,* 77.

46. Winegarten, *Black Texas Women,* 20–22; Boles, *Black Southerners,* 140–46.

47. Winegarten, *Black Texas Women,* 21–22; Donald G. Mathews, *Religion in the Old South* (Chicago: University of Chicago Press, 1977).

48. Brown, "Material Culture," 110–16; Malone, *Women on the Texas Frontier,* 30–31; Winegarten, *Black Texas Women,* 20–21; Stevenson, *Life in Black and White,* 228; Campbell, *Empire for Slavery,* 123.

49. Campbell, *Empire for Slavery,* 231–51.

JAMES M. SMALLWOOD
and BARRY A. CROUCH

2. Texas Freedwomen during Reconstruction, 1865–1874

Although much as been written on varied aspects of Reconstruction, until recently little in-depth research has appeared in print regarding the lives of freedwomen in Texas after the Civil War; it is an oversight that needs to be corrected.[1] At the end of the Civil War approximately 85,000 to 90,000 slave women resided in Texas, as did only a few free black women, nearly 150, who were forced to live with most of the constraints of slavery. But on "Juneteenth"—June 19, still celebrated by blacks in the state—General Gordon Granger, speaking in Galveston, read the official Emancipation Proclamation for Texas. The bondspeople were supposedly freed, although some slaveholders worked their chattels for years after Granger's announcement. Census figures for 1860 divulged that 182,921 African Americans resided in the Lone Star State, with women numbering 91,551 (approximately 50.1 percent).[2] Questions arise. What did freedom mean to black women? How did they adjust? How did conditions change for the women and for their families? How did they make social and economic adjustments? How did whites react? How did black women deal with white attempts to thwart their aspirations?

Allen Trelease, in *White Terror*, has been among those who have noted what freed people wanted after emancipation. Generally, they expected the same freedoms that Anglos enjoyed, with similar prerogatives and opportunities. Among other things, educated blacks wanted full and immediate political and civil rights, while the masses wanted land redistribution and educational opportunity. African Americans— women as well as men—also hoped that emancipation meant a new home, a new job, a new social life, complete religious freedom, and the right of unrestricted travel: to seek better employment or to locate lost family members. They desired to have legal marriages, and sought family stability. Emancipation had yet another definition for women who had been field hands. Many believed that they, like white mistresses, should now be exempt from field labor; that they should engage in housework only, reserving free time for rearing children, for visiting friends and family, and for shopping. Female domestics felt the same way.[3]

Some freedwomen allegedly refused to work outside the home. They spent so much time in town shopping that they reportedly "enraged their husbands." Perhaps they were like Cassie Middleton's mother who now chose to remain in the family home—in Jasper County—cooking and making home manufactures. So many black women quit the fields that they drew vociferous complaints from employers, mostly yeomen farmers and planters who went before the Freedmen's Bureau agents, trying to pressure them to force black women to work.[4]

Typically, when women first heard about emancipation, they thought not of themselves but of their children. On gaining their freedom, some mothers immediately began planning for their offspring, wanting them to have the same benefits as whites, including the right to an education and to be exempt from work. Some even thought of simple things like dress. They wanted their children to dress the same way as free whites.[5] The reaction of Harriet, a domestic slave hired out to Amelia Barr of Austin, was perhaps typical. After the local sheriff read General Granger's proclamation, Amelia informed Harriet that she was free. Whereupon Harriet "darted to her child, and throwing it high, shrieked hysterically, 'Tamar, you are free. You are free, Tamar! She did not at the supreme moment think of herself. Freedom was for her child; she looked in its face, at its hands, at its feet. It was a new baby to her—a free baby."[6] Then Barr said, "Harriet, you are free [—] from this hour [you are] as free as I am. You can stay here or go."[7] Harriet quickly agreed to stay and to work for wages of six dollars per month, but like most other slaves, daily contacts with an ex-master or mistress who expected total, undue deference troubled Harriet. Further, Harriet reconsidered Barr's offer of wages, after which Harriet asked for eight dollars a month. The ex-slave believed that she was worth more now that she was a free laborer. When Barr refused the raise, Harriet left Barr's home three days later to find a new employer.[8]

For some freedwomen, as well as for freedmen, emancipation became a time of confusion. One slave report, for example, from the James Davis plantation in San Jacinto County, held that "there was lots of crying and weeping when they [slaves] were set free. Lot's [*sic*] of them didn't want to be free because they knew nothing and had nowhere to go."[9] Minerva Bendy, a slave in Woodville, Texas, remembered that she was at first upset by freedom because she was just turned out with "no food, no nothing."[10] On other plantations and farms, some ex-slaves, shocked and unsure about their new status, still asked for passes when they left.[11]

For most slaves, however, joy replaced temporary confusion. In rural and urban areas, scenes of jubilation became common as the new freedpeople alternately sang, danced, and prayed. Some women expressed joy simply because they believed that emancipation meant an end to physical punishment.[12] As Sarah Ford commented, "We sure were happy because the bright light done come and there was no more whippings."[13] As Margrett Nillin put it, "In slavery I owned nothing and never owned anything. In freedom I own a home and raise a family. All this cause me worriment and in slavery I had no worriment, but I'll take the freedom."[14] Although most African Americans wanted to celebrate their new condition immediately after learning about emancipation, they had to exercise care, lest they upset whites, many of whom were prone to violence. For example, in Huntsville during a celebration, some local whites rode into the midst of a jubilee, and one Anglo who wielded a knife disemboweled a freedwoman whose body was then pitched into a wagon and hauled away.[15]

On gaining emancipation, most women, like Harriet, left their old master. Most could not bear the often-painful contact with ex-masters because it reminded the ex-slaves of bondage. Moreover, like Mistress Barr of Austin, most ex-masters demanded total deference. For example, Harriet Caulfield's owner told his slaves that they could stay but that if they did not "mind" him, he would give them whippings just as in the slave days. Hearing that, Harriet and her family struck out for Waco where they intended to find jobs that would be free of physical punishment. In Tyler, freedpeople Frank and Miranda, husband and wife, and Amanda belonged to local Confederate hero George Chilton. Although they had apparently been treated well, all three chose to leave. According to Chilton's son Horace, most area slaves left, for to stay reminded them too much of slavery. After traveling south to a farm about 15 miles from Tyler, the three contracted with a new employer. However, some slaves happily stayed with their former masters. Evaline Groesbeck, aged thirteen in 1865, had belonged to a Doctor Phillips of Austin almost since her birth. She grew up with Phillips's children, was well cared for and well clothed, and was educated by her master. Understandably, Groesbeck decided to stay with Phillips after emancipation and happily worked for him as a domestic.[16] Likewise, Betty Bormer, ex-slave of M. T. Johnson of Tarrant County, remembered that her ex-master tried to help the newly emancipated freedpeople. He gave a cow or mule to each family who left, and he hired for wages those who stayed. Betty Bormer chose to stay and to work as a nanny for Johnson's children. Yet another woman, Millie Forward, remembered that after emancipation she stayed with her ex-master who treated his workers well. For youngsters like Millie, he established a night school and taught it himself.[17]

Not all slaves were freed in 1865, and women were no exception. A young girl, Tempie Cummins, was a slave on the William Neyland place near Jasper, Texas, but the owner did not free his slaves in June of 1865. Doubtless he wanted to wait at least until his crops were in. But Tempie's mother overheard Neyland telling his wife about General Granger's proclamation. Tempie's mother then quickly spread the word to all in the slave quarters, whereupon all of them prepared to leave. Neyland became so enraged when he learned that his bondspeople were leaving that he shot at and tried to kill Tempie and her mother for letting the secret out. Nevertheless, all ex-slaves escaped.[18]

In a similar case, the owner of Nancy Hardeman told all his slaves that if they left, they would starve; hence, Nancy's mother told the ex-slaveholder that she was taking her children and leaving, anyway, saying that "if we starve, we'll starve together."[19] In yet another case, "Marse Tom" of Navarro County wanted to keep the underaged son of "Mammy," but she ran to her boy to warn him and to tell him to travel to the nearby place of "Miss Mary," a white woman who told every slave on "marse Tom's" place that they could stay with her until "We figurates a way for you [all] . . . to make your own way."[20] Still, many slaveholders bragged to the editor of *Flake's Daily Bulletin* in Houston that they were still holding slaves as late as December of 1865.[21]

In Bowie County in far northeastern Texas, Joseph Hiram testified in July of 1867 that a white ex-mistress, Jessie Paxton, held his sister Mary York unlawfully in a state of slavery. The same month

another Bowie County African American, Amanda Hayes, testified
that plantation owner William Hayes took her son Henry on a cattle
drive from Bowie County to Johnson County but did not free him
after the return trip. And, once again, in Bowie County yet another
freedwoman complained the same year that her daughter was still being held in illegal bondage.[22] From Austin, Freedmen's Bureau agent
Byron Porter complained that Washington Ake and his wife lost all
four of their children—Isaac, Francis, Mary, and Henry, the eldest being only eleven years old—to John E. Chisholm who refused to release
them after emancipation. The kidnapper moved from the state capital to Grayson County in North Texas where he held the children for
more than eighteen months after Juneteenth.[23]

Likewise, in Wharton County, a white, W. Brooks, held the wife
and the children of Simon Brooks. Agent Porter, then in Houston,
had to intervene to secure their release. An ex-Confederate major,
Matt Gaud of Rusk County kept his slaves and forced them to toil on
his plantation for a full year after Juneteenth. In July of 1867, a bureau
agent in Austin reported that he had just recently rescued two underaged freedgirls from planter William Greenwood. No one released the
slaves of Alex Simpson, a horse thief, until he was hanged in 1868, after
which authorities searched his place and found men, women, boys, and
girls, all chained to prevent any escapes.[24] In a most extreme case, Katie
Darling's owner kept her enslaved for six full years before Darling's
brother secured her release. Katie later said that "When Massa come
home from the War[,] he wants to let us loose, but Missy wouldn't do
it . . . Missy whip me after the War just like she did before."[25] Such
reports were prevalent throughout the rest of the state.[26]

Two particular sources of confusion, which some whites exploited,
were the harsh Texas apprenticeship statute and the Contract Labor
Code—two of the state's black codes. In October of 1865, the Texas legislature passed a child apprenticeship law. It assured that whites would
control the segment of the African American labor pool that was underaged. It provided that parents could bind their young to employers
until minors reached twenty-one years of age or until children married. If fourteen years or older, a minor could, without parental consent, apprentice himself or herself. Further, white county judges could
also apprentice youngsters. All that was necessary under the law for
such a maneuver was to place a notice in county newspapers. Because
most ex-slaves remained illiterate, they often learned of the apprentice-

ships of their young only after the courts had already acted. Such a black code, many observers believed, created a "second slavery."[27]

The Anglo practice of forcefully separating African American children from their parents became an obvious factor in the process of family disintegration. Possibilities of sexual exploitation of freedgirls drove many Anglos on, as did hopes of securing a cheap source of labor. They refused to free youngsters when their parents were freed. They exploited the apprenticeship laws or simply resorted to kidnapping.[28]

Freedwomen Margaret Heard and Nancy Sneed, both from Travis County, lost children when several whites took the children away under false pretenses. The whites took the children to deep East Texas and refused to let them return home. From throughout the state, bureau agents reported similar cases as they complained about the apprenticeship code.[29]

Other black codes framed in 1865 also entrapped women. The most heinous was the aforementioned Contract Labor Code. It meant to ensure, as white politician W. C. Dalrymple said, that the ex-slaves would remain "hewers of wood and drawers of water."[30] Thus did the Texas legislature pass a labor law designed to "freeze" ex-slaves into a system of indentured servitude. Under the law, after "voluntarily" choosing an employer, laborers had to sign written contracts if their work lasted longer than one month. Once workers signed agreements, they could not leave their employers (new "masters") during the contract period. The law further cautioned laborers to act politely, to obey orders, and to take care of all livestock, equipment, and tools belonging to the employers, who could deduct "reasonable" sums from wages if their property were damaged. Virtually given judicial powers, landlords could "hold court" and impose fines on any workers guilty of disobedience and on those who lost work time because of unapproved absence. The new employers could also administer corporal punishment, as they deemed necessary. Of course, this law affected women as well as men because an agreement with any male head of a family bound all family members. Women who were family heads had to sign contracts just as men did. Further, many employers preferred that freedwoman sign contracts, apparently believing that the women were more reliable than their husbands or brothers.[31]

Often, employers did not pay women and girls who were under contract. Mike Moore contracted with Huntsville freedgirl Mary Hunter in 1868 and took her to his home in Tyler. She worked as a domestic, but her dissatisfaction came fast because Moore worked her but refused to pay her. Moore would neither honor the contract by paying the young woman her due, nor would he release her. He kept Mary in illegal bondage until mid-1868. Ultimately the girl's mother, who still lived in Huntsville, complained to a Freedmen's Bureau agent. He secured the girl's release and her return to her mother.[32]

Other cases were more extreme. One D. Sanders of Robinson County forced Josephine Wesley of Millican to sign a labor contract. Once she began work, he frequently beat her and cut into her ribs, sides, and legs with a leather strap, assaulting her apparently because he believed that she should work harder. Then he tried to kill her by slashing her throat with a knife. He next told her as she was recovering from her wounds that if he caught her trying to run away, he would shoot her. Only through an act of tremendous courage did Wesley escape. She went to the nearest bureau agent and received protection after complaining about her attacker. On yet another occasion, ex-slave Lucy Thomas reported that in Harrison County the widow of one "Colonel" Haggerty kept a freedgirl chained to a loom for more than one year after emancipation, giving her no contract and continuing to treat her as a slave. Such exploitation eventually forced the bureau to act. In 1867, its higher officials told the field agents to void unfair contract or apprentice codes and to frame new contracts that would be fair to black men, women, boys, and girls alike.[33]

As late as 1880, many whites were still refusing to pay the crop shares that freedwomen and freedmen had coming. Louisiana freedman Henry Adams toured East Texas and reported that "I have seen colored children barefooted, half naked[,] and even starved on their way to school . . . the white people rob the colored people out of two-thirds of what they make . . . from the mouth of the Red River to Jefferson, Texas, no difference can be seen." Continuing, Adams related that he asked black Texans, "don't you live well?" They told him "No, the whites take all we make and if we say anything about our rights they beat us."[34]

In addition to the problem of defrauding the freedpeople, blacks, including women, had to suffer much violence at the hands of whites, violence that could spring forth at any time. For example, the domestic servant Lucy Grimes of Harrison County had a particularly brutal death in 1866. Two white men alleged that Grimes's young son had committed theft of money and demanded that Lucy punish him. Grimes said no. She explained that he was too young to even know what he did; he only played with the money as a child would a toy. Refusing to accept Lucy's appeal, the two brigands seized her, took her to a wooded area outside Marshall, stripped her, possibly raped her, and then beat her to death. The killers went unpunished for their gruesome deed because a local judge flatly refused to hear a case brought by a black person, who in this case happened to be Lucy's oldest son. About the same time, two ex-Confederates from Smith County beat a black woman to death but went free because the only witnesses were freedpeople; the judge in the case simply would not accept their testimony.[35]

Freedmen's Bureau records are replete with white-on-black violence during Reconstruction. Consider, for example, the action of James Wise of Houston, a white who was convicted of whipping and gouging the eyes of freedwoman Emily Graves. The white woman Margaret Jones, also of Houston, was convicted for whipping Eliza Elders and then pounding the woebegone freedwoman with stock wood and a shovel. In yet another case, one in which, inexplicably, no legal action was taken, John Fogarty of Limestone County—whom one bureau agent called "an inhuman monster"—cut off the ears of Minerva Maid and then set her on fire, burning her arms "to a crisp." A man only known as Jones assaulted and tried to rape freedwoman Jenny Goodfellow, but he was not successful in his attempt, perhaps because he was impotent and could not perform the deed.[36] More serious, on one occasion in mid-1867, the desperado Elisha Guest, who was drunk at the time, attacked a freedwoman who was "in a family way[,] cut out her womb with its living contents [still inside,] and exhibited [the fetus to others] in his drunken glee."[37]

Yet another account of a gruesome crime against freedwomen occurred in the spring of 1869. Six members of the Bob Lee gang accosted freedman Jerimiah Everhart in his rural home in Grayson County. The pillagers took the freedman's six-gun and a small amount of money. Then, while Everhart's family looked on, the villains calmly shot the man to death. They next turned to Everhart's young daughter, apparently a comely girl, whom they savaged. All six men—Dick Johnson, Simp Dixon, William Penn, and Dow Witt, along with men known only as Chase and Clark—viciously had at the girl, raping her repeatedly until they were totally spent and could no longer perform, and they did so "in the most brutal manner[,] each and every one of them participating in this inhuman act."[38] Notably the man who reported

the murder and the multiple rapes was none other than freedman
A. M. Bryant of Grayson County, a leader of his people who had just
returned from Austin where he had been a delegate to the Texas Con-
stitutional Convention.[39] Similar cases of murders and rapes of freedwomen became commonplace in Reconstruction Texas.

Freedwomen, like the freedmen, were also forced to contend with
organized terrorist attacks. Klan-like terrorist groups began organizing
in East-Northeast Texas as early as 1865. Shortly after the war, Colonel
George A. Custer was assigned a command that included much of settled Texas. He told of a "brotherhood" of whites in Freestone County
that had sworn not to allow blacks to be employed in their county, that
vowed to whip any freedpeople who tried to contract with whites, and
that also planned to whip any whites who contracted with the ex-slaves.
By the end of 1866, there were at least seventy-eight Klan-like terrorist
groups in the settled portion of Texas, and they targeted black women
as well as black men; the groups had no gender-related mercy when
they dealt out their savagery. For example, in Smith County, Klansmen
gathered late on most nights to attack the homes of the area's freedpeople. They robbed the homes and gave both men and women floggings,
sometimes not stopping until their arms became tired. They showed
the female sex no more mercy than they granted the men.[40]

As well, outlaw gangs flourished in post–Civil War Texas, and
many of those groups posed as defenders of the "Lost Cause," helped
the Klansmen control the blacks, and also plundered black homes,
while raping and killing an untold number of freedwomen and freedgirls. The more infamously noted desperados included Cullen Baker,
Ben Bickerstaff, Bob Lee, Pomp Duty, Elisha Guest, and "Indian" Bill
English. All were known as "nigger killers."[41]

Daily, it seemed, black women faced a variety of forms of intimidation and violence. For example, in Tyler on July 19, 1868, a race-related
altercation took place on a Sunday morning just after both a white and
black church ended services. A local white congregation met a local
black congregation on a sidewalk. When neither party would give way,
tempers erupted, the result being that two women, one white, one
black, ended up wrestling in the street and ruining their clothes. Soon,
the white George Kennedy intervened. He beat the freedwoman with
his cane while shouting, "Now, God Damned you, after this [the beat-
ing he was giving her] give the sidewalk to the ladies."[42]

In the midst of trying to eke out a living and to fight off white attempts to reenslave or even kill them, many blacks, the women in par-

ticular, tried with great difficulty to locate lost family members after emancipation. However, only a fortunate few had success, they became the exception, not the rule. One African American woman from East Texas, known only as Judy, sought out bureau agent W. B. Pease in Houston in 1867 and inquired about her children who were sold to a white man named James McCoy in 1853. After the war, from 1865 to 1867, Judy tried in vain to locate her children and appealed to the agent as a last "resort" to find her offspring. Unfortunately, she was unsuccessful. The same year, a woman from Galveston, Petsey Ball, asked Agent Abner Doubleday to help find her husband whom her ex-master had sold in 1849. Doubleday had no success.[43]

Yet another woman, Lucinda Ott, who had been taken illegally from Louisiana to California after the war, came to Columbus, Texas, in 1867. She was searching for her three children who had been left in the Lone Star State. From most areas of Texas came similar stories about women who sought in vain to find lost family members. In one particularly pathetic case, a new owner brought Julia Washington from West Virginia to Galveston during the war, while her husband, mother, and two children had been sold to different owners, all of whom lived near Springfield, West Virginia. Washington appealed to Agent Doubleday to help find her kin. Ultimately the story had a happy ending; Doubleday was successful this time. In 1867, Julia was reunited with her family. Mary Armstrong was also successful. After searching for two years, she found her mother in Warton, where the two, when united, alternately sang and cried.[44] Thus the more fortunate women located and were reunited with their lost families, while those whose kin were lost forever evidently learned to live with their emotional pain.

The importance of finding family members notwithstanding, the most urgent problem the new freedwomen faced was supporting themselves and their children, a task compounded by gender discrimination. Women who after emancipation were forced to continue to work alongside men in the fields suffered wage differentials. The pay of male hands ranged from $2 to $15 a month while women received from $2 to $10. Fluctuations depended on availability of and need for labor, on the national and regional economy, and on the amount of material subsistence that landlords constantly tried to reduce without increasing the pay they gave workers. In the system, men averaged about $5 per month and women, $3, although all sorts of fluctuations continued to exist. One planter near Austin, for example, paid a freedwoman who was head of a household $10 per month and also gave her a place to stay, but she paid back $2 per month to feed her three children. Additionally, the woman clothed her own family and paid all family medical bills.[45] Freedwomen who worked in the grain and lumber industry in East Texas received approximately the same pay, $10 per month. However, even in these industries there was discrimination. Men doing the same jobs earned an average of $14 per month.[46]

Women who worked the fields, either with menfolk or alone, had one other great disadvantage. They and their families became the victims of greedy landlords. After the Texas legislature passed the black codes, many owners exploited both the labor code and the vagrancy code. In Harrison County, by 1867 many African American women worked as sharecroppers, and their employers promised them shares at the end of harvest. But once they had the crops in, owners whipped the women and forced them from the land. In Grayson County the same thing happened, with blacks who refused to leave being murdered. And, of course, once freedpeople were off the land, owners simply asserted that they had just "run off" and had, therefore—under the labor code—forfeited all their rights to the crops. Sometimes, landowners even hired outlaws to run the freedmen off. James McCleery, a bureau agent who toured Northeast Texas in 1869, asserted that the above pattern prevailed in literally "hundreds of places."[47] Other reports from across the state confirmed McCleery's account. Moreover, even those who stayed on the job and received crop shares were often victimized by unscrupulous landlords who inflated charges in account books to such an extent that uneducated workers ended a season owing more than they had owed at the beginning. Thus did employers force freedwomen, along with their men, into the economics of peonage, into a type of debt slavery.[48]

Regarding their workaday world, freedwomen and girls in rural areas engaged in strenuous labor much like their menfolk. Women helped their husbands or fathers plant, cultivate, and harvest crops. Most also performed all household chores. They supervised less strenuous farm work such as milking, feeding chickens and hogs, and gathering eggs. Women made clothing, dried and preserved fruits and vegetables, made molasses and preserves, and collected nuts. Young girls, particularly if they attended school, found themselves exempt from some of the hard work; yet they still had light daily chores such as cleaning house, milking, churning, and gathering eggs. Many older girls performed all these tasks and helped with all other farm work as well.[49]

Freedwomen in both rural and urban areas who engaged in domestic work received salaries roughly the equivalent of, or perhaps a little higher than, female field-workers. Domestics' pay ranged from $2 to $10 per month, but the average was closer to $5. Again, employers constantly tried to reduce the pay of household workers to keep them on the subsistence level. Issabella Boyd remembered that in her first job after emancipation she continued to work as a cook for $5 a month for her old master, Gus Wood of Beaumont. Yet pay for domestics as well as field hands suffered wide fluctuations. Harriet Barrett, who had belonged to Steve Glass of Walker County, also stayed and worked as a cook, but she received only $2.50 a month. Because pay was low, many domestics took full advantage of the "pan," which became a Southern tradition—one practiced by whites who sympathized with the blacks' plight—that lasted well into the twentieth century. Domestics cooked as much food as the employer would permit, and usually they were allowed to take the "pan" of leftovers home. For many black families, food acquired in this way was their major source of nourishment.[50] On his plantation near Austin, Thomas Blackshear originally paid his household help $10 per month plus room and board. But in 1868, while bemoaning his declining economic position, he cut domestic wages to $5 per month shortly before he made a $1,000 addition to his law library. Needless to say, all the women working for Blackshear left him after he cut wages, but they had recently signed new contracts (under pressure), and authorities forced them to return to fulfill their "agreements."[51] Despite low pay, domestics abounded. By 1870, 10,603 women worked as domestics, and almost all were black. The numbers increased in subsequent years. For example, in Dallas, black women comprised 104 of the 130 women working as domestics as of 1870. The total number grew to 527 by 1880, and black women still made up the great majority.[52]

Some women who worked as domestics after the war evidently began testing their new freedom by becoming more assertive with white employers. Many apparently wanted a new working relationship, one with at least tacit recognition of their freedom. Some, however, ran afoul of Southern customs requiring black deference. "The Negroes [servants] are becoming insufferable," Amelia Barr of Austin complained in 1867. They "demand a bedroom in the house and a seat at

your table."[53] Consequently, some white women employed white domestics, but they paid dearly for their choice. Barr hired a white but
had to pay her $20 a month, a sum more than three times what she had
offered Harriet, her slave-days domestic, to stay on.[54]

In urban areas, particularly, women who could not secure work
as domestics faced a dire existence unless they had husbands or other
male kinsmen to care for them. An exception to that rule involved
the laundresses; many women took work in the home, washing and
ironing for more affluent whites. Or they would do their work in the
homes of whites where they might also serve as cooks and nannies.
Between 1870 and 1880, the number of laundresses in Texas grew
from 1,107 to 4,643, with the great majority being black. By the latter
date, in Dallas, 70 percent of the black wives washed and ironed for
whites. In some towns, black laundresses developed a sense of solidarity and took action, like those in Galveston who struck for a pay raise
to $1.50 per day. Laundresses there also protested because, increasingly,
Chinese immigrants were cutting into their business. A few freedwomen, luckier than most, secured work as seamstresses who either
remained self-employed or who worked for local dress shops. However,
destitution forced some urban freedwomen to become rag pickers who
fished cast-off clothing or bits of cloth out of trash cans and sewers and
dried and cleaned them for sale.[55]

A handful of black women moved westward and became frontiers-
women. A woman remembered only as "Aunt 'Melia" accompanied a
white family to Haskell County where she continued to work as a nurse
and midwife. Cindy Carter moved to Mobeetie, where she did practi-
cally the entire town's laundry. Martha, an ex-slave, accompanied the
white Dennis Murphy family to the Texas Panhandle. Martha worked
on the J A Ranch doing housework and other of the ranch's chores. A
few black women accompanied the buffalo soldiers to the Texas frontier where their husbands served in garrisons like Fort Concho and
Fort Davis. Others came as cooks, maids, and camp followers. Ellen
Lynch joined her husband who was stationed at Fort Concho in the
latter 1870s, while George Custer's wife Elizabeth hired freedwoman
Eliza Brown to work as the family's maid and cook during their Texas
years.[56]

Some freedwomen, especially the younger ones, were reduced to
practicing prostitution to make financial ends meet. Most major towns
in Reconstruction Texas had a "red-light" district where both white

and black courtesans sold their bodies to make more money than they otherwise could have—and they earned more than either domestics or farmhands. By 1880, black women comprised 40 percent of all the prostitutes in Austin, while they were also numerous in places like Dallas, Houston, and Galveston. Risking disease, arrest, violence, and perhaps an early death, black women usually worked entirely for themselves or in segregated brothels, but some were like freedwoman Celia Miller who ran an integrated whorehouse in Galveston. As well, in Dallas a newspaperman bemoaned the fact that white women were working in "negro dens." As of 1880, 40 percent of all courtesans in Austin were black. Regardless of where they worked, black prostitutes were more likely to be arrested and jailed than their white or Hispanic counterparts, and they also made less money.[57]

Some women, perhaps alone and uncared for, faced such destitution that they had to depend on city or county aid or help from the Freedmen's Bureau; yet, such aid was almost nonexistent. Federal law charged the bureau with extending relief and medical assistance to needy freedpeople, but in 1865 it issued rations to only sixty-four black Texans, about one-half of that number women. Because of widespread want and some cases of starvation, increased rationing began in 1866. Still, only a small percentage of the needy received aid. Then, without explanation, an order came to suspend rationing. And as for medical care, the bureau established only one hospital in the state, at Galveston, but it never employed more than five doctors at any one time, and it was disbanded in September of 1866.[58]

With few rations issued by the bureau, observers noted the pitiful plight of many freedwomen. Fannie Campbell, an American Missionary Association (AMA) teacher who had been sent to Austin in 1866, said that when the bureau stopped rationing, the elderly of both sexes, particularly the blind and the crippled, were reduced to a hopeless state—as were young orphans. Campbell requested aid from the AMA for such people but did not receive it. She did, however, encourage the African American community in Austin to begin a "self-taxing" plan that provided a fund for relief of indigents.[59] Likewise, ex-slaves in San Antonio and Houston established mutual aid societies for the less fortunate. In Houston black leaders asked workers to pay a $2.50 "initiation" fee and to further contribute $.25 per week to an indigent fund. Reverend Elias Dibble became president of the new society and quickly collected $80, but the funds were just as quickly distributed, leaving the coffer empty. Typically, more black women than men worked as volunteers in such community self-help efforts.[60]

Many city and county offices, usually in the hands of ex-rebels, refused to help destitute African Americans. F. P. Wood, a bureau agent working in Brenham, reported that his district had many black indigents and paupers; yet the county court refused in all cases to help. The court was "unanimous" against the agent when he asked for assistance. Wood could only report that the "people are actually suffering and I wish some remedy or relief for them."[61] Another agent, W. B. Pease, headquartered in Houston, reported on the similar plight of his area's black community, noting particularly that older women were in desperate need.[62] Still, local authorities exhibited little concern. In February of 1867, Charles Rand, bureau agent at Marshall, Harrison County, discovered four black orphans, two boys and two girls, all less than eight years old. They had literally been wandering the streets, digging in garbage for food. Rand asked civil officers to admit them to the county's poor (alms) house. But one county commissioner, John Munden, told Rand that the board "ignored all the Goddamned Radicals and that the damned niggers would not be allowed the benefits of the poor."[63] Rand also noted that the county would not care for elderly African Americans; yet he was powerless to act for his orders commanded him to turn such cases over to the chief justices of his district's counties.[64]

In Harrison County, then, indigent women as well as men, and young boys and girls, too, were turned out into the streets, literally with nothing but the clothes they wore. But because of Rand's continuing protests, ultimately many elderly freedwomen were finally admitted to the poor houses of the county. There, they faced much less than a desired fate. The almshouses remained self-sustaining, but prison labor was mixed in with the indigents. The convicts often verbally and physically abused the indigents, and they had neither the strength nor the youth to resist. One local source called the poor farm "unfit, unhealthy, uncomfortable." The source went on to exclaim that "the quarters of these poor people, mostly colored, are filthy beyond endurance; they are often in times of cold without fire, and at other times [they are] crying piteously for food . . . and for water. . . . [T]hey are mostly old persons, who are unable to help themselves."[65] Thus did dire fate consign the elderly freedwomen of Harrison County to such a horrible place to wait for oncoming death. Never had they expected freedom to bring them to such terrible circumstances.

Other African American expectations raised by "the bright light" of emancipation "come down" rarely came to fruition. Certainly they had believed that they were to be equal with whites before the law, but the ex-slaves soon learned the meaning of "justice" in the white-controlled legal system. Like freedmen, black women seldom received justice in courts, where Anglos remained ever ready to believe and to rule in favor of their fellows and to discount any black testimony. However, there were unusual exceptions. Phillis Oldham, a slave of Major William Oldham, CSA, was a light-skinned mulatto who cohabited with her owner both before and after the war. She had several children by him while they lived on his farm in Burleson County. But he was shot in 1868 and died in a hospital in Austin. Because Oldham left no will, his white relatives laid claim to his property. The upset Phillis then petitioned for homestead rights to the house and farm. The judge apparently had little sympathy for her, but Federal troops stationed in nearby Caldwell may have influenced his decision: He granted Phillis's petition, and she and her children remained secure in their home and farm.[66] The case, most unusual, was not duplicated in many places in Texas. Most freedwomen in similar circumstances were turned out with nothing but the clothes on their backs.

However, a few more became landowners. Some received property from their ex-masters. Her ex-owner, the Butler family, gave Hattie Roonie's grandmother 125 acres near Goliad because Hattie had "always been so good."[67] Matilda Boozie's ex-master gave her 1,500 acres in Washington County. In Matilda's case, such largesse came because "young mawster" had fathered one of Matilda's children when she was just a young teenager. Apparently, "mawster" was guilt-ridden and sought to ease his mind. The owner of John Sneed's mother gave her 70 acres near Austin in addition to a wagon, two horses, and a pair of cows. Although the Texas Homestead Act excluded blacks, freedwoman Hannah Perryman nevertheless laid claim to 80 acres in Polk County and, apparently, was able to keep it.[68]

Meanwhile, some black women who were suspected of crimes usually received short shrift from white judges and juries. Judges sentenced many of them to jail terms for such offenses as petty theft (chicken stealing). The authorities sent some to the state penitentiary, an obviously discriminatory application of justice since white women committing the same offenses received only jail time. By August of 1866, the state penitentiary housed 264 felons, including 117 black men and seven unfortunate black women. By February of 1867, a judicial "crackdown" upped the count to 411, of whom 211 were African American males and fourteen were freedwomen, all of whom had been sentenced for theft. Discrimination was rife according to Freedmen's Bureau inspector general William Sinclair, who held that African Americans, particularly the women, were innocent in most cases but were victims of white "frustration and hatred" over the lost war and lost slaves.[69]

Stubbornly refusing to permit embittered whites to shatter their shining image of freedom, younger women searched for ways to better their condition—for themselves, for their families, for their progeny, and for blacks in general. They sought education. Some women had acquired rudimentary literacy either in slave times or in the early Freedmen's Bureau schools. During Reconstruction, they managed to improve themselves and rise in the African American social and economic hierarchy by becoming teachers. In fact, Texas superintendent of education for the bureau, Edwin Wheelock, maintained that black teachers were "very important" because, as he said, they were content with "scanty support" and could "penetrate where white teachers could not go."[70]

Consequently, many women—like Jeptha Choice of Henderson—became instructors while also continuing to help on their husbands' farm. Caroline Poe of Marshall began instructing a class of thirty-five youths in 1867, this in addition to her farm chores. Like Eunice Smothers, some freedwomen taught in private academies. Smothers was a long-time faculty member at Dallas Institute, a private school for blacks.[71] Most of the early black teachers were male, but by 1880, 274 females out of a total of 1,379 black teachers staffed Afro-American schools around the state.[72]

Like their male counterparts, the women teachers usually had to face a hostile white community that contained elements who did not want ex-slaves to receive an education. Moreover, many whites, once they realized that African Americans were going to be taught, demanded that fellow whites do the teaching to eliminate dangerous ideas about freedom and equality. Because freedwomen who were teachers often remained vulnerable and unprotected, they became easy targets for violence. For example, at Circleville, near Georgetown, an Afro-American woman opened a bureau school in 1868, but before six months had elapsed, a group of whites burned the place to the ground.[73]

A number of black women entered professions other than teaching. Possibly the first black photographer in the United States, Mary Warren had a studio in downtown Houston by 1866. A number of freedwomen became professional nurses. Others like Jane J. Calloway became businesswomen. Calloway owned, developed, and operated a coal business in Dallas. As mentioned, many became expert seamstresses, their number including Dallas's Delia Jones and Mary Waters, both of whom were self-employed, and Bettie White, who worked for the Thompson Theater making costumes.[74] Like black women teachers, however, the more successful professionals and businesswomen became, the greater the white hostility toward them, for they were "rising above caste."

The conflicts black women teachers, along with black women professionals and artisans, had with white society mirrored the racial climate of the entire state. Everywhere, whites frowned upon, and sometimes committed violence upon, African Americans who behaved as free people. Some women who might have otherwise had much trouble adjusting to new freedom in an atmosphere of hostility created by whites used lessons learned during slave times to help them survive. Many who had learned accommodating roles in slavery did not internalize those roles but continued that outward behavior after the war. Others apparently did internalize the "lessons": Ex-slave Philles Thomas of Brazoria County reported, "We were lucky with the troubles. I guess it was because we knew how to behave. When I was young my mammy taught me how to behave and where I belonged; so, the patterollers and the Ku Klux never bothered us."[75]

Although Philles Thomas found a role to play wherein she could "please" Anglos, other women refused to acquiesce and sometimes had problems dealing with whites. One such woman was Susan Macklin, wife of Soloman Macklin of Houston. In March of 1867, she had an argument with an Anglo that resulted in assault. The fray began in a typical way. A white, George Jackson, stopped Susan's son on the street one day and demanded that the youth run an errand. But the child said no; he was in a hurry to do something for his mother. Enraged by the boy's refusal to obey, Jackson unleashed his vicious dog upon the youngster who ultimately beat the animal away. Then Jackson attacked Susan's son with a cane. From a window of her home, Susan finally noticed the altercation and rushed to her son's defense. The Anglo, now completely irate, "cussed her and then like a 'chivalric son' of the

South [and] threw a brick at her, striking her on the back of the neck." Freedmen's Bureau authorities later tried to arrest Jackson but could not find him.[76]

Thus, socially, economically, and educationally, the white community showed much determination to deprive ex-slaves of first-class citizenship. Included in their efforts was an immediate drive toward further segregation.[77] In all areas of life, the races were separated rapidly after emancipation, but not all black women meekly accepted second-class citizenship. In the mid-1870s, for instance, years after the "color line" was drawn in Texas, three separate incidents occurred wherein freedwomen tried to integrate the ladies' circles of opera houses in Sherman, Waco, and Galveston. The state was back in Democratic hands, and segregation was the norm, yet the women persisted, trying to attain their rights to equal accommodations.[78] More typically, freedwomen did not argue when forced to accept second-class status because complaining accomplished little. Thus, in places like Austin, Waco, and Sherman, as in all Texas communities, whites segregated black women—and their male counterparts—in all theaters, inns, and other places of public accommodation.[79]

Nevertheless, some women led the fight in demanding equal accommodations on railroads. The "unreconstructed" Texas legislature in 1866 provided separate cars for freedpeople, but Radical Republicans repealed the law in 1871, substituting one that prohibited public carriers from making racial distinctions in accommodating passengers. Generally, railroad officials observed neither law, instead forcing all African Americans to ride in the smoking car. After Congress passed the Civil Rights Act of 1875, some Texas freedwomen became vociferous in their demands to ride in the ladies' car while freedmen also demanded first-class accommodations.[80] Ultimately a test case reached the state courts in 1877 when a black woman brought charges. The judge affirmed her right to ride in the ladies' car if no other space was available. He went on to state, however, that if "equal" cars were provided, races—and sexes—might be separated.[81] Although the railcar issue was not ultimately settled until the ruling in *Plessy v. Ferguson* in 1896, in practice freedpeople in Texas never received the right of equal accommodations on public carriers. Emphatically, the "white" position was stated time after time but was perhaps best illustrated by an incident that occurred in the early 1880s. The wife of Walter Burton, state senator from Fort

Bend County, was thrown off a moving train, head first, after she refused to leave the ladies' coach.[82]

Effectively blocked from equal economic, educational, and social advantages by embittered whites, many freedwomen became actively involved in church work, work that also related to education and to community solidarity. Most quickly withdrew from white churches where they had been segregated, and they helped form their own black congregations. A large majority became either Baptists or Methodists (with fewer belonging to the Presbyterian or other churches), as they enjoyed one of the few means of self-expression that freedpeople had. Black churches became the center of freedwomen's social life and provided the "moral underpinnings" of a righteous, just community.[83]

Perhaps typical was Mariah Robinson, an ex-slave who was taken from Georgia to Waco in 1857. After freedom, she married Peter Robinson, who later became a state legislator. Soon after the war, the Robinsons acquired a small farm near Meridian, Bosque County. There, they helped to organize the first Afro-American church in the area—the Colored Cumberland Presbyterian Church of Meridian. Typically, women were more active in church than their men. For example, after the African Congregational Church was organized in Paris, Texas, in March of 1868, 174 members immediately joined, 122 were female.[84]

Church work led many freedwomen into the related field of social work. They became founders of homes for the aged, orphanages, and other benevolent organizations. They fed the hungry; they nursed the sick. They cooperated with most any benevolent drive to uplift the black community, its children and/or its adults, but direct church work remained a constant.[85]

Occasionally, as was true in the white world, Afro-American churches became scenes of uproarious events. In 1875, a deacon of the Corpus Christi Congregational Church, George Guilmenot, accused his wife Caroline and pastor George Swann of adultery. Vociferously denying the charge, the embarrassed Caroline faced other women while Swann faced a church jury, which could have removed him as preacher and expelled him from the church. Much to Caroline's relief, the court found Swann innocent and indirectly cleared woebegone Caroline's name as well.[86]

Not all freedpeople left white churches after emancipation. For example, the owner of slave Hannah Carr allowed her to attend the

Methodist Church in Matagorda, the church she continued to attend during Reconstruction. Voluntarily, she also cleaned the interior and kept it in "perfect order." In a similar case, at the Union Baptist Church in Nacogdoches, whites had always permitted blacks to attend services on a segregated basis before the war. After emancipation, many continued to do so. And they proved to be not much different from whites in terms of piety or sin. Most were "faithful," but sometimes discipline became necessary. The white leaders of Union Baptist found it necessary to expel temporarily "several" freedwomen from church on charges of adultery. But such unfortunate events and serious charges could be explained by the familial dislocations that came after emancipation as some African American women left old slave-days mates, who had been forced on them, and found new partners with whom they settled and married.[87]

In areas of southern Texas where Catholicism gained a foothold, whites allowed blacks to attend segregated Catholic services. In Goliad, freedgirls entered the convent and attended school on a segregated basis. Likewise, Catholic schools in Victoria also accepted young black women who attended services and classes.[88]

The churches (Protestant and Catholic) thus became instrumental in providing women with "values" and with "normal" marital and familial patterns to follow in creating the free African American family. As well, most black churches remained firm in enforcing moral codes. In 1872 and 1873, the African Congregational Church in Paris excommunicated eleven members and temporarily suspended fifteen more for "moral" reasons.[89] And, indeed, the black family apparently needed help because emancipation brought changes. But one noticeable trend, the rapid disintegration of some families because one of the mates desired a new partner, proved to be a temporary one.

Sometimes women took the initiative by leaving their husbands. Aaron Black's slave-days "wife," Caroline Robinson, deserted their East Texas home, migrated to Austin, and began cohabiting with an Anglo. She refused to leave her new mate, but because she remained kindly disposed toward Black, she loaned money to her then-penniless ex-husband. Accepting the loss of his erstwhile wife, Black settled near Austin and remarried, thereby shattering an apparently understanding relationship with Caroline. Learning that he had another wife, she became enraged, confronted him, demanded immediate repayment of the loan, and beat the dejected Aaron with a club. Yet her independent behavior proved exceptional.[90] More often, separation occurred when husbands "just ran off," deserting wives and children to marry other women. Early reports indicated that wayward husbands were the biggest threat to the stable development of the free family, as bureau agents time and again heard complaints of men leaving their wives and children destitute.[91]

Although some white observers castigated African Americans for weaknesses of character and morality, other factors, most of them rooted in slavery, explained the disruption of black homes. Some form of home life always existed in slavery, but family structure remained weak. In Texas, as in all southern states, many slaveholders allowed the separation of families whenever it proved profitable. Some owners forced compulsory breeding upon slave women. Others forced slaves, men and women alike, to mate quickly and gave them little time to be selective. Such practices increased the likelihood of unhappy unions. To produce more offspring, still other owners encouraged frequent mate changes. Moreover, slave marriage had no legal basis, and owners recognized such "unions" only as long as it suited their whim. Miscegenation also strained family ties. Such treatment often left psychological if not physical scars on black women. Children also suffered because their day care often devolved upon a nanny while slaveholders sent their real mothers back to the fields. Only at night in the quarters could parents assume the traditional roles that might have been expected of free people.[92]

In some cases the marital behavioral patterns and values forced upon chattels by their owners extended into the postbellum period. The white community's refusal to treat slave unions with the same reverence as Anglo marriages affected the new freedpeople. Some who had more than one partner during slave times placed a premium on pleasure, not responsibility, and believed that frequent change was normal. As historian John Blassingame notes, blacks appeared to develop fewer inhibiting sexual guilt complexes than whites because they had not been enslaved by a "puritanical [sexual] code."[93]

White observers of the freedpeoples' community handily tossed around references to illicit relations and "fornication," but such criticisms often amounted to a matter of semantics as the ex-slaves applied the definition of "marriage" that they had learned in antebellum times. For some women, "marriage" still consisted of jumping over the broomstick and then living with their men. Equally, for some "divorce" consisted simply of leaving the old mate and choosing another. In the immediate postwar years the break-up of many unions was explicable because, once emancipated, many women as well as men who had been forced to endure unhappy, perhaps forced, slave unions chose a new partner at first opportunity. Some women, like Caroline, even scandalized white society by choosing a white mate.[94]

As had happened in the antebellum period, the actions of some Anglos undermined the stability of the black family and particularly of women. Many Anglo males still believed that they could take liberties with freedwomen. Frequently the women or their husbands or fathers lodged charges of rape. In December of 1865, for instance, a freedman from Houston reported that two whites had raped his wife and robbed her of $20. In less than a week, another white Houstonian raped another freedwoman. However, even when authorities caught rape suspects, black women seldom received real justice. Usually, their attackers never spent a day in jail. Often, white offenders were allowed to "buy" their way out of a charge by paying off a freedwoman's father—or husband, if she were married. Alternately, white juries would simply return a not-guilty verdict.[95]

In other instances whites used economic rather than physical power to force intimate relations with freedwomen. Threatening them with the loss of their jobs if they complained, some employers openly conducted affairs with the wives and daughters of black men. One white, Robert Moore of Panola County, frequently "visited" a freedgirl for sex, but her father, one of Moore's sharecroppers, complained to the bureau. When Moore found out, he threatened to shoot the father and, indeed, did drive him from his crops.[96] In another case, A. W. Warrymore, who lived near Marshall, had frequent sex with a freedwoman's daughter but was eventually caught in the act by her indignant parents who asked Warrymore to end the affair. Responding like Moore, the Marshallite threatened to kill the girl's father and drove the family away from their fields.[97]

Although such factors as mentioned above weakened family ties, many countervailing forces worked to strengthen the African American family after emancipation—forces that finally dominated. Even in slave times, family life always existed, subject to the interests or whims of slaveholders. After emancipation, which imposed at least some limits on white control over black institutions, family ties became stronger. Mariah McElroy and her husband Jesse were both happy and even bragged about the fact that they received the first marriage license given to "coloreds" in Henderson County. However, many black couples suffered because most county clerks refused to give them marriage licenses, deciding instead to bombastically castigate blacks for immoral behavior and for living together out of wedlock. Importantly for the self-respect of freedwomen, the U.S. Congress legalized slave marriages in March of 1865, and the Freedmen's Bureau applied this law to Texas approximately one year later. Bureau policy recognized as married any African Americans who previously had lived together. Others wishing to marry would, like whites, secure a license and take vows in either civil or religious ceremonies.[98] Because women had never been able to have a marital ceremony during slave times, many placed a premium on a "real" wedding after emancipation. Josie Brown remembered that at age fifteen, during Reconstruction, she had a "real" wedding ceremony that left an impression on her the rest of her life. To clarify the legal muddle about black marriages, slave marriages were legalized in the Texas Constitution of 1869, a document that recognized children born of black parents as legitimate.[99]

In addition to enforcing congressional action that legalized marriages, the bureau helped strengthen the black family in yet other ways. Most local agents worked tirelessly to secure the release of those, adults and children, whom whites held illegally. They also acted as marital counselors. With threats of fines and even jail sentences, agents impressed upon freedpeople the virtues of monogamous relationships. An agent in Cotton Gin reported an amazing decline in adultery among ex-slaves in his district after he fined a husband the unreasonable sum of $196.50 for the offense. Another agent sentenced a husband to three days in jail on bread and water after his wife proved that he had visited another woman's home and had allowed her to sit on his knee.[100] Bureau men meted out similar punishment for women who committed adultery. In Columbia, Mary Ann Francis frequently fornicated with a white, John Bruelsen, but when bureau agent James Hutchinson learned of the affair, he fined both parties $100 each. He also fined freedwoman Adelaide Spencer for cohabitating with an Anglo and later fined yet another black woman (known only as Rebecca) for adultery.[101]

Local agents also ordered men who left children destitute to begin supporting them, made males responsible for breach of promise and children born out of wedlock, and continued to punish fornicators, especially if both races were involved. In many instances when whites used economic pressure to exploit African American women sexually, agents warned employers to stay away from them. When forceful rape occurred, agents continued to order Anglos to pay damages of up to $150 per offense when blacks could secure no redress in white courts. Such strong action regulating sexual indiscretions, duplicated by most agents throughout the state, helped reduce incidents of adultery, miscegenation, and rape and thus strengthened family ties.[102]

Afro-American schools and the newly emerging black churches also helped strengthen family structure. Schoolteachers included morality lessons in their day, night, and Sabbath classes and left ex-slaves with definite impressions of how free people "should" behave. Likewise, both black and white preachers stressed sobriety, monogamy, and responsibility, while condemning the vices that might disrupt families. The American Missionary Association sponsored continuing temperance drives. Although they risked retribution that included assassination, some teachers and preachers used their community positions to investigate conditions of apprenticeships. If they uncovered evidence of illegal bondage or of mistreatment of children, official investigations followed that sometimes resulted in returning children to their parents.[103]

Usually, African Americans needed instruction in morality less than Anglos supposed. After the brief period of flux during which ex-slaves left partners with whom they had been forced into unhappy, forced "marriages," families grew more stable. Most freedpeople strongly desired to "do the right thing" and thereby to "prove" that they were worthy of freedom.[104] Certainly, sample census statistics suggest that the Afro-American family in Texas had achieved a remarkable degree of stability by 1870, and comparisons of data on black families and white families reveal far more similarities than differences.

Indeed, with some exceptions, census data confirmed that the African American families in Reconstruction Texas tended to mirror those in white society. Particularly, the Afro-American family became more patriarchal, and that development changed the lives of freedwomen. Although a majority continued to work outside the home, more remained at home, and all had more time to devote to their husbands and especially to their children. Knowing that they had at least a modicum of protection from white control, they became more secure. The mere fact that the law and society recognized African American marriages as legal encouraged faithfulness and responsibility among black women.[105]

By 1870 the black family in Texas had acquired a remarkable degree of stability. Although a high percentage of black women and children worked, and varied occupational patterns based largely on racial lines emerged, the black family closely resembled the white. Households and individual families were approximately the same size with the same percentage headed by men. The trend toward male domination in the house also evolved into the norm in Reconstruction Texas.

Nevertheless, despite the apparent "health" of the family, in retrospect, emancipation for freedwomen in Texas was a disappointment. They faced a hostile white society determined to deny them even a modicum of equality. Forced into deprivation and want by Anglo masters who drove them out with nothing but the clothes on their backs, elderly African American indigents existed filthy and hungry in abominable almshouses, finding their "bright light come down" only in their dreams. Other women, a bit more fortunate, labored at low-paying jobs and "made do" as best they could. Denied justice in the courts and equal access to public accommodations, freedwomen did what they had done for survival in slave times: they adjusted. One of the few outlets for their pent-up frustrations and rage was the church. Many became actively involved in their congregations, for there they were important and mattered. There, they could make decisions and could be themselves, casting aside for a time the subservient image necessary to escape the brunt of white hostility.

A few African American women secured an education, thus partially rising above "caste." Most important, the ex-slave family became more stable after emancipation, demonstrating that women worked hard to create successful marriages, to raise children, and to teach them to survive in a hostile white world. As freedwomen strove to overcome the handicaps laid upon them by whites, they either perished or became strong. These women became the foundation of the family, the church, and the black community. Despite the constant humiliation and actual physical abuse meted out to them during the Reconstruction era, the freedwomen protected their families, worked outside the home to help their fathers and husbands, swelled the ranks of their churches, and secured a rudimentary education, as possible. Most innately knew their worth as human beings; most never lost their inner pride and dignity, legacies they passed down to future generations.

Notes

Abbreviations used in the notes section:

AMA   Archives, American Missionary Association, Dillard University, New Orleans
BRFAL   Bureau of Freedmen and Abandoned Lands (the Freedman's Bureau)
NA   National Archives, Washington, D.C.
RG   Record Group, NA
5th MD   Fifth Military District
DT   Department of Texas, 5th MD
TSL   Texas State Library, Austin, Texas
UTL   Archives, University of Texas at Austin Library

1. Various books, broad in scope, contain brief comments about Southern freedwomen during Reconstruction. Examples include Dorothy Sterling's *We Are Your Sisters: Black Women in the Nineteenth Century* (New York: W. W. Norton, 1984) and Jacqueline Jones's *Labor of Love, Labor of Sorrow* (New York: Basic Books, 1985), but neither author contributed much on Texas freedwomen in particular. For a thorough discussion of African Americans in Reconstruction Texas, see James Smallwood, *Time of Hope, Time of Despair: Black Texans during Reconstruction* (Port Washington, N.Y.: National University Publications, 1981).

Relatively speaking, little Texas historical literature has devoted space to fleshing out the story of the Lone Star State's black women during Reconstruction. Few studies focus specifically on freedwomen. However, some exceptions include: Barry A. Crouch's "The 'Cords of Love': Legalizing Black Marital and Family Rights in Postwar Texas," *Journal of Negro History* 79 (1994): 334–51; "Seeking Equality: Houston Black Women during Reconstruction," in *Black Dixie: Afro-Texan History and Culture in Houston,* ed. Howard Beeth and Cary D. Wintz (College Station: Texas A&M University Press, 1992), 54–73; and [with Larry Madaras], "Reconstructing Black Families: Perspectives from the Texas Freedmen's Bureau Records," *Prologue: Quarterly of the National Archives* 18 (1986): 109–22. See also James Smallwood's "Black Texas Freedwomen after Emancipation: The Texas Experience," *Prologue: Quarterly of the National Archives* (1995): 303–17, and "Emancipation and the Black Family: A Case Study in Texas," *Social Science Quarterly* 57 (1977): 849–57. Ruthe Winegarten's *Black Texas Women: 150 Years of Trial and Triumph* (Austin: University of Texas Press, 1994) has a chapter on freedwomen, and she has relative documents in her *Black Texas Women: A Sourcebook: Documents, Biographies, and Time Line* (Austin: University of Texas Press, 1996).

2. U.S. Bureau of the Census, *Ninth Census of the United States, 1870: Population* (Washington, D.C.: Government Printing Office, 1872), 612–13.

3. Allen W. Trelease, *White Terror: The Ku Klux Klan Conspiracy and Southern Reconstruction* (New York: Harper and Row, 1971), xvii; and see James M. Smallwood, "Blacks in Reconstruction Texas: First Freedom," *East Texas Historical Journal* 14 (Spring 1976): 9–10.

4. P. F. Duggan to James T. Kirkman, August 1, 1867, Letters Sent, vol. 78, Sub-Assistant Commissioner, Columbia, Texas, BRFAL, RG 105, NA; Winegarten, *Black Texas Women: 150 Years of Trial and Triumph,* 43.

5. H. Donald Henderson, *The Negro Freedman* (New York: Schulman, 1952), 28–29.

6. Amelia Barr, *All the Days of My Life: An Autobiography* (New York: D. Appleton, 1913), 251.

7. Barr, *All the Days of My Life,* 251.

8. Ibid., 252; Winegarten, *Black Texas Women: A Sourcebook,* 46.

9. Statement of Will Adams, Federal Writers' Project, "A Folk History of Slavery in the United States from Interviews with Former Slaves" (Washington, D.C., 1941), Texas Narratives, XVI, part 1: 3, NA, hereafter abbreviated as "Slave Narratives," Texas, NA.

10. Statement of Minerva Bandy, "Slave Narratives," Texas, XVI, part 1: 69.

11. B. A. Botkin, ed., *Lay My Burden Down: A Folk History of Slavery* (Chicago: University of Chicago Press, 1945), 236–37.

12. Statement of William M. Adams, "Slave Narratives," Texas, XVI, part 1: 11, NA; statement of Armstead Barrett, ibid., 47–48, NA; statement of Tom Holland, ibid., part 2: 144–47, NA.

13. Statement of Sarah Ford, ibid., part 2: 46, NA.

14. Botkin, *Lay My Burden Down,* 267.

15. Statement of Armstead Barrett, "Slave Narratives," Texas, XVI, part 1: 47, NA; statement of Tom Holland, ibid., part 2: 146, NA. Both Barrett and Holland confirmed the Huntsville incident mentioned in the text.

16. James Oakes to J. Kirkman, May 30, 1867, Letters Sent, vol. 49, Sub-Assistant Commissioner, Austin, Texas, BRFAL, RG 105, NA.

17. Statement of Betty Bormer, "Slave Narratives," Texas, XVI, part 1: 109–11, NA; statement of Millie Forward, ibid., part 2: 47–49, NA; Vicki Betts, ed., "The Memoirs of Horace Chilton: Part 1," *Chronicles of Smith County, Texas* 30 (Summer 1991): 13; James M. Smallwood, *Born in Dixie: The History of Smith County, Texas,* 2 vols. (Austin: Eakin Press), 1: 272–73; Winegarten, *Black Texas Women: 150 Years of Trial and Triumph,* 42.

18. Statement of Tempie Cummins, "Slave Narratives," Texas, XVI, part 1: 263–65, NA.

19. Statement of Nancy Hardeman's mother quoted by Winegarten, *Black Texas Women: 150 Years of Trial and Triumph,* 42.

20. William Moore, quoted in Winegarten, *Black Texas Women: A Sourcebook,* 45.

21. *Flake's Daily Bulletin,* December 3, 1865.

22. William G. Kirkman to [ ] Hawskins, July 19, 1867, W. Kirkman to Philip Howard, July 16, 1867, Letters Sent, vol. 67, Sub-Assistant Commissioner, Boston, Texas, BRFAL, RG 105, NA.

23. Byron Porter to Albert Evans, December 28, 1866, Letters Sent, vol. 48, Sub-Assistant Commissioner, Austin, Texas, BRFAL, RG 105, NA. The Freedmen's Bureau was charged, generally, with helping the ex-slaves make their transition from slavery to freedom. For more on the bureau in Texas, see Barry A. Crouch, *The Freedmen's Bureau and Black Texans* (Austin: University of Texas Press, 1992); "The Freedmen's Bureau in the 30th Sub-District of Texas: Smith County and Its Environs during Reconstruction," *Chronicles of Smith County, Texas* 11 (Spring 1972): 15–30; "The Freedman's Bureau in Beaumont," *Texas Gulf Historical and Biographical Record* 28 (1992): 8–27; and "Guardians of the Freedpeople: Texas Freedmen's Bureau Agents and the Black Community," *Southern Studies* 31 (1992): 185–201. And see William Richter, *Overreached on All Sides: The Freedmen's Bureau Administrators in Texas, 1865–1868* (College Station: Texas A&M University Press, 1991. "'The Revolver Rules the Day!': Colonel DeWitt C. Brown and the Freedmen's Bureau in Paris, Texas, 1867–1868," *Southwestern Historical Quarterly* 93 (1990): 303–32; "Who Was the Real Head of the Texas Freedmen's Bureau? The Role of Brevet Colonel William H. Sinclair as Acting Assistant Inspector General," *Military History of the Southwest* 20 (Fall 1990): 121–56. Also see James Smallwood, "The Freedmen's Bureau Reconsidered: Local Agents and the Black Community," *Texana* 11 (1973): 309–20 and "Charles E. Culver: A Reconstruction Agent in Texas: The Work of Local Freedmen's Bureau Agents and the Black Community," *Civil War History* 27 (1981): 350–51.

24. Porter to W. Brooks, January 27, 1866, Letters Sent, vol. 100, Sub-Assistant Commissioner, Houston, Texas, Porter to Albert Evans, December 28, 1866, Letters Sent, vol. 48, Sub-Assistant Commissioner, Austin, Texas, James Oakes to J. Kirkman, "Monthly Report," July 11, 1867, Letters Sent, vol. 49, BRFAL, RG 105, NA.

25. Katie Darling, quoted in Winegarten, *Black Texas Women: A Sourcebook,* 46; Winegarten, *Black Texas Women: 150 Years of Trial and Triumph,* 42.

26. Smallwood, "Blacks in Reconstruction Texas: First Freedom," 15; *Flake's Daily Bulletin* (Galveston), December 3, 1865. And see James Oakes to J. Kirkman, July 31, 1867, Letters Sent, vol. 49, Sub-Assistant Commissioner, Austin, Texas, BRFAL, RG 105, NA.

27. H. P. N. Gammel, comp., *The Laws of Texas, 1822–1897,* 10 vols. (Austin: Gammel Book Company, 1898), 4: 979–81; Charles E. Culver to J. Kirkman, August 15, 1867, Letters Sent, vol. 78, Sub-Assistant Commissioner, Cotton Gin, Texas, BRFAL, RG 105, NA; for more on the black codes, see Barry A. Crouch, "'All the Vile Passions': The Texas Black Code of 1866," *Southwestern Historical Quarterly* 97 (1993): 13–34 and Smallwood, *Time of Hope, Time of Despair,* 54–59, 64, 123–24, 130–31.

28. For more discussion of black codes and their effect in reducing freed-

people to semislavery, see James M. Smallwood, "Perpetuation of Caste: Black Agricultural Workers in Reconstruction Texas," *Mid-America* 61 (January 1979): 5–23; and see A. G. Malloy to J. Kirkman, September 2, 1867, Letters Sent, vol. 134, Sub-Assistant Commissioner, Marshall, Texas, BRFAL, RG 105, NA.

29. James Oakes to J. Kirkman, "Monthly Report," July 31, 1867, Richardson to A. M. Bryant, September 27, 1867, Letters Sent, vol. 49, Sub-Assistant Commissioner, Austin, Texas, David L. Montgomery to Matthew and Samuel Rogers, March 30, 1867, Letters Sent, vol. 162, Sub-Assistant Commissioner, Tyler, BRFAL, RG 105, NA; Smallwood, *Time of Hope, Time of Despair*, 113.

30. Charles W. Ramsdell, "Presidential Reconstruction in Texas," *Quarterly of the Texas State Historical Association* 11 (April 1908): 301.

31. Gammel, *Laws of Texas, 1822–1897*, 5: 994–97; Winegarten, *Black Texas Women: 150 Years of Trial and Triumph*, 45.

32. James Butler to D. S. Montgomery, March 17, 1868, Letters Sent, vol. 163, Sub-Assistant Commissioner, Huntsville, Texas, "Complaint Book," 1866–1868, vol. 58, Millican, Texas, BRFAL, RG 105, NA; Winegarten, *Black Texas Women: 150 Years of Trial and Triumph*, 42.

33. Butler to Montgomery, March 17, 1868, Letters Sent, vol. 163, Sub-Assistant Commissioner, Huntsville, Texas, Huntsville, Texas "Complaint Book," 1866–1868, vol. 58, Millican, Texas, General Order no. 2, January 3, 1867, "Special and General Orders, 1865–1869," vol. 9, Assistant Commissioner, Texas, BRFAL, RG 105, statement of Lucy Thomas, "Slave Narratives," Texas, XVI, part 4, 90, NA.

34. Henry Adams, quoted in Winegarten, *Black Texas Women: A Sourcebook*, 51.

35. U.S. House of Representatives, *House Reports*, 39th Cong, 1st sess., 1866, report no. 30, 46–47, 77; Smallwood, *Born in Dixie*, 1: 275.

36. Winegarten, *Black Texas Women: A Sourcebook*, 57.

37. *Flake's Semi-Weekly Bulletin*, July 24, 1867; Col. William H. Sinclair to AAAG J. T. Kirkman, July 2, 1867, Texas Assistant Commissioner, Letters Received, BRFAL, RG 105, NA. Both the *Bulletin* and Sinclair mentioned Guest's disemboweling of the pregnant freedwoman. The quote is from *Flake's*. For more on violence, also see Barry A. Crouch, "A Spirit of Lawlessness: White Violence; Texas Blacks, 1865–1868," *Journal of Social History* 18 (1984): 217–32.

38. A. M. Bryant to Rev. Thadeous McKae (private secretary to Governor Elisha Pease), March 1, 1869, Letters Received, E. Pease to Gen. E. R. S. Canby, March 16, 1869, Letters Sent, Governor's Papers, Archives, TSL.

39. Bryant to McKae, March 1, 1869, Letters Sent, Pease to Gen. Canby, March 16, 1869, Letters Sent, Governor's Papers, Archives, TSL.

40. John E. Thompson to Andrew Jackson Hamilton, October 8, 1865, D. J. Baldwin to Hamilton, n.d., Governor's Papers, Archives, TSL; for more on terrorist groups, see Smallwood, *Time of Hope, Time of Despair*, passim; James Smallwood, "When the Klan Rode: White Terror in Reconstruction

Texas," *Journal of the West* 25 (October 1986): 4–13; Smallwood, *Born in Dixie,*
1: 293; *New Orleans Tribune,* September 1, 1866; Barbara Clayton, "The Lone
Star Conspiracy: Racial Violence and the Ku Klux Klan Terror in Post–Civil
War Texas" (unpublished master's thesis, Oklahoma State University, 1980).
The tremendous extent of Klan violence is replete in the records of the Freed-
men's Bureau and in the records of the Fifth Military District; both collections
are in the National Archives. See, for example, Vernon to Gregory Barrett,
July 13, 1868, Letters Received, Barrett to Vernon, August 14, September 2,
30, 1868, Montgomery to J. Kirkman, June 15, 1867, Letters Sent, vol. 162,
Sub-Assistant Commissioner, BRFAL, RG 105, NA.

    41. For an in-depth example, see Barry A. Crouch and Donaly Brice, *Cul-
len Montgomery Baker: Reconstruction Desperado* (Baton Rouge: Louisiana State
University Press, 1997), passim. In addition, the records of the Freedmen's Bureau and the Fifth Military District in the National Archives contain much
material on desperados and their relationship with organized terrorist groups.
See also Smallwood, *Time of Hope, Time of Despair,* 61, 35–136, and passim.

    42. John T. Carrier, "Bullets, Ballots, and Bayonets," *Chronicles of Smith
County, Texas* 13 (Summer 1974): 8. Carrier used the term "Race War" to de-
scribe the turmoil in Smith County. Also see William Barrett to Charles
Vernon, July 21, 26, Barrett to Horace Jewitt, September 26, 1868, Sub-
Assistant Commissioner, Tyler, Letters Sent, vol. 162, BRFAL, RG 105, NA.

    43. W. B. Peace to James McCoy, April 15, 1867, Letters Sent, vol. 102,
Sub-Assistant Commissioner, Houston, Texas, Abner Doubleday to Sub-
agent, Charleston, South Carolina, February 10, 1867, vol. 93, Letters Sent,
Sub-Assistant Commissioner, Galveston, Texas, BRFAL, RG 105, NA.

    44. J. Kirkman to E. M. Harris, Letters Received, Sub-Assistant Com-
missioner, Columbus, Texas, J. P. Richardson to A. M. Bryant, September 27,
1867, Letters Sent, vol. 49, Sub-Assistant Commissioner, Austin, Texas, Doubleday to Sub-Agent, Springfield, West Virginia, Doubleday to J. Kirkman,
May 18, 1867, Letters Sent, vol. 93, Sub-Assistant Commissioner, Galveston,
Texas, BRFAL, RG 105, NA; Winegarten, *Black Texas Women: 150 Years of
Trial and Triumph,* 42.

    45. See, for example, John Hill, labor contracts, December 29, 1865, Au-
gust 14, 1867, John Hill Papers, Thomas Blackshear, Memo Book, January–
April, 1868, Thomas Blackshear Papers, Archives, UTL; Smallwood, "Perpetuation of Caste," 5–6.

    46. Esther L. Thompson, "The Influence of the Freedmen's Bureau on
the Education of the Negro in Texas" (unpublished master's thesis, Texas
Southern University, 1956), 34.

    47. *Harrison Flag* (Marshall, Texas), May 2, 1867; James McCleery to
J. W. Alvord, September 7, 1869, Letters Sent, vol. 440, Superintendent of
Education, Louisiana and Northeast Texas, BRFAL, RG 105, NA.

    48. Daniel Dumit to Harris, January 12, 1867, Letters Received, Sub-
Assistant Commissioner, Columbus, Texas, W. Kirkman to J. P. Richardson, November 14, 1867, Letters Sent, vol. 67, Sub-Assistant Commissioner,

Boston, Texas, BRFAL, RG 105, NA; and see Smallwood, "Perpetuation of Caste," 17–18.

49. Hattie M. York, "Reminiscences, 1860–1940," Archives, Cooke County Museum, Gainesville, Texas.

50. Statement of Issabella Boyd, "Slave Narratives," Texas, XVI, part 1: 114–16, NA; Statement of Harriet Barrett, ibid., 49–50, NA; Winegarten, *Black Texas Women: 150 Years of Trial and Triumph*, 48.

51. Thomas Blackshear, Memo Book, January–April 1868, Thomas Blackshear Papers, Archives, UTL.

52. Winegarten, *Black Texas Women: 150 Years of Trial and Triumph*, 47–48.

53. Amelia Barr to Jennie, June 3, 1866, Amelia Barr Papers, 1861–1916, Archives, UTL.

54. Barr, *All the Days of My Life*, 251; Winegarten, *Black Texas Women: 150 Years of Trial and Triumph*, 47.

55. Mary A. Lavender, "Social Conditions in Houston and Harris County, 1869–1872" (unpublished master's thesis, Rice Institute, 1950), 259–60; Janelle DuPont Scott, "Married Women at Work: Dallas, Texas, 1880–1900" (unpublished master's thesis, University of Texas at San Antonio, 1979), 66, 68, 89; *Galveston Daily News*, August 1, 1877; Winegarten, *Black Texas Women: 150 Years of Trial and Triumph*, 48–49; Winegarten, *Black Texas Women: A Sourcebook*, 53–54.

56. Willie Newbury Lewis, *Between Sun and Sod: An Informal History of the Texas Panhandle* (College Station: Texas A&M University Press, 1976), 93–94; Bill Green, *The Dancing Was Lively: Fort Concho, Texas: A Social History, 1867–1882* (Fort Concho, Tex.: Fort Concho Sketches Publishing, 1974), 55–84; John M. Carroll, comp. and ed., *Custer in Texas: An Interrupted Narrative* (New York: Sol Lewis, Liveright, 1975), 12, 99, 100–101, 151–52; Winegarten, *Black Texas Women: 150 Years of Trial and Triumph*, 51–52; and see Ann Patton Malone, "Black Women," in *Women on the Texas Frontier: A Cross-Cultural Perspective* (El Paso: Texas Western Press, 1983), 26–52, 63–78.

57. Richard F. Selcer, *Hell's Half Acre: The Life and Legend of a Red-Light District* (Fort Worth: Texas Christian University Press, 1991), 21–23, 138–45; David G. McComb, *Galveston: A History* (Austin: University of Texas Press, 1971), 108; David C. Humphrey, "Prostitution and Public Policy in Austin, 1870–1915," *Southwestern Historical Quarterly* 86 (April 1983): 473–516; Winegarten, *Black Texas Women: 150 Years of Trial and Triumph*, 51.

58. Circular no. 16, June 18, 1866, Special and General Orders, 1865–1869, vol. 9, Assistant Commissioner, Texas, W. Pease to J. Kirkman, May 18, 1867, Letters Sent, vol. 102, Sub-Assistant Commissioner, Houston, Texas, BRFAL, RG 105, NA.

59. Fannie Campbell to George Whipple, November 24, 1866, Texas Correspondence, Archives, AMA.

60. Ibid.; B. Porter to William Sinclair, September 1, 1866, Letters Sent,

vol. 100, Sub-Assistant Commissioner, Houston, Texas, BRFAL, RG 105, NA; *Houston Tri-Weekly Telegraph*, October 6, 1865.

61. F. P. Wood to J. J. Reynolds, April 27, 1868, Letters Sent, vol. 64, Sub-Assistant Commissioner, Brenham, Texas, BRFAL, RG 105, NA.

62. W. P. Pease to J. Kirkman, May 18, 1867, Letters Sent, vol. 102, Sub-Assistant Commissioner, Houston, Texas, BRFAL, RG 105, NA.

63. Charles F. Rand to J. Kirkman, February 11, 1867, Letters Sent, vol. 134, Sub-Assistant Commissioner, Marshall, Texas, BRFAL, RG 105, NA.

64. Rand to O. Hendrick, March 21, 1867, Letters Sent, vol. 134, Sub-Assistant Commissioner, Marshall, Texas, BRFAL, RG 105, NA.

65. *Marshall Tri-Weekly Herald*, October 26, 1875.

66. Catherine C. Alford to Deolece Parmelee, August 28, 1972, in "Fort Oldham," Vertical File, Archives, Texas State Historical Commission, Austin, Texas.

67. Jackie L. Pruett and Everett B. Cole, *As We Lived: Stories by Black Story Tellers* (Burnet, Tex.: Eakin Press, 1982), 15; Winegarten, *Black Texas Women: 150 Years of Trial and Triumph*, 53.

68. Winegarten, *Black Texas Women: 150 Years of Trial and Triumph*, 53.

69. W. Sinclair to J. Kirkman, February 26, 1867, Letters Received, Assistant Commissioner, Texas, BRFAL, RG 105, NA.

70. Edwin Wheelock to Alvord, April 28, 1867, Letters Received, Superintendent of Education, Texas, BRFAL, RG 105, NA. For education, see also James Smallwood, "Black Education in Reconstruction Texas: The Contributions of the Freedmen's Bureau and Benevolent Societies," *East Texas Historical Journal* 19 (1981): 17–40, and "Early Freedom Schools: Black Self-Help and Education in Reconstruction Texas: A Case Study," *Negro History Bulletin* 41 (1978): 790–93, and *Time of Hope, Time of Despair*, 68–95.

71. Jeptha Choice, "Slave Narratives," Texas XVI, part 1: 217–19, NA; Malloy to Charles Garretson, September 30, 1867, Letters Sent, vol. 134, Sub-Assistant Commissioner, Marshall, Texas, BRFAL, RG 105, NA; Winegarten, *Black Texas Women: 150 Years of Trial and Triumph*, 50.

72. U.S. Bureau of the Census, *A Compendium of the Tenth Census, June 1, 1880* (Washington, D.C., 1883), 1640–41.

73. See James M. Smallwood, "Black Texans during Reconstruction," (Ph.D. diss., Texas Tech University, 1974), 118–57. For more discussion of the powerful Ku Klux Klan in Texas and the violence its members committed against the black community, see James M. Smallwood, "When the Klan Rode: White Terror in Reconstruction Texas," *Journal of the West* 25 (October 1986): 4–13.

74. Jeanne Moutoussamy-Ashe, *Viewfinders: Black Women Photographers* (New York: Dodd, Mead, 1986), 10–11, 146; *Austin American Statesman*, October 27, 1974; Elizabeth Enstam, "The Frontier Woman as City Worker: Women's Occupations in Dallas, 1856–1880," *East Texas Historical Journal* 18 (1980): 22; Winegarten, *Black Texas Women: 150 Years of Trial and Triumph*, 50.

75. Statement of Philles Thomas, "Slave Narratives," Texas, XVI, part 4: 94, NA; and see John Blassingame's *The Slave Community: Plantation Life in the Antebellum South* (New York: Oxford University Press, 1972) for discussion of the "Sambo" image and whether slaves "internalized" the role.

76. Pease to J. Kirkman, March 2, 1867, Letters Sent, vol. 102, Sub-Assistant Commissioner, Houston, Texas, BRFAL, RG 105, NA.

77. See James M. Smallwood, "The Woodward Thesis Revisited: The Origins of Social Segregation in Texas," *Negro History Bulletin* (1984): 6–9; also see Barry A. Crouch and L. J. Schultz, "Crisis in Color: Racial Separation in Texas during Reconstruction," *Civil War History* 16 (1970): 37–48.

78. *Brenham Weekly Banner,* March 6, 1875; *Galveston Daily News,* March 13, April 29, 1875; *Marshall Tri-Weekly Herald,* April 5, 1877, January 24, 1885; *Bastrop Advertiser,* April 30, 1875.

79. *Daily Austin Republican,* July 21, 1868; Smallwood, "Social Segregation in Texas," 6–9.

80. Lawrence Rice, *The Negro in Texas, 1874–1900* (Baton Rouge: Louisiana State University Press, 1971), 145–46.

81. *United States v. Dodge,* Federal Case No. 14 796 (WD Texas), 1877.

82. *Colorado Citizen* (Colorado, Texas), March 23, 1882, September 27, 1883; *Longview Democrat,* March 24, 1882. And see Smallwood, "Social Segregation in Texas," 6–9.

83. See James M. Smallwood, "The Black Community in Reconstruction Texas: Evolution of the Negro Church," *East Texas Historical Journal* 16 (Fall 1978): 16–28; see also Winegarten, *Black Texas Women: A Sourcebook,* 58.

84. Botkin, *Lay My Burden Down,* 77–79; "Report of the African Congregational Church of Paris, Texas," September 30, 1873, Archives, AMA.

85. Winegarten, *Trial and Triumph,* 62; and see Smallwood, *Time of Hope, Time of Despair,* passim.

86. George Guilmenot to J. E. Streiby, December 30, 1875, G. W. Swan to Streiby, January 24, 1876, Mitchell Thompson to Streiby, March 3, 1876, Archives, AMA.

87. Winegarten, *Black Texas Women: 150 Years of Trial and Triumph,* 61; A. J. Holt, "A Brief History of Union Baptist Church," ed. Jerry M. Self, *East Texas Historical Journal* 9 (March 1971): 60–71.

88. Thompson to Streiby, September 27, 1877, Archives, AMA.

89. "Report of the African Congregational Church of Paris, Texas," September 30, 1873, Archives, AMA.

90. Complaint, August 20, 1867, Austin Complaint Book, vol. 52, Sub-assistant Commissioner, Austin, Texas, BRFAL, RG 105, NA.

91. See Smallwood, *Time of Hope, Time of Despair,* 95–96.

92. See James M. Smallwood, "Emancipation and the Black Family: A Case Study in Texas," *Social Science Quarterly* 57 (March 1977): 849–50; Blassingame, *Slave Community,* for a longer survey.

93. Blassingame, *Slave Community,* 85; Smallwood, "Emancipation and the Black Family," 850.

94. Smallwood, "Emancipation and the Black Family," 850; and see Blassingame, *Slave Community*.

95. Complaints, December 25, 30, 1865, Houston Complaint Book, 1865–1868, vol. 109, BRFAL, RG 105, NA.

96. See Malloy to Richardson, October 31, 1865, Letters Sent, vol. 134, Sub-Assistant Commissioner, Marshall, Texas, BRFAL, RG 105, NA.

97. Ibid.

98. Circular no. 9, March 23, 1866, Special and General Orders, 1865–1869, vol. 9, BRFAL, RG 105, NA.

99. Statement of Josie Brown, "Slave Narratives," Texas, XVI, part 1: 163–65, NA; Winegarten, *Black Texas Women: 150 Years of Trial and Triumph*, 54.

100. David Beath to Charles Alernion, September 18, 1868, Letters Sent, vol. 78, Sub-Assistant Commissioner, Cotton Gin, Texas, Complaint, June 12, 1867, Millican Complaints Book, 1866–1868, vol. 58, BRFAL, RG 105, NA.

101. James Hutchinson to J. Kirkman, April 30, 1867, Letters Sent, vol. 78, Sub-Assistant Commissioner, Columbia Texas, BRFAL, RG 105, NA.

102. See Smallwood, "Emancipation and the Black Family," 851–52.

103. See Complaint, September 29, 1869, Post of Austin, "Report of Scouts, Indian Depredations, and Crimes," Fifth Military District, 1867–1870, RG 393, NA, Washington, D.C.; Thompson to E. M. Cravath, March 24, 1874, W. B. Lacy to Cravath, April 10, 1874, Archives, AMA; and see James M. Smallwood, "The Black Community in Reconstruction Texas: Readjustments in Religion and the Evolution of the Black Church," *East Texas Historical Journal* 16 (Fall 1978): 16–28.

104. *New Orleans Tribune*, May 26, 1969.

105. For comparative "profiles" of the white and black families drawn from census returns, see Smallwood, "Emancipation and the Black Family."

REBECCA SHARPLESS

3. *"Us Has Ever Lived De Useful Life"*

AFRICAN AMERICAN WOMEN
IN TEXAS, 1874–1900

As the dust of Reconstruction settled in 1874, Texas freedpeople found themselves largely dependent upon their own resources. More than 250,000 African Americans lived in Texas, comprising almost a third of the state's population, and more were arriving from the southeastern United States every day. They were overwhelmingly poor, having become free with almost no material resources. They were still largely illiterate. More than half of them were female.

By 1900, the African American population of Texas would more than double, to 620,722. Even as the number of African American Texans rose, however, the number of white immigrants flooding the state increased at even greater rates, and the proportion of African Americans in the state's population declined to 20 percent in 1900.[1] At the turn of the twentieth century, African Americans could point to significant progress in several areas, although conditions remained difficult. Wealth increased throughout the 1880s and 1890s, as a few African Americans owned property. Literacy rates grew significantly. Urbanization provided more economic opportunities. Texas became urban faster than any other southern state, and while 85 percent of all Texans still lived in rural areas by 1900, the population in the cities had grown to more than half a million people.[2] On the negative side, nineteenth-century Texans of African descent lived in a world of increasing segregation. Racial boundaries, somewhat fluid in the confusion of Reconstruction, solidified throughout the 1880s and 1890s, culminating in the *Plessy v. Ferguson* decision of 1896, declaring racial segregation legal. Continuing racial violence intimidated even some of the bravest souls.

Economic opportunities in the countryside stagnated, with the crop-lien system becoming ever more firmly entrenched. Texans, black and white, were learning to negotiate their way in a world without slavery.

African American women actively participated in the social ne-gotiations of freedom. They maintained traditional roles for women, as mothers and wives. The majority of them participated in agricul-tural work, just as their mothers and grandmothers had done. Some moved to town, finding paid employment primarily as domestic work-ers but also as teachers. Others became full-time housewives. African American women resisted intimidation and segregation, and they banded together to improve their lives and those of others. All in all, they strove, in the words of former slave Mariah Robinson, to live "de useful life."[3]

As women have throughout history, most African American women in Texas centered their lives around their families, forming re-lationships with men and bearing children. Those relationships could sometimes prove complicated and transitory, while others could create lasting bonds.[4] Betty Powers of Fort Worth spoke fondly of her hus-band, Boss Powers, whom she married in 1870: "We'uns lives on rent land nearby for six years and has three chillen and den he dies. . . . I never took de name of Ruffins [her second husband], 'cause I's dearly love Powers and can't stand to give up he name." Boss Powers did his best to provide for his young wife in life and in death. Betty Powers ob-served: "Powers done make de will and wrote on de paper, 'To my be-loved wife, I gives all I has.' Wasn't dat sweet of him?"[5] Many African Americans gladly embraced the traditions and legal institutions of white American society.

Although it is impossible to know how many people in Texas mar-ried, a study of African Americans nationwide estimated that, at the turn of the twentieth century, 95 percent of them married at some point before their forty-fifth birthday.[6] In Central Texas in 1900, the aver-age age at marriage for women in rural areas was nineteen years.[7] A woman, therefore, could expect to spend much of her adult life in a re-lationship with a man. Couples often celebrated their marriages follow-ing traditional Anglo customs. Minerva Bendy, living near Woodville, recalled, "I's a June bride 59 years ago when I git married [ca. 1878]. De old white Baptist preacher name Blacksheer put me and dat nigger over dere, Edgar Bendy, togedder and us been togedder ever since."[8] A wedding portrait of Tom and Nancy Stewart Jones taken in Bonham in 1900 depicts a serious, well-dressed couple. Her arm is through his. She is wearing a jacket with a short waist, a filigree pin on her high-necked blouse, and a flat-brimmed hat. Clearly the Joneses commemorated the occasion of their marriage with formalities and purpose.[9] Julia Blanks recalled her 1877 wedding with delight: "I was fifteen years old the first time I married. I was married in San Antonio. My first husband's name was Henry Hall. My first wedding dress was as wide as a wagon sheet. It was white lawn, full of tucks, and had a big ruffle at the bottom. I had a wreath and a veil, too. The veil had lace all around it." She remembered the festivities: "We danced and had a supper. We danced all the dances they danced then: the waltz, square, quadrille, polka, and the gallopade—and that's what it was, all right—you shore galloped. You'd start from one end of the hall and run clear to the other end. In those days, the women with all them long trains—the man would hold it over his arm."[10]

Marriage, however, was a fragile institution in the late nineteenth century for African Americans and whites alike. Both death and divorce severed marriages. The 1880 census showed that 51.2 percent of African American families in Waco had two parents, while 27.8 had only a mother.[11] In Harrison County at the same time, 13.4 percent of the heads of African American households were female, an identical proportion to whites.[12]

The threat of death hung over every relationship, with the life expectancy of an African American male at around forty years in 1900, and far more marriages ended in death than in divorce.[13] Texas kept no mortality statistics until 1930, but the memories of women show them as grieving widows. Health problems, aggravated by brutally hard work and very limited medical care, took the lives of some Texas men. Elsie Reece married her first husband, John Love, in 1865, when she was eighteen. They bought land and built a house in Navasota, having four children together. Reece recalled, "He died in 1881, 'way from home. He's on his way to Austin and draps dead from some heart mis'ry. Dat am big sorrow in my life."[14] The violence of Texas society in the postbellum period also ended some husbands' lives. Annie Row lived in Rusk in the early 1870s. She remembered, "I marries Rufus Jackson and on Saturday we marries and on Monday we walks down de street and Rufus accident'ly steps on a white man's foot and de white man kills him with a pistol."[15] Life expectancy for women was no better, due in large part to the dangers of childbirth. A man could just as easily find himself widowed, although very few men attempted rearing children alone.[16]

African American women were surprisingly forthright about discussing the abusive relationships in which they found themselves. Two years after Rufus Jackson's death, Annie Row married Charles Row. She recalled, "I marries 'gain after two years to Charles Row. Dat nigger, I plum quits after one year, 'cause him was too rough. Him jealous and tote de razor with him all de time and sleep with it under him pillow. Shucks, him says he carry on dat way 'cause him likes me. I don't want any nigger to show his 'fection for me dat way, so I transports myself from him."[17] Tillie Powers complained about her former husband, whom she married in 1880: "I works 'round a while and gits married to John Daniels in 1880. Dis nigger was better off in slavery dan with dat nigger. Why, him wont work and whips me if I complain. I stood dat for six year and den I's transported him. Dat in Roberts County [North Carolina]. Marster Race Robinson brought dat no good nigger and me, with 'bout 50 other niggers, here to Texas. We'uns share cropped for him till I transported dat ornery husban.'"[18] Powers, in a new state, far away from her birthplace, nonetheless found the courage to "transport" her abusive husband.

Indeed, a number of women spoke about their decisions to leave their husbands, and women appear to have exercised a good bit of initiative in leaving unsatisfactory relationships. Eliza Holman lived in Jacksboro from the time that she left her former master in about 1872. In 1874, she married, to her unhappiness: "I marries Dick Hines at Silver Creek and he am a farmer and a contrary man. He worked jus' as hard at his contrariness as him did at his farmin.' Mercy, how distressin' and worryment am life with dat nigger! I couldn't stand it no longer dan five year till I tooks my getaway."[19] Leithean Spinks sent her husband packing in no uncertain terms: "I marries Sol Pleasant in 1872 and us has two chillen. Us sep'rate in 1876. De trouble am, he wants to be de boss of de job and let me do de work. I 'cides I don't need no boss, so I transports him, and says, 'Nigger, git out of here and don't never come back. If you comes back, I'll smack you down.'"[20] Mollie Taylor, from Hunt County, found herself unlucky twice: "I marries Tom Gould and move to McLennan County. But he so mean I didn't stay with him very long, and 'bout six months of his foolishness and I ups and leaves him. After two years I marries George Taylor and I lives with dat man for 12 years and took 'nough of his foolishness, so I leaves him."[21] Louise Mathews recalled with great relief the departure of her second husband: "I marries Jim Byers in 1885 and he am lazy and no 'count. He leaves on Christmas Day in de mornin,' and don't come back. Dat de only present he ever give me! He am what you calls de buck passer. I does de washin' and ironin' and he passes de bucks I makes."[22]

As these narratives indicate, both widows and divorced women often remarried. When Rosina Hoard's second husband died, leaving her with five children, she married his brother, Jim Hoard.[23] Families stretched as needed. Elizabeth Peterson lived in Brazos County in an extended family. The 1880 census, when Elizabeth Peterson was twenty-seven years old, enumerated Elizabeth's husband, Ned; Elizabeth herself; seven children ranging in age from twelve years to one year; an eighty-year-old widow; a single twenty-one-year-old farmhand; and Ned Peterson's widowed twenty-three-year-old sister.[24]

Most women could count on becoming a mother numerous times. In Harrison County in 1880, 69 percent of African American households had at least one child aged five to seventeen.[25] In 1900, the average African American woman in the rural South bore about seven children. In Central Texas, the average was around five. Of those five children, about four would survive.[26] Because of the mortality of parents as well as children, families stretched and bent to take in children without parents. Josie Brown of Woodville reared ten biological children as well as a group of orphans: "'Sides dat, I raises six or seven dat I pick up on de street 'cause dey orfume and hab nobody to care for dem."[27]

The number of children born out of wedlock is a source of considerable debate in historical circles. Women in their old age talked openly about the fathers of their children whom they had never married. Millie Forward of Jasper told a tale of a young man who not only stole the family farm but also left her with a son: "After us git free a long time, me and Susan and Tom us work hard and buy us de black land farm. But de deed git burnt up and us didn't know how to git 'nother deed, and a young nigger call McRay, he come foolin' 'round me and makin' love to me. He find out us don't have no deed no more and he claim dat farm and take it 'way from us and leave me with li'l baby boy what I names Joe Willie McRay. But never 'gain. I never marries."[28] Betty Bormer of Tarrant County had two husbands, but "I'se never married to the father of my only chile."[29] Families worked out their differences and blended their patchwork families. Rubin

Hancock, a Travis County landowner, and Rosetta Williams, who was not his wife, were the parents of Martha Ann Hancock. According to family members, Martha Ann was treated as a member of the Hancock family and enjoyed good relationships with her father's wife, Elizabeth Hancock, as well as her half sisters.[30]

For African Americans, marriage was both feasible and desirable, and it contributed to the ability to be effective agricultural workers.[31] Although Texas was urbanizing rapidly in the late nineteenth century, more than 80 percent of African American Texans lived in rural areas in 1900.[32] Brought to Texas as agricultural laborers, most African Americans continued to work the land. Farming in nineteenth-century Texas provided a meager living; in Hunt County in 1880, the average African American household had only 3 percent of the wealth that an average white household did, and only 6 percent in 1890.[33] Betty Farrow, living in Tarrant County, remembered: "We'uns stayed right dere en de farm, 'cause it was de only home we knew and no reason to go. I stays dere till I's twenty-seven years old, den' I marries and my husban' rents land. We'uns has ten chillun and sometimes we has to skimp, but we gets on."[34] Hard work and perseverance were required for Texas African American farm families to "get on."

In 1900, most of the African American population of Texas lived in the valleys of the Colorado, Brazos, Trinity, and Neches rivers, as well as in the old plantation lands along the Louisiana border, just as they had during slavery. Indeed, in seven counties, African Americans made up more than 50 percent of the population.[35] The majority of African Americans in Texas followed the agricultural routine of planting and harvesting cotton in much the same way they had done before the Civil War. Cotton production expanded with the coming of the railroads, and it held unbroken sway over the economy of rural Texas.

By 1874, the crop-lien system was well established in Texas. A system of tenancy had existed among white farmers before the Civil War, and the crop-lien served a dual purpose in providing a means for landless farmers to acquire land to farm and giving landowners a source of agricultural labor without paying cash.[36] For a variety of strongly debated reasons, the crop-lien system kept the people of the South, white as well as black, in poverty until World War II.

Very little documentation exists on the farm work of women between the Civil War and 1900; those who would learn about rural African American women's work must rely on a combination of the Former Slave Narratives, census returns, and the oral tradition of families. Each source proves problematic in its own way. Census returns appear to underrepresent substantially the farm labor of African American women. Keith Krawczynski found that the census recorded only 7 percent of African American women age seventeen and over working as full-time farm hands in 1880 in Bexar, Galveston, Panola, Rusk, and Smith counties.[37] The words "full time" may account for this low figure, which is surely an undercount. Women in the early twentieth century participated most fully in the chopping and planting seasons and probably did so in the late nineteenth century as well.[38] The labor of women was absolutely crucial in bringing in the cotton crops.

Circumstances permitting, women also worked diligently to grow food for their families. Every meal that they could provide through their own labor kept down the debt at the furnishing merchant. In the early twentieth century, slightly more than half of African Americans kept gardens. Kyle Wilkison's studies of Hunt County indicate that food production fell in the latter part of the nineteenth century as families became enmeshed in tenancy, concentrating increasingly on the cash crop, cotton. Cow ownership, sweet potato production, and even hog ownership plummeted as cotton production rose.[39] But women grew vegetables, which lasted only for the short growing season; canning technology was not widespread until around World War I. They raised chickens by the score, for both eggs and meat. Some had cows, milking twice a day and turning milk into butter.[40] And they cooked two hot meals a day, sometimes in an open fireplace and sometimes on a wood stove.

Even as African Americans remained in large numbers in the countryside, the black population of the state's growing cities swelled as well. The period from 1870 to 1900 saw tenfold growth in the urban population of Texas, from 59,521 people to 520,759, increasing from 4.4 percent of the state's population to 15.5 percent.[41] The counties experiencing the most rapid growth of African American population included the relatively urbanized Harris (Houston), Bexar (San Antonio, the largest city in the state), Galveston, Dallas, Travis (Austin), Brazos (Bryan), McLennan (Waco), and Tarrant (Fort Worth).[42] Clearly, the cities attracted freedpeople and offered new opportunities. In McLennan County, for example, the percentage of African Americans living in the county seat of Waco increased from 30 percent in 1870 to 40 percent in 1900, substantially greater than the statewide average of 19 percent.[43]

For women, the move from farm to town created immense changes in their lives. Economic opportunities, while still quite limited, were significantly more diverse than in the countryside. The chances to meet and socialize with other people nearby were much greater. And the possibility of receiving an education was greatly enhanced by city life. Young people, realizing the situation, moved to town in large numbers. Philles Thomas relocated from Brazoria County to Galveston in 1877. She reminisced: "I stays with mammy till I's seventeen and help dem share crop. Den I leaves. . . . I marries in Galveston, to dat old cuss, settin' right dere, William Thomas am he name and I's stood for him ever since. . . . Dat cullud gen'man of mine allus bring in de bacon. We'uns am never rich, but allus eats till de last few years."[44] Thomas found true love in the big city as well as financial security and freedom from sharecropping.

What African American women did not find was freedom from work outside the home. Elizabeth Enstam compiled exhaustive statistics on African American women's employment in Dallas. She discovered that in 1880, 76 percent of the African American women aged sixteen and over in Dallas worked for pay, in comparison to 13.8 percent of the white women. African American women, comprising only 23 percent of the female population, made up 68 percent of the female labor force.[45]

In studies of Waco and Dallas, the occupations of African American women remained constant in the late nineteenth century. The largest group worked as laundresses and the next largest as domestics—cooks, maids, servants. Some found employment as nurses or as nursemaids, while others labored as seamstresses. Only a handful had the necessary education to work as schoolteachers or in other professions, such as medical doctors. And a tiny percentage earned wages in the sex trade.[46]

Many domestic servants lived in the household with the families for whom they worked. A sample of 190 domestic workers in Waco in 1896 reveals that 71 percent of them "lived in"; in Dallas, the figure reached 80 percent. In Galveston, domestic servants lived in many back buildings behind Galveston houses.[47] Sharing a domicile with a white family could bring great difficulty for an African American woman, who lost her privacy and sometimes received pay in the form of leftover food and old clothes rather than the cash that she might have preferred. House servants also worked extremely long hours, sometimes on call twenty-four hours a day. I. H. Kempner, son of a very wealthy Galveston family, reminisced fondly about the servants in his parents' home. The cook, coachman, and the housemaid all lived in the quarters at the back of the Kempner property with their "numerous children." In the 1870s, the Kempners paid the women servants ten dollars a month and the men, fifteen dollars, plus living accommodations and food.[48]

The classification of women's domestic work is difficult, given the many different ways of enumeration. Ellen Beasley traced the career of Sarah Bennett through the Galveston city directories. Bennett migrated from Alabama to Galveston in 1870, when she was seventeen years old. In 1875–76, she was working as servant for Christopher Dart, clerk of the U.S. District Court. By 1882–83, Bennett was a cook for M. H. Royston, clerk of the criminal court, and remained there through 1888–89. "The next three directories find her working for three different people, all in the same neighborhood, and in two instances definitely living on her employer's property." In 1898, she was listed as a "laundress," presumably working for herself.[49] It is impossible to know how Bennett's tasks changed from location to location, but the nomenclature of her work shifted by the year. No matter what they were called, many African American women worked as domestics in white homes. In Dallas in 1880, 15 percent of the households had some sort of domestic worker.[50] Rural women, too, almost surely did domestic work for pay along with their work in the fields, as they did in the twentieth century, but little evidence discusses this before 1900.[51]

Laundress was the most common urban employment for African American women. In most nineteenth-century homes, laundry remained a matter of boiling clothes in a pot over an open fire, rubbing them on a rub board, and wringing them before hanging them to dry and then ironing them with flat irons. It was hot, heavy work, which women uniformly dreaded. Many African American women challenged their physical strength and stamina in this line of work. In 1880, Dallas had a self-employed laundress for every 37.1 persons, or approximately every 6.6 households. Half of these women were married and worked at home whenever possible.[52] Despite the arduousness of the work, there was no stigma attached to the physical labor. Clarissa Stayten Rayner, wife of politician John B. Rayner, took in laundry as the only source of steady income for their family; otherwise, the family relied on contributions from Rayner's well-wishers.[53] A number of laundresses saved enough from their slender wages to purchase real estate. In 1900, thirty-nine "washwomen" in Waco were property owners.[54] A

small fraction of African American women also worked in the manufacture of clothing, with their occupations listed as "seamstress." [55]

Elsie Reece, from Navasota, remembered well her two stints working as a cook. She recalled that she began as a young, single woman,
immediately following her freedom: "My folks stays nearly two years
after 'mancipation. Den us all move to Navasota and hires out as cooks.
I cooks till I's eighteen and den marries John Love." After Love's death
in 1881, she resumed her career: "There I is, with chillen to support, so
I goes to cookin' 'gain and we has some purty close times, but I does
it and sends dem to school. I don't want dem to be like dey mammy, a
unknowledge person." [56] Reece most likely worked very hard as a cook.
In the Kempner household in Galveston, the cook served the father of
the house toast and coffee before six A.M. The father then returned for
breakfast between 9:30 and 10:00. The evening meal would be served
between five and seven P.M. The cook would be on duty from the wee
hours of the morning, therefore, until early evening. [57]

Like many women, Mandy Morrow took great pride in her cooking and her employment as the cook of the Texas governor's mansion for James Stephen Hogg. She told her WPA interviewer, "I stays
in Georgetown 'bout 20 years and den I goes to Austin and dere I
works fer de big folks. After I been dere 'bout five year, Gov'ner James
Stephen Hogg send for me to be cook in de Mansion and de best cook
job I's ever had. De gov'nor am mighty fine man and so am he wife.
She am not of de good health and allus have de misery, and befo' long
she say to me, 'Mandy, I'se gwineter 'pend on you without my watchin.'
Massa Hogg allus say I does wonders with dat food and him proud fer
to have him friends eat it. . . . I works for de Gov'nor till he wife die
and den I's quit, 'cause I don't want bossin' by de housekeeper what
don't know much 'bout cookin' and am allus fustin' 'round." [58] Morrow
treasured the autonomy that Sallie Stinson Hogg allowed her in running her own affairs, considering it valuable enough to quit rather than
lose it. Some cooks also did well enough financially to purchase real
estate. [59]

African American women also found employment caring for the
young and for the sick; both positions carried the title of "nurse," although the duties were different. A little girl as young as six years old
might find work as a nursemaid for an infant. [60] Adults cared for children as well; I. H. Kempner wrote, "I recall the fidelity to my parents of my old Negro mammy, Aunt Eveline." [61] Minerva Bendy, from

Woodville, rejoiced in the children whom she had cared for, despite her own childlessness: "Us never have chick or chile. I's such a good nuss I guess de Lawd didn't want me to have none of my own, so's I could nuss all de others and I 'spect I've nussed most de white chillen and cullud, too, here in Woodville."[62] As Lillian Smith pointed out, the racial lines remained muddled as African American women gained the love of white children who were to grow up to subjugate them.[63]

African American women also served as midwives, delivering or helping to deliver even the most elite of Galveston babies. Margaret Sealy Burton recalled her mother's midwife, "Aunt Maria": "My mother had Aunt Maria for all her babies, and many a time the old mammy was seen with a basket on her arm, covered with snow white linen, in which she insisted that she was carrying new babies to the young mothers." I. H. Kempner remembered "Aunt Isabel," who assisted with the births of "several" of his brothers.[64] In Meridian, Mariah Robinson also delighted in "help[ing] de doctors with de babies."[65] Nursing careers extended beyond midwifery. Mary Armstrong moved to Houston in 1871 and immediately found work with a local physician: "I gets me a job nussin' for Dr. Rellaford and was all through the yellow fever epidemic. I 'lects in '75 people die jes' like sheep with the rots. I's seen folks with the fever jump from their bed with death on 'em and grab other folks. The doctor saved lots of folks, white and black, 'cause he sweat it out of 'em. He mixed up hot water and vinegar and mustard and some else in it."[66] For most women, nursing was as close as they came to being a health care professional. Only one African American female physician, Dr. Mary S. Moore, served in Texas in the nineteenth century. One of the first women to graduate from Meharry Medical College, Moore was in practice in Galveston by 1900.[67]

Other women found employment delivering comfort of another sort; an undetermined number of African American women worked as prostitutes in Texas cities. The *Galveston Daily News* complained about "the negro prostitutes that nightly prowl about our streets," and at least nine African American women were arrested in a raid of "women of disreputable character, corralling some 25 or 30 of the residents of Tin-can and Fat alleys." The Waco censuses of 1880 and 1890, respectively, enumerated six and eleven African American prostitutes.[68]

At the other end of the spectrum of respectability was teaching school. In the nineteenth century, educational opportunities for African Americans expanded dramatically, and teaching became an occupation for the best-educated and most ambitious women. An 1881 Texas law gave cities and towns permission to levy taxes for public education, giving a boost to urban schools. All-white school boards distributed the county's share of state funds to African American and white schools. In Harrison County, African American schools received only half of the funds to which they were entitled. African American schools grew nonetheless; by 1883, thirteen cities and towns had thirty-two schools for African American students. Galveston chartered Central Public High School, the first high school for African Americans in Texas, in 1885, and it graduated its first class in 1890. By 1900, Texas had nineteen African American high schools.[69] Nineteenth-century rural schools, which probably went no further than the eighth grade at best, are extremely underdocumented. They likely had shortened school years, to fit the needs of the cotton crop, and were probably mostly scarce and small. Diligent research is needed to uncover the history of these important outposts of education.

As elsewhere in the United States, the percentage of women teaching increased in the late nineteenth century; in Waco in 1880, 50 percent of the teachers were women, and in 1900, the number had increased to 65 percent.[70] Galveston had seven African American women teachers by 1887, and Dallas had eleven by 1889. A Dallas woman became principal of a "colored" school by 1900.[71] African American women found themselves at the lowest rung of the pay scales. In Harris County, the average teacher's annual salary for the period 1882–84 was $72 for white males, $47.80 for white females, $42 for African American males, and $35 for African American females. Ten years later, African American women had gained considerably but still lagged behind, with white males earning $292, white females, $260, African American males, $252; and African American females, $205.[72]

The women who taught school clearly represented some of the urban elite. In Waco in 1896, the teachers at the First District School included Maggie C. Denham, the wife of an African Methodist Episcopal (AME) minister, and Anna L. Quarles Vandavell, the widow of physician Dr. J. M. Vandavell. At the Old East Waco School no. 27, teacher L. M. Sublett had the formal assistance of Anne E. Sublett, his wife. The Second District School employed Cornelia Henry, wife of another schoolteacher, Benjamin Henry; Georgia G. Majors, married to Monroe A. Majors, a local physician; and Mary E. Moore, the wife of the school principal, A. J. Moore. Teaching also offered opportunity for unmarried women. Mabel Mofford and Alice Banes, teachers at the same Waco school, boarded at the same house near the school. There was no one else with the same surnames living in Waco, indicating that these women were living independently of their relatives.[73]

African American women who wanted to become teachers often endured arduous paths to higher education. Josie Briggs Hall, born in Waxahachie in 1869, attended Bishop College but did not graduate. She went on to teach school in the communities of Canaan, Ray, and Mexia. Mattie Ella Holman Durden began school in Refugio in a one-room, one-teacher school with a very limited curriculum. She moved to Austin to attend Tillotson Collegiate and Normal Institute in 1896, when she was fifteen. Examinations for grade placement put her in the fifth grade, but through diligent study and reexamination she placed in the eighth grade. Durden managed to remain at Tillotson for two years, until financial difficulties forced her to leave. In 1899, Durden took her county teachers' examination, passed, acquired a teaching certificate, and began teaching in Refugio County.[74]

Education of African Americans in Texas made extraordinary progress in the years between 1874 and 1900. The overall African American illiteracy rate dropped from 75.4 percent in 1880 to 38.2 in 1900, the lowest in the South. By 1900, 70 percent of the women in rural Central Texas under the age of forty-five knew how to read, and 66 percent could write.[75] By 1880, most African American urban schools divided into elementary, intermediate or grammar, secondary, and college. Elementary and grammar schools taught the three Rs, geography, and history. Secondary school curriculum was divided into college prep and normal. Classical studies were common in the denominational schools, including Latin, Greek, math, science, philosophy, modern language, and theology.[76]

African American higher education flowered with a large number of institutions: Paul Quinn College in Waco, 1872; Wiley College in Marshall, 1873; Tillotson College in Austin, 1875; Prairie View A&M in Prairie View and Samuel Huston College in Austin, 1876; Bishop College in Marshall, 1881; Guadalupe College in Seguin, 1884; Mary Allen Seminary in Crockett, 1886; Texas College in Tyler, 1894; and St. Philip's College in San Antonio, 1898.[77] All of these schools except Prairie View were founded by church groups, and all of them admitted women from the beginning. In the early days, the curriculum was firmly committed to liberal arts instruction, prompting criticism from those who believed that African Americans needed vocational instruction rather than classical studies. The schools gradually added industrial courses to the curriculum, offering such topics as agriculture, carpentry, printing, cutting, and "practical housekeeping," which included cooking, dressmaking, millinery, and other "useful arts."[78]

The schools founded by African American religious denominations, Texas College, Paul Quinn College, and Guadalupe College, had African American personnel in all teaching capacities in the nineteenth century. Those schools founded by whites gradually desegregated their faculties, and Wiley and Samuel Huston had African American personnel by the 1890s.[79] The faculty of Paul Quinn in 1896 had four male teachers and two females: Miss Emma A. Reynolds, M.D., "lady principal, matron, and instructor in nurse training dept.," and Miss Beatrice F. Rochon, teacher of music. Both Reynolds and Rochon lived on campus.[80]

Beginning with nothing at emancipation, African Americans in Texas gradually accumulated some property and wealth. From the time of freedom, African Americans wanted to have land of their own. Mollie Dawson of Navarro County, who sharecropped with her husband, discussed their hunger for land: "George and me worked hard on dis little farm all de time and had hopes of owning it some day. We had done lots of work there, we built a good log crib and built more fences and cleared up more land down in de bottom, part of it was bottom land, part was hillside but about that time we was gittin where we could buy us a little home of our own, George took typhoid fever and died."[81]

By 1900, a third of African American farmers in Texas owned their land.[82] Women played an active part in acquiring land. Martha Taylor employed one of the more unusual methods. The white landowner of the Prairie Bottom community in McLennan County instigated a race among the African American settlers: "The first man, woman or child that gets to the bottom; point to a clump of trees, and cuts the Youpon bush, I will give a home." Taylor won the race, and she and her husband, Quincy Taylor, cleared the land and established their home.[83] Although the white owners' actions of pitting the settlers against one another, possibly for his own amusement, might be suspect, the Taylor family benefited from the competition.

The path taken by Pete and Mariah Young of Bosque County was more traditional. The family left their former mistress in Georgia and headed for Texas, rootless. Mariah Young remembered: "After leavin'

Miss Joe us move here and yonder till I gits tired of sich. By den us have sev'ral chillen and I changes from de frivol'ty of life to de sincereness, to shape de dest'ny of de chillens' life. I tells Pete when he comes back from fiddlin' one night, to buy me de home or hitch up and carry me back to Missy Joe. Dat lead him to buy a strip of land in Meridian. He pays ten dollar de acre." The Young family thrived: "We has a team of oxen, call Broad and Buck, and we done our farmin' with dem. Pete builds me a house, hauls de lumber from Waco. Twict us gits burnt out, but builds it 'gain. Us makes de orchard and sells de fruit. Us raises bees and sells de honey and gits cows and chickens and turkeys. Pete works good and I puts on my bonnet and walks behind him and draps de corn. He gits in organizin' de fust cullud church in Meridian, de cullud Cumberland Presb'terian Church. Us has ever lived de useful life."[84] By working actively together, working behind plodding oxen, and diversifying their production, Pete and Mariah Young managed to buy a home of their own.

A number of women owned property independently. Some bought it outright; in 1883 Dorcas Gregg bought 12 acres of Travis County land from Rubin and Elizabeth Hancock. Hannah Perryman homesteaded an 80-acre homestead in Polk County, having her land surveyed in 1874.[85] Most female landowners, however, were most likely widows who inherited their husbands' parts of their estates. Their holdings were small but treasured. When Fanny Cribbs of Liberty County died in 1887, she carefully parceled out her possessions to neighbors and friends. Cribbs directed that her nine cattle, five horses, four hogs, and 8.5 acres of land be equally divided between Antony Dodson, who lived on a farm outside of Liberty, and her neighbor, Henderson Montgomery. She left a heifer to Lettie Dodson and split her household goods and furniture and all seven of her beehives between Lettie Dodson; the daughter of a neighbor, Rebecka Brown; farmer's wife Laura Bullock; and Bullock's neighbor Louiza Anderson. With her kitchen goods, Cribbs's entire estate was valued at $262.50.[86]

Mary Lawrence Carrington, also from Liberty County, inherited 18 acres of land and her home place when her first husband died. In 1880, her property was valued at $350 with $150 worth of stock: hogs, a horse, two milk cows, and eight other cattle. Carrington produced 2 bales of cotton, 50 bushels of corn, 20 pounds of honey, 5 pounds of wax, and 15 bushels of sweet potatoes worth $110.[87] The 1880 enumeration of Brazos County listed other female African American smallholders: Marlinda

Whitehead, the owner of 5 acres, one cow, and eight chickens; Elizabeth Small, with 3 acres and five chickens; and Harriet Satterwith, 10 acres, one horse, and two chickens.[88]

A few women controlled substantial amounts of land. Ann B. Welch of Brazos County owned 70 acres, with five horses, forty-six cows, a hog, and twenty-five chickens.[89] After her husband's death in the late 1880s or early 1890s, Jane Johnson Endsley managed her family's 100-acre farm in Dallas County, where it had been assessed at a value of $15,150 in 1882. Endsley was independent by the standards of the day, regularly delivering her own cotton to the local cotton gin and defending her property with a cotton hook when a white man attempted to steal a bale of cotton from her.[90]

As noted, women also owned property in town. The most remarkable African American female landowner in Texas was Hope Thompson. Thompson worked as a laundress in Dallas. In the early 1870s, "her family wanted to buy a small piece of property at the corner of Live Oak and Elm streets for fifty dollars." Thompson negotiated a loan from Captain W. H. Gaston, a client who was also a banker. He agreed to let her repay the debt by washing his clothes. Thompson's wealth brought difficulty, however. Her husband left in 1872 and moved to Collin County, and she continued on as a single woman. From the 1870s until at least the mid-1880s, Thompson was involved in a number of lawsuits over the property, but she succeeded in retaining title to it. The land increased rapidly in value, and in September 1885 Thompson's real estate was appraised at about $35,000. She sold the land in various parcels, dealing and trading her real estate.[91]

Despite considerable gains, African Americans continued to suffer from the legacy of racism in the American South. The racial violence that plagued the entire South in the late nineteenth and early twentieth centuries is well documented. Terrorism and lynching abounded, as much in Texas as anywhere else. Their sex did not exclude women from the miasma of violence that covered the South. In his exhaustive study of violence in Central Texas through World War I, William Carrigan found several examples of women losing their lives to organized violence. He reported that at least forty-five people died at the hands of mobs in Central Texas between the end of Reconstruction and the turn of the century. Thirty-two of the victims were African American. Three were women, all of whom were African American. Two of the women were killed for allegedly committing murder. In July 1874, the

San Antonio Express reported that "Nathanel Burges and his wife were lynched by a mob of five men in central Texas for 'no provocation.'" The only motive, Carrigan concluded was "racial prejudice."[92] In addition to mob violence, African American women were also subjected to terrorism. Mary Phillips and her three children were killed by a dynamite bomb at their house in Falls County in July 1895. The bombing followed the death of Phillips's husband, Abe Phillips, in a gun battle with a white neighbor over an unspecified dispute. A local newspaper reported that the explosion was so powerful it killed birds in the area. The bombers were not identified.[93] Additionally, there was individual violence, such as that reported by Annie Row, whose husband was shot for stepping on a white man's foot.[94]

Racial tensions sometimes caused difficult lives to become impossible. African American women occasionally sought extreme solutions to bad conditions. Carrigan found scattered examples of African American women doing violence to themselves or others: "In 1877, a local black woman named Eliza Jackson attempted to take her own life by swallowing morphine. A year later, a poor black woman attempted to drown herself in the Brazos river. . . . In 1888, a black mother sought to save her newborn baby from the travails of life by killing her child."[95]

Most Texas African American women dealt with the difficulties of life not with violence but with perseverance and resignation. Some actively contested the racial boundaries that were springing up like hedgerows across the Texas landscape in the late nineteenth century. After the passage of the U.S. Civil Rights Act of 1875, women sought to occupy equal space. One area that women wished to occupy was the theater. In Galveston, Waco, and Sherman, African Americans tried to desegregate the seating. In Galveston, Mary Miller sued for damages in federal court after being forcibly ejected from the "white ladies circle" of the Treemont Opera House in Galveston. The court ruled that the owner of the opera house was guilty of depriving Miller of her civil rights and fined him five hundred dollars. The judge, however, undercut his ruling by saying that he wished the fine could be one cent and later dismissed it completely. The outraged Galveston African American community held a mass meeting to denounce the judge's actions.[96]

The segregation of transportation facilities alarmed African American women. Trains were one area of contestation. Milly Anderson won a suit in U.S. District Court in 1875 against the Houston and

Texas Central Railroad for denying her admission to a railroad car. The judge ruled that a female passenger had a right to sit in the only car for ladies alone. Isabella E. Mabson, a teacher in Galveston's West District School, also sued in district court. She received humiliating treatment while traveling from Kansas City to Galveston aboard the Missouri, Kansas and Texas Railway Company. She bought first-class tickets in Kansas City, and she and her children rode in the "palace car" until they reached Denison, Texas, where they were ejected to a "dirty, common coach provided for negroes." The disposition of her case is unknown.[97]

Steamships were another area of difficulty and potential segregation. In 1883, two African American Galveston women bought first-class tickets from Key West to Galveston on the Mallory line, but on the second day at sea the attendants humiliated them. Told to leave their first-class table in the dining area, they were forcibly removed, forbidden to return, and not given the first-class accommodations for which they paid. The women sued for damages but presumably lost their case.[98]

Other women used their physical presence as protest. Adelina Dowdie Cuney, the daughter of a white planter and his mulatto slave, married African American Galveston politician Wright Cuney in 1871. Adelina and Wright Cuney expressed their views on the racial situation by naming their son Lloyd Garrison, after the abolitionist. In 1886, before Texas had passed a separate coach law, Adelina Cuney "tried to board the train to Houston. She was barred from entering the first-class car by a conductor who locked the door. Noting the racially motivated act, she simply asked her brother-in-law Joseph for a lift, climbed into the train through the window, and rode undisturbed to Houston."[99]

The protests became moot in 1883, when the U.S. Supreme Court declared the public accommodations section of the Civil Rights Act of 1875 to be unconstitutional, and Texas began passing a series of restrictive laws.[100] With the passage of *Plessy v. Ferguson* in 1896, "separate but equal" became the law of the land for another fifty years.

With the walls of segregation hardening, African Americans turned instead to their institutions of their own making for support. Foremost among these was the church.[101] In Texas, as elsewhere throughout the South, freed slaves moved quickly to develop their own churches. African American Baptists left the churches of their masters, forming their own congregations. Methodist missionaries from the African Methodist Episcopal (AME) and the Methodist

Episcopal churches moved into Texas and founded congregations; the Colored Methodist Episcopal (CME) church formed in 1870. Seven Presbyterian congregations formed the Negro Presbytery of Texas in 1874. Although none of these congregations allowed women to serve as pastor, women outnumbered men "by a considerable margin."[102]

While no overall study of Texas African American churches exists, one may draw some conclusions about the makeup of the church in the late nineteenth century. In a study of churches across the South in 1950, researcher Ralph Felton found that of 481 rural congregations, 18 percent were organized in the 1870s, 14 percent in the 1880s, and 14 percent in the 1890s. Half of the congregations traced their beginnings to the thirty-five-year period starting in 1865.[103] By 1900, Galveston had at least fourteen African American congregations.[104] Clyde McQueeney's study of 375 historic African American churches in Texas found that 68.4 percent of the churches were Baptist; 11.7 percent AME, 4.5 percent CME, 0.3 percent Methodist Episcopal, and 14.1 percent United Methodist; 0.5 percent Catholic; and 0.3 percent Church of Christ.[105]

Women undoubtedly played a major role in creating and sustaining church congregations. A history of St. Paul AME in Waco observes that former pastor A. W. Jones was the "first African American preacher in town. His wife, Nanie T. Jones, assisted him greatly." A listing of the charter members of almost any church included more female names than male.[106]

Churches served as a base for women to address community needs. In the 1880s and 1890s, churchwomen founded benevolent aid societies to nurse the sick and care for orphans and the aged. As Josie Brown noted, orphans needed care. Most were simply taken in by kin, but African American women created organizations to care for the children in Gilmer and Houston.[107] The African American churches also played an active role in fostering higher education in Texas.

Another method of caring for one another and for society at large was through women's clubs. Although the largest number of women's clubs were created after 1900, some had roots in the nineteenth century. By 1901, the African American Eastern Star order, one of the female auxiliaries to the Masons, had thirty-three chapters in Texas. The Grand Order, Court of Calanthe, founded in Texas in 1897 by Mrs. S. H. Norris of Dallas, was "the only fraternal insurance organization owned and controlled by black women." It grew rapidly, with thirteen courts being organized in 1902 alone. By 1903, seventy-seven chapters existed in sixty-five towns, hamlets as well as county seats. Calanthean club minutes reveal the difficulty of organizing groups in the days before easy transportation. M. A. Johnson of Marshall complained, "This has been a very rainy spring in these parts. Therefore the club could not meet as often as they desired." E. Ida R. Smith of Houston observed, "The Court I set up at Cold Springs is twelve miles from any railroad, which distance must be made by vehicle. I did not hesitate for this and other inconveniences, but went forth at duty's stern command." Women were willing to sacrifice much for the Calanthean cause. In return, they received a chance to join together in grand ways; the suggested regalia for officers was "white plush collars trimmed with gold lace."[108]

Most clubwomen were members of the rising middle class. Among the Calantheans, both state officeholders from Waco were schoolteachers. They had accepted standards of behavior, resolving that any member "guilty of acting disorderly at any public place or gathering or drinking in public places shall be fined not less than $5."[109] African American clubwomen, like their white counterparts, highly valued respectability.

Without suffrage, the political activities of African American women were limited, but they did take an interest in affairs of national significance. Isabelle Smith, wife of reformer R. L. Smith, worked with him to found the Farmers Improvement Society (FIS) in 1889, with membership open to men and women. As president of FIS's Ladies' Auxiliary, Smith addressed a meeting of five hundred male and female delegates in Hempstead around 1900. She stressed the need for a practical education for boys and girls and declared that "the negro woman had much to do with fixing the status of the negro in this country." African American women also worked with the temperance movement. Frances Willard established the first two Texas chapters of the Women's Christian Temperance Union (WCTU) in Paris, one for white and one for African Americans, in 1882. The African American union met in an African American church and was presided by over the pastor's wife. By 1886, there were six African American temperance unions in Texas. The state organization of the Colored Division of WCTU formed in Dallas in 1897 and began growing rapidly after the 1898 election of Mrs. Eliza Peterson, a music teacher from Texarkana. In Houston in April 1900, officers held a meeting at the African Methodist Episcopal church on Wall Street to organize a chapter.[110]

As African American women faced the new century, they could

point to a mixed balance sheet. They had gained much since Reconstruction: literacy, churches, colleges, organized activities, and economic opportunities in town. For many women, however, life remained much the same, with excruciatingly hard work on the region's cotton farms, racial violence, and increasing segregation. Surely they looked ahead with a mixture of hope and resignation.

Notes

1. Robert A. Calvert and Arnoldo De Leon, *The History of Texas* (Arlington Heights, Ill.: Harlan Davidson, 1990), 156; Lawrence D. Rice, The Negro in Texas, 1874–1900 (Baton Rouge: Louisiana State University Press, 1971), 162.

2. Calvert and De Leon, *The History of Texas*, 156.

3. "Born in Slavery: Slave Narratives from the Federal Writers' Project, 1936–1938," Mariah Robinson, Texas Narratives, vol. 16, part 3, 255, http://memory.loc.gov/ammem/snhtml/snhome.html. Henceforth, all "Born in Slavery: Slave Narratives" are available at this site.

4. For a discussion of the heated theoretical debates surrounding the structure of the African American family, see Steward E. Tolnay, *The Bottom Rung: African American Family Life on Southern Farms* (Urbana: University of Illinois Press, 1999), 100–106.

5. "Born in Slavery: Slave Narratives," Betty Powers, Texas Narratives, vol. 16, part 3, 192.

6. Michael Haines, "Western Fertility in Mid-Transition: Fertility and Nuptiality in the United States and Selected Nations at the Turn of the Century," *Journal of Family History* 15 (1990); quoted in Tolnay, *The Bottom Rung,* 53.

7. Rebecca Sharpless, *Fertile Ground, Narrow Choices: Women on Texas Cotton Farms, 1900–1940* (Chapel Hill: University of North Carolina Press, 1999), 18.

8. "Born in Slavery: Slave Narratives," Minerva Bendy, Texas Narratives, vol. 16, part 1, 69.

9. Pat Stephens, comp. and ed., *The Black Community of Bonham, Texas: Forgotten Dignity: A Photographic History, 1800–1930* ([Bonham, Tex.]: Progressive Citizens, 1984), 20.

10. "Born in Slavery: Slave Narratives," Julia Blanks, Texas Narratives, vol. 16, part 1, 99.

11. Jiangjiang Xie, "The Black Community in Waco, Texas: A Study of Place, Family, and Work, 1880–1900" (master's thesis, Baylor University, 1988), 48.

12. Randolph B. Campbell, *A Southern Community in Crisis: Harrison County, Texas, 1850–1880* (Austin: Texas State Historical Association, 1983), 369.

13. Tolnay, The Bottom Rung, 97, 106–107.

14. "Born in Slavery: Slave Narratives," Elsie Reece, Texas Narratives, vol. 16, part 3, 235.

15. "Born in Slavery: Slave Narratives," Annie Row, Texas Narratives, vol. 16, part 3, 261.

16. Tolnay, The Bottom Rung, 17; Xie, "The Black Community in Waco, Texas," 48.

17. "Born in Slavery: Slave Narratives," Annie Row, Texas Narratives, vol. 16, part 3, 261.

18. "Born in Slavery: Slave Narratives," Tillie Powers, Texas Narratives, vol. 16, part 3, 194.

19. "Born in Slavery: Slave Narratives," Eliza Holman, Texas Narratives, vol. 16, part 2, 150.

20. "Born in Slavery: Slave Narratives," Leithean Spinks, Texas Narratives, vol. 16, part 4, 60.

21. "Born in Slavery: Slave Narratives," Mollie Taylor, Texas Narratives, vol. 16, part 4, 77.

22. "Born in Slavery: Slave Narratives," Louise Mathews, Texas Narratives, vol. 16, part 3, 66.

23. "Born in Slavery: Slave Narratives," Rosina Hoard, Texas Narratives, vol. 16, part 2, p. 142.

24. Shawn Bonath Carlson, *African American Lifeways in East-Central Texas: The Ned Peterson Farmstead (41BZ115), Brazos County, Texas* (College Station: Center for Environmental Archaeology, Texas A&M University, 1995), 38.

25. Campbell, *Southern Community in Crisis*, 369.

26. Tolnay, *The Bottom Rung*, 17; Sharpless, Fertile Ground, Narrow Choices, 40.

27. "Born in Slavery: Slave Narratives," Josie Brown, Texas Narratives, vol. 16, part 1, 165.

28. "Born in Slavery: Slave Narratives," Willie Forward, Texas Narratives, vol. 16, part 2, 48.

29. "Born in Slavery: Slave Narratives," Betty Bormer, Texas Narratives, vol. 16, part 1, 111.

30. Marie E. Blake and Terri Myers, *After Slavery: The Rubin Hancock Farmstead, 1880–1916* (Austin: Texas Department of Transportation, 1999), 21.

31. Tolnay, *The Bottom Rung*, 72.

32. Alwyn Barr, *Black Texans: A History of Negroes in Texas, 1528–1971* (Austin: The Jenkins Company, 1973), 164.

33. Kyle Grant Wilkison, "The End of Independence: Social and Political Reaction to Economic Change in Texas, 1870–1914" (Ph.D. diss., Vanderbilt University, 1995), 63.

34. "Born in Slavery: Slave Narratives," Betty Farrow, Texas Narratives, vol. 16, part 2, 34.

35. Historical U.S. Census Data Browser, http://fisher.lib.virginia.edu/

census/. The counties with the highest number of African Americans were Harrison, Harris, Robertson, Smith, Washington, McLennan, Grimes, Dallas, Travis, and Falls. The seven counties with the highest percentage of African American population were Harrison, 68.0 percent African American; Fort Bend, 65.3 percent; Brazoria, 55.3 percent; Grimes, 54.8 percent; Robertson, 53.1 percent; Walker, 52.6 percent; and Wharton, 51.4 percent.

36. The literature on the crop-lien system is voluminous. For discussions of the system in Texas, see Samuel L. Evans, "Texas Agriculture, 1880–1930" (Ph.D. diss., University of Texas, 1960), 308–43; Wilkison, "The End of Independence," 1–96; and Neil Foley, *The White Scourge: Mexicans, Blacks, and Poor Whites in Texas Cotton Culture* (Berkeley: University of California Press, 1997), 17–39.

37. Keith Krawczynski, "The Agricultural Labor of Black Texans as Slaves and as Freedmen" (master's thesis, Baylor University, 1989), 92; Carlson, "African American Lifeways in East Texas," 38.

38. Sharpless, *Fertile Ground, Narrow Choices,* 164–66.

39. Wilkison, "The End of Independence," 48–52.

40. Blake and Myers, After Slavery, 34; Carlson, *African American Lifeways in East Texas,* 131, citing the 1880 Productions of Agriculture, Enumeration District 20, Brazos County.

41. Calvert and De Leon, *The History of Texas,* 156.

42. Figures extrapolated from Census Browser and Campbell, *Empire for Slavery,* 264–66.

43. Census Browser; Xie, "The Black Community in Waco, Texas," 22.

44. "Born in Slavery: Slave Narratives," Philles Thomas, Texas Narratives, vol. 16, part 4, 92–93.

45. Elizabeth York Enstam, *Women and the Creation of Urban Life: Dallas, Texas, 1843–1920* (College Station: Texas A&M University Press, 1998), 65. See also tables on pages 215 and 216, demonstrating the changes in African American women's employment between 1880 and 1890.

46. Xie, "The Black Community in Waco, Texas," 63; Enstam, *Women and the Creation of Urban Life,* 66, 77–78; Ruthe Winegarten, *Black Texas Women: 150 Years of Trial and Triumph* (Austin: University of Texas Press, 1995), 49.

47. *Morrison & Fourmy's General Directory of the City of Waco, 1896–97* (Galveston: Morrison and Fourmy, 1896), sample; Enstam, Women and the Creation of Urban Life, 66; Ellen Beasley, *The Alleys and Back Buildings of Galveston: An Architectural and Social History* (Houston: Rice University Press, 1996), 7.

48. I. H. Kempner, *Recalled Recollections* (Dallas: The Egan Company, 1961), 2–3; quoted in Beasley, *The Alleys and Back Buildings of Galveston,* 29.

49. Beasley, *The Alleys and Back Buildings of Galveston,* 44.

50. Enstam, *Women and the Creation of Urban Life,* 214.

51. Sharpless, *Fertile Ground, Narrow Choices,* 70–71, 102, 104–105, 148, 244.

52. Enstam, *Women and the Creation of Urban Life,* 66, 214.

53. Gregg Cantrell, *Kenneth and John B. Rayner and the Limits of Southern Dissent* (Urbana: University of Illinois Press, 1993), 218–19.

54. Xie, "The Black Community in Waco, Texas," 70.

55. Ibid., 63; Krawzynski, "The Agricultural Labor of Black Texans," 92.

56. "Born in Slavery: Slave Narratives," Elsie Reece.

57. Kempner, *Recalled Recollections*, 2–3; quoted in Beasley, *The Alleys and Back Buildings of Galveston*, 29.

58. "Born in Slavery: Slave Narratives," Mandy Morrow, Texas Narratives, vol. 16, part 3, 139–40.

59. Xie, "The Black Community in Waco, Texas," 70.

60. Winegarten, *Black Texas Women: 150 Years of Trial and Triumph*, 47.

61. Kempner, *Recalled Recollections*, 2–3; quoted in Beasley, *The Alleys and Back Buildings of Galveston*, 29.

62. "Born in Slavery: Slave Narratives," Minerva Bendy, Texas Narratives, vol. 16, part 1, 69.

63. Lillian Smith, *Killers of the Dream* (New York: W. W. Norton, 1949), 28–29.

64. Elizabeth Hayes Turner, *Women, Culture, and Community: Religion and Reform in Galveston, 1880–1920* (New York: Oxford University Press, 1997), 259; Kempner, *Recalled Recollections*, 2–3; quoted in Beasley, *The Alleys and Back Buildings of Galveston*, 29.

65. "Born in Slavery: Slave Narratives," Mariah Robinson, Texas Narratives, vol. 16, part 3, 255.

66. "Born in Slavery: Slave Narratives," Mary Armstrong, Texas Narratives, vol. 16, part 1, 30.

67. Turner, *Women, Culture, and Community*, 25.

68. Beasley, *The Alleys and Back Buildings of Galveston*, 31, 34; Xie, "The Black Community in Waco, Texas," 63.

69. Winegarten, *Black Texas Women: 150 Years of Trial and Triumph*, 92–93, 95; Turner, *Women, Culture, and Community*, 244.

70. Xie, "The Black Community in Waco, Texas," 72.

71. Turner, *Women, Culture, and Community*, 23; Enstam, *Women and the Creation of Urban Life*, 66, 77.

72. Winegarten, *Black Texas Women: 150 Years of Trial and Triumph*, 95.

73. *Waco City Directory, 1896–97*, 46, 126; Garry H. Radford Sr., *African American Heritage in Waco, Texas* (Austin: Eakin Press, 2000), 103, 104.

74. *The Handbook of Texas Online*, http://www.tsha.utexas.edu/handbook/online/: s.v. "Hall, Josie Briggs," by Paul M. Lucko; "Durden, Mattie Ella Holman," by Olive Durden Brown.

75. Winegarten, *Black Texas Women: 150 Years of Trial and Triumph*, 91; Sharpless, *Fertile Ground, Narrow Choices*, 194.

76. Michael R. Heintze, *Private Black Colleges in Texas, 1865–1954* (College Station: Texas A&M University Press, 1985), 47–48.

77. *Texas Almanac 2000–2001* (Dallas: Dallas Morning News), 548; *The*

Handbook of Texas Online, http://www.tsha.utexas.edu/handbook/online/: s.v. "Guadalupe College," by Anne Brawner; "Mary Allen Junior College," by John R. "Pete" Hendrick; "Paul Quinn College," by Douglas Hales; "Prairie View A&M University," by George Ruble Woolfolk; "St. Philip's College," by John S. Gray III; "Samuel Huston College"; "Texas College," by Nancy Beck Young; "Tillotson College"; and "Wiley College," by Sallie M. Lentz and Gilbert Allen.

78. Heintze, *Black Private Colleges in Texas,* 58, 68.

79. Ibid., 90–91.

80. *Waco City Directory 1896–97,* 48.

81. Carlson, *African American Lifeways in East Texas,* 38, quoting slave narrative of Mollie Dawson, District 8, D–F.

82. Barr, *Black Texans,* 88.

83. *Mt. Olive Missionary Baptist Church, Downsville, Texas, 100th Year Anniversary, 1884–1984* (N.d., n.p. In The Texas Collection, Baylor University, Waco, Texas), 6.

84. "Born in Slavery: Slave Narratives," Mariah Robinson, Texas Narratives, vol. 16, part 3, 255.

85. Blake and Myers, *After Slavery,* 19; Winegarten, *Black Texas Women: 150 Years of Trial and Triumph,* 53.

86. Debra Ann Reid, "Farmers in the New South: Race, Gender, and Class in a Rural Southeast Texas County, 1850–1900" (master's thesis, Baylor University, 1996), 134–35.

87. Reid, "Farmers in the New South," 131.

88. Carlson, *African American Lifeways in East Texas,* 131, 137.

89. Ibid., 139.

90. *The Handbook of Texas Online,* http://www.tsha.utexas.edu/handbook/online/: s.v. "Endsley, Jane Johnson," by Teresa Paloma Acosta.

91. Winegarten, *Black Texas Women: 150 Years of Trial and Triumph,* 49; *The Handbook of Texas Online,* http://www.tsha.utexas.edu/handbook/online/: s.v. "Thompson, Hope," by Mary M. Standifer.

92. William Dean Carrigan, "Between South and West: Race, Violence, and Power in Central Texas, 1836–1916" (Ph.D. diss., Emory University, 1999), 223, 224.

93. Carrigan, "Between South and West," 242.

94. "Born in Slavery: Slave Narratives," Annie Row, Texas Narratives, vol. 16, part 3, 261.

95. Carrigan, "Between South and West," 244.

96. Winegarten, *Black Texas Women: 150 Years of Trial and Triumph,* 71, 75; Turner, *Women, Culture, and Community,* 235.

97. Winegarten, *Black Texas Women: 150 Years of Trial and Triumph,* 73–75; Turner, *Women, Culture, and Community,* 235.

98. Turner, *Women, Culture, and Community,* 235.

99. Ibid., 229–30.

100. Winegarten, *Black Texas Women: 150 Years of Trial and Triumph*, 73.

101. For an overview of the development of the African American church, see Albert J. Raboteau, *Canaan Land: A Religious History of African Americans* (New York: Oxford University Press, 2001).

102. William E. Montgomery, "The Formation of African American Churches," introduction to *Black Churches in Texas: A Guide to Historic Congregations* by Clyde McQueen (College Station: Texas A&M University Press, 2000), 10, 11, 13, 14.

103. Ralph A. Felton, *These My Brethren: A Study of 570 Negro Churches and 1,542 Negro Homes in the Rural South* (Madison, N.J.: Department of the Rural Church, Drew Theological Seminary, 1950), 78.

104. Turner, *Women, Culture, and Community*, 240.

105. Clyde McQueen, *Black Churches in Texas: A Guide to Historic Congregations* (College Station: Texas A&M University Press, 2000), xviii.

106. Radford, *African American Heritage*, 11, 13, 17; Winegarten, *Black Texas Women: 150 Years of Trial and Triumph*, 61.

107. Winegarten, *Black Texas Women: 150 Years of Trial and Triumph*, 62.

108. *Minutes of the Sixth Annual Session, Grand Court of Texas, Independent Order of Calanthe, K. of P., Jurisdiction, N.A., S.A., E., A., A. and A., held at San Antonio, Texas, June 9–13, 1903* (Dallas: Dallas Express Print, 1903), 40.

109. *Minutes of the Sixth Annual Session*, 40; *Directory of the City of Waco, 1902–1903* (Galveston: Morrison and Fourmy Directory Co., 1902), 159, 211. The two Wacoans were Mary Moore, discussed above, and Lota B. Waites.

110. Winegarten, *Black Texas Women: 150 Years of Trial and Triumph*, 76, 77.

BRUCE A. GLASRUD

4. Time of Transition

BLACK WOMEN IN EARLY TWENTIETH-CENTURY TEXAS, 1900–1930

By 1900, African American women in Texas endured slavery, achieved a limited degree of freedom during Reconstruction, and adapted to their particular role in Texas society in the generation after Reconstruction. The succeeding thirty years would be a "time of transition," in which changes occurred in the lives of numerous black Texas women. The impact and the resultant direction of the efforts of black Texas women have led other writers to describe this period, at least on the national scene, by using phrases such as "Lifting As We Climb," "No Mountain Too High," and "They Carried Their Freedom Bags." In fact, these depictions, in light of the bleak status of black Texas women in 1900, probably seem overly rosy.

For too many women, 1900 seemed to bring little more than mere survival. Deep-rooted racism, an extensive system of segregation, potential rape, long and dreary hours of tedious work for little pay, no voting or other political rights, and inadequate food offered little scope for more. Historians have described these years of the early twentieth century as the nadir of race relations. At the same time, however, these slogans do apply to the determined effort of black Texas women to enhance and protect themselves, their families, and their communities during these years. By 1930 a growing African American middle class, migration to urban areas, community-based activities, and the right to vote provided new considerations and opportunities for women.

The black population in Texas increased from 670,722 in 1900 to 854,964 in 1930. Despite the apparent gain, by 1930 the percentage decline of the African American population in Texas from 20.4 percent to 14.7 percent presaged a decline that continued for the duration of the twentieth century. Although little studied by historians as yet, the decline appeared to lessen white fears of blacks while at the same time reducing black political influence. Concurrently with the percentage decline of black population during this thirty-year period was migration from rural to urban Texas. Staggering poverty and difficult daylong labor coupled with harsh racial conditions in rural Texas fueled this migration. In 1900, the proportion of Afro-Texans residing in urban areas was 19.2 percent; by 1930 the movement resulted in 38.6 percent of African Americans in the Lone Star State residing in urban centers.[1]

Despite the urbanization trend the economic plight of black women improved little during the period from 1900 to 1930. The vast majority of black Texas women faced grim economic straits, featured by working in agriculture and dominated by the economics of tenant farming. Even by 1910, over one-half of all black Texas women worked in agriculture and another one-third in domestic work and laundry. With little change, this situation continued through 1930. Women in agriculture endured a long hard life of unremitting labor. They had access to almost no laborsaving devices. They worked in the fields (especially during planting and picking seasons), did chores, and oversaw the family—caring for children, washing, ironing, canning, and cooking. As agricultural workers they averaged ten hours a day in fields during planting and picking time (whether they worked on their own farm or for someone else).[2]

Some of the rural black women during these years lived in one of several hundred "freedom colonies," independent communities established by blacks on the fringes of white settlement in the decades after the Civil War. Life in these settlements had both favorable and unfavorable aspects for black Texas women in the three decades after 1900. They were free of the more stringent Jim Crow laws and attitudes but at the same time they worked long and tedious hours for minimal return.[3]

A substantial part of the nonagricultural menial labor force in Texas was made up of African American women, indicating the economic position of black Texans during this period. Black women were required by necessity to work, compared to the number of white women who were gainfully employed, and their wages were much lower. They supplemented the meager wages of black males; whites expected them to work; and they were sometimes the heads of households. In 1900, black female workers outnumbered white women employed; by 1930 working white women outnumbered blacks, but black women were still a larger proportion of their respective work force than white women.[4]

Most of the women employed outside of agriculture could be found in domestic and personal service; others were seamstresses or dressmakers (not in factories), and by 1930 over one thousand were listed as nonspecified laborers. Of the approximately 84,000 black women employed in domestic and personal service in 1930, most were either servants or laundresses. Although black women were not alone in domestic service, many white employers preferred to hire African American maids, perhaps because of the low wages they commanded. Terribly exploited, most black domestic workers preferred day work to living-in. Not all women's work was menial; over four thousand females were employed as schoolteachers in 1930, far exceeding the number of black males in education.[5]

Some black women owned or operated businesses. Usually they were service businesses that required little initial capital and that catered primarily to African Americans. Among the businesses were beauty parlors, dressmaking shops, mortuaries, and nightclubs. An area of black businesses ran along Central Track in downtown Dallas; some Deep Ellum drinking establishments in that area were run by women called "landladies." The Park Theater in downtown Dallas opened in March 1912, it was operated by former South Carolina residents Ella B. Moore and her husband. In 1924, they opened a second theater, the Ella B. Moore, the showplace of the Southwest. Mrs. A. W. Rysinger operated Rysinger's Central Millinery Emporium in Austin from 1900 to 1919. In 1925, Isabell H. Williams opened the first school of embalming for black Texans, the Hampton Williams School of Embalming; she also operated the Dallas Mortuary and Funeral Home.[6]

A few black Texas women were pioneers in the field of medicine. A graduate of Howard Medical School, Dr. Carrie Jane Sutton from San Antonio was the first black female to practice medicine in Texas. She worked in San Antonio during the 1920s. Dr. Thelma Patten Law practiced medicine in Houston beginning in 1923. Dr. Ollie L. Bryan graduated from Meharry Dental College in 1902, began her dental practice in Dallas in 1905, and served there until 1915. Another dentist, Dr. Sarah Howland Shelton, practiced in Austin from 1913 to 1920. Georgia Williams graduated from Meharry Medical College with a degree in pharmacy and opened Williams Pharmacy in Tyler in 1926.[7] The increase of black hospitals in the state led to the demand for African American nurses, and by 1930 the census listed 158 (including midwives). Beginning in 1922, Annie Maie Mathis worked for the Texas State Board of Health.[8] For the most part, though, the professions in Texas were closed to women of any race, and it would be years before black women were able to overcome the employment barriers and participate fully in the economic life of the state.

Standing almost alone in this period of limited opportunity are a few women whose perseverance and ability led to careers unusual for women of the day. Atlanta and Waxahachie native Bessie Coleman, an aviator and barnstormer, was the world's first licensed black pilot. Coleman received her license in France but tragically later fell out of a plane in 1926 while in Florida. She refused to land at Waxahachie until they desegregated the airport. Her last Texas exhibition was in 1925 in Houston. San Antonio–born Ellie A. Walls Montgomery, prominent educator and social scientist in Houston, received a master's degree from Columbia University in 1913 and returned to Texas in 1915. Montgomery taught high school and ultimately at the Houston College for Negroes. Mary Evelyn V. Hunter, appointed as one of first two black agricultural extension agents in 1915, continued in her post until 1931.[9]

Black Texans eking out an existence between 1900 and 1930 faced job discrimination, segregation, lack of experience and education, racism, and exploitation by landlords and employers. Black women were frozen into low-paying, dead-end, and uncertain employment that continued even as education and training became more open for other Texas women. The economic and employment difficulties faced by black Texas women were both a result of Texas' Jim Crow society and a factor in its continuation.

Although employment opportunities and work determined the possibilities of eating and living and surviving for black Texas women, those factors also mandated roles and responsibilities for black women regarding their primary focus, their family. The majority of Afro-Texas women worked outside the home during the day, and children either went with them to the fields or were cared for by extended family members, by neighbors, or by others in the community. Males were often absent from the community, either searching for employment or working. Their too often meager wages meant that black women must work in order to ensure family survival and sustenance. Despite criticism of the matriarchal structure of the black family by some twentieth-century specialists, the black family held together while facing the fragmenting potential presented by slavery. Once free of slave restrictions in Reconstruction and the ensuing years of Jim Crow, African American families sought legal marriages and togetherness while creating a stable familial environment.

By the beginning of the twentieth century in Texas, the time of transition, two developments increasingly affected black Texas families. The migration from rural to urban centers meant a change in employment for black women from working in the fields or performing at-home work such as laundry to wide-scale entry into domestic service. The growth of the African American middle class meant a family structure more similar to that of the white middle class, where both parents resided with children at home, and middle-class black women sought to emulate the situation of white women who were not expected to work. However, even in the black middle class, women often continued working because of the limits on black males in professions, clerical posts, businesses, or other normally secure jobs. These developments were neither uniform across the state nor widespread. Even by 1930, the majority of black families resided in the rural areas of the state. The black woman continued to bear responsibility for holding the family together, at the same time as she was "making community."[10]

Recent scholars have taken us a long way toward understanding the black family, not by comparing the black family to middle-class white family structure, but by looking at African American families to ascertain how they functioned. Overall, children in black families grew up with two parents present. For a minority, the father was absent at times looking for work or working; sometimes the father died young, and occasionally the father left home. Perhaps the first scholar to effectively study the black family was Herbert G. Gutman, who, in *The Black Family in Slavery and Freedom, 1759–1925*, debunked earlier myths surrounding the black family. More recently, Jacqueline Jones, *Labor of Love, Labor of Sorrow: Black Women, Work, and the Family, from Slavery to the Present*, detailed the dual responsibilities of African American women not only as breadwinners but also as guardians of family and community stability. Families remained the central aspect of black women's lives. Although most who had families preferred not to work outside the home, they needed to supplement the salaries of the males, or were in some instances, the sole wage earner.[11]

The economic pressures on black family women in Texas were strong ones. Ruth Allen, in "The Negro Woman," pointed to the bleak circumstances of life for the residents imposed by the cotton culture, the poverty, the lack of amenities, the bare homes, and the drudging employment. Rebecca Sharpless stepped beyond the bleakness, noting that homes and families were places of pride, and she portrayed the interactions created by these exceptionally committed black women despite their difficult lives. The community provided a social life outside work. Neighbors visited, children played and courted, and special occasions such as quilting bees or fairs offered escape and relaxation. Churches and schools fostered support, encouragement, and social activities as well as educational and religious opportunities.[12]

African American women during the thirty-year period from 1900 to 1930 lived, worked, and relaxed in a Jim Crow society based on a rigid separation of the races. Segregation in Texas traced its roots to the first arrival of non-Hispanic whites (generally from the southern United States) to the territory that became Texas. By 1900 the system of segregation governed most areas and incidents of black/white relations in the state, including the side of the street used, what to do when approaching whites, and how to address whites. Transportation was segregated, miscegenation laws forbade interracial marriage, public accommodations separated the races or excluded African Americans, places of residence were separated, state-operated institutions provided separate or no care for blacks.[13] During the first third of the twentieth century whites expanded the detested system even more with both de jure and de facto embellishments.

In the early twentieth century, state laws, city ordinances, and custom further dictated the extent of Jim Crow in Texas society. The legislature in 1907 declared that all forms of transportation for the public must include separate coaches, compartments, or seating. That same year the legislators determined that an amusement place could either supply separate areas for black patrons or refuse to admit them. Although no state law called for residential separation, in fact most communities maintained separate living districts for black and white. In 1909, the legislature provided that white prisoners be kept apart in all respects from black inmates. No black Texan could use a white swimming pool or rest room. Water fountains for whites could not be used by Afro-Texans. Texas cities enacted legislation preventing intimate relations between black and white. In Fort Worth it was unlawful for any white and any black person to have sexual intercourse with each other in the city limits. In Texarkana white males could not visit the homes of black females. Houston forbade African American and Caucasian races to live together. The state legislature (1907) provided that no white couple could adopt a black child and that no black couple could adopt a white child.[14] The horrid irony of these laws is that a black male could be lynched (many were) for alleged sexual overtures to a white female, but no white male was lynched or convicted for sexually molesting a black female. Terminology was offensive as well, white newspapers insultingly referred to black women as "negresses." Overall, with the exception of master/servant relationships, whites, either by law, violence, or custom kept Texas African Americans from intermingling with whites.

In response to this stringent Jim Crow society, black women protested, protected their families, adapted, and developed their own institutions, separate communities, education, religion, and lodges. In Austin (as in other Texas cities) black women boycotted a 1906 law that required separate compartments on streetcars; domestic workers told employers that they would quit rather than ride Jim Crow streetcars. Later in the 1920s a white policeman accosted a black Houston woman as she was selling copies of the *Houston Informer,* and ordered her to leave the district. She was arrested and charged with disturbing the peace when she failed to move as rapidly as the white enforcer deemed appropriate. Her black employer, *Informer* publisher Clifton F. Richardson, ultimately succeeded in having the charges dropped. Wealthy whites aided in disrupting the segregation ordinance in Houston as well when they insisted their maids and other servants must ride on nonsegregated buses in order to get to work on time.[15]

The disadvantages of being black in this segregated society were noticed in the lack of public care and institutions for African Texans. Some facilities for African Americans existed, insane asylums, juvenile rehabilitation schools (for males), and deaf, dumb, and blind schools were supported by the state. The state provided no orphanage for blacks until 1929, though six private orphanages existed. Lack of separate facilities led black girls convicted of wrongdoing to be jailed in the prison for black women. This lack became a cause of the Colored Women's Club; in 1923 the Club gave a parcel of land to the state for a facility that would serve as a home and a training school for juvenile women, but no support came from the state. In 1927, the legislature authorized construction of a home for black girls but did not appropriate any money. It was not until 1945 that state funds were provided. The state also neglected black epileptics and tuberculars during the first third of the century until finally in 1935 the state provided financial funding.[16]

A consequence of the segregated society was that Afro-Texans developed all-black communities in the rural areas of the state. In these locales, separated from whites, they were able to work together for mutual benefit and protection. Thad Sitton and James H. Conrad, in *Freedom Colonies,* depict the independence that resulted from these black colonies. African Americans did not face lynching, mob violence, rape, or other racist behavior from whites as they did in other rural communities of the state. Rebecca Sharpless, in *Fertile Ground, Narrow Choices,* pointed to the greater opportunities and advantages open to black women in separate black communities.[17] Similar benefits could be noticed in segregated districts in major cities such as Dallas, Houston, and San Antonio.

Family and community were sources of relief and pride, and African American women could relax and enjoy special events and holidays with their families and friends. State and county fairs generally held special days for the black community, and blacks sponsored their own fairs on occasion. Black Houstonians organized De-Ro-Loc in 1909, a special fall carnival modeled after a white event. The National Negro Progressive Society of El Paso hosted a fair in Fort Worth in the late 1920s. Juneteenth, the day in 1865 when black Texans learned of the abolition of slavery, provided a holiday to visit, celebrate freedom, and relax in a venue of friendship, games, and speech-making. Black History Week, established in 1926 by Carter G. Woodson, provided another opportunity to discuss history, politics, and racial pride. Schoolteachers, mainly women, became especially vital to its celebration. In urban areas, recreational facilities were available for black youths. In Houston, the Colored Branch of the Houston Public Library offered a spot to read and visit. Dance halls and theaters provided attractions in the evening and on the weekends.[18]

Much of the potential, as well as the reality of life, for black Texas women derived from education. As with other aspects of Texas life, the educational systems were segregated from the beginning. Early educational struggles by black Texans resulted in some successes; by 1900 Texas' illiteracy rate for African Americans was the best in the South. Over the succeeding thirty years, other accomplishments were achieved. Teacher salaries for blacks, though they remained lower than for whites, increased. The illiteracy rate was reduced even more. By

1925 over 150 black high schools operated in Texas even though only seven were accredited.[19]

Low teacher salaries especially affected black women, as teaching was largely a female occupation. For African American women, educational and professional training was a means to improve their status in life, as well as to escape unskilled labor, and black women persevered in that goal despite inferior textbooks and facilities. By 1930 three-fourths of black schools in Texas remained one-room, one-teacher schools.[20] Deficient as they were, the black high schools served as one of the central institutions in black communities, and along with churches their importance cannot be overstated.

Texas' higher education efforts also began in the nineteenth century with the start of eleven privately funded black colleges. Coeducational, they overlapped with high schools and provided industrial and agricultural courses, teacher training, and home economics. Although most African American collegiate students attended private colleges, public institutions eventually opened in the state. The primary public institution, Prairie View A&M, opened in 1878 and eventually offered programs in sewing, cooking, music, and classics for its female students. In 1901, the legislature allowed Prairie View to offer classical and scientific studies. As late as the 1920s, however, Prairie View taught elementary courses up to a university curriculum. In 1927, another public educational institution arrived when Houston established the only public junior college for black students.[21]

Black women played a vital part in African American education, both as students and as educators. The strong commitment to education passed from one generation to the next. Women were encouraged and supported in their educational quests by their families; parents and siblings worked and saved to send the students to high school and college. Many hard-working and energetic black women educators succeeded. Inez B. Prosser, dean and registrar at Tillotson College in Austin from 1921 to 1930, became the first black female from Texas to earn a doctorate when in 1931 she graduated in educational psychology from the University of Cincinnati. Born in Hempstead, Fannie A. Robinson joined the Colored Teachers' State Association of Texas in 1901 and served as its secretary from 1918 to 1926; she received a bachelor's degree from Prairie View A&M. Early in the century (1902) Georgia-born Artemesia Bowden was named head of St. Philip's School in San Antonio. When it became St. Philip's Junior College in 1927 Bowden became president, the first African American woman college president in Texas.[22]

One school established solely for black women, Mary Allen Seminary in Crockett, was a precursor of later educational avenues for black women. After difficult beginnings, the Seminary, with support from the Presbyterian Church, USA, opened its doors in 1886, and in 1889 the school acquired 300 acres of adjacent land. Mary Allen Seminary was established to help improve the harsh lives endured by black women in East Texas as well as to evangelize among African Americans. From 1910 to 1924 Mary Allen Seminary survived a fire, lack of funds, and declining enrollments. Restructured in 1924, with a black administrator and all-black faculty, the school grew and achieved accreditation as a junior college.[23] Private black colleges such as Mary Allen Seminary received aid from and depended upon the major support institution in African American life, the church.

The focal point of African American religious and social life, the churches also provided a structure for the development of black leaders. The Baptists were the largest of the denominations, followed by three Methodist churches, and then by a number of dependent black churches such as Roman Catholic, Congregationalist, and Presbyterian. In the cities, the process of urbanization stimulated the growth of Holiness, Spiritualist, and Pentecostal groups. Black Pentecostals in Texas exhibited a dual commitment to spiritual and intellectual growth, members of the Church of God in Christ (COGIC), for example, emphasized social uplift and educating their community.[24]

Generally, men held positions of power and leadership in the churches, but women comprised most of the membership and devoted their time and efforts to the church and its outreach. The churches offered women more freedom than other aspects of Texas' segregated society. In 1926, State Mother Hannah Chandler raised nearly $3,500 for the COGIC. A black Catholic order, Sisters of the Holy Family, entered Texas in 1898 and established schools early in the century in Houston, San Antonio, and Ames with an emphasis on nurturing African American respect. Black women avidly participated in camp meetings and revivals.[25]

The "four pillars of Afro-Christian tradition" iterated by Cheryl Townsend Gilkes—prayer, music, testimony, and preaching—strengthened and supported the spiritual beliefs and efforts of black Texas women. Maud A. B. Fuller, born in Lockhart, taught in Seguin and elsewhere for years while at the same time using her skills for the Baptists. Residing in Austin, in 1926 she accepted a national leadership post, and shortly (1928) became president of the National Baptist Convention's Women Auxiliary, where she placed an emphasis on children's organizations. Another teacher, Baptist Eliza Davis from Taylor, used her educational training to develop and establish Liberian mission schools, one of which she helped found in 1912. There existed also a vibrant female spiritual heritage in Texas. Some spoke at services, and Elderess O. A. Laws preached at Texas revivals in the 1920s. Faith healer Annie Webb Buchanan, known as the "Seer of Corsicana," used her skills to heal, provide advice, and support the needy. She gave money to schools and churches. A spiritual healer, Sadie Baylor from Caldwell County, taught that to learn spiritually, one's life must be centered on spiritual things.[26]

Other important social and civic organizations were the Lodges. Women and men joined the lodges for social and economic reasons. The lodge organizations performed three functions critical to the black community: social relaxation, civic improvement, and provision of insurance and death benefits. Lodges organized for black women included the Heroines of Jericho, Sisters of Mysterious Ten, and the Household of Ruth. Two of the larger and more successful of the orders were the Female Masons, the Order of the Eastern Star; and the Grand Court, Order of the Calanthe. By 1930 the Court was financially secure and able to lend money to Paul Quinn College among other projects. Mrs. A. D. Key, who served as grand worthy counselor of the Grand Court from 1902 to 1925 was able to use her lengthy tenure to restructure the organization and to increase the allowed amounts of insurance policies.[27]

The sororities that college women joined, and in many instances continued to support after graduation, similarly gave scope to the educational elite of black women. One of the sororities established by black Texas women, Delta Sigma Theta, began in 1913 at Howard University when Fredericka Chase Dodd and a group of Texas friends chartered the sorority. The sorority supported able young women seeking educational advantages away from home. One of Dodd's Texas friends, Myra David Hemmings, became president of the new organization. Hemmings later returned to Texas and became a prominent educator in San Antonio.[28]

Barred by segregation laws from participation in the white-dominated social and cultural activities in Texas, black women worked through their separate institutions to provide avenues for education, spiritual care, and a social structure to their community despite the neglect and animosity demonstrated by lawmakers in Texas. Their achievements are testimony to their belief in family and community. Many used these same experiences and traits in the political realm.

Politically, at the turn of the twentieth century, black Texas women, as all Texas women, were disenfranchised. The Texas Constitution prevented women from voting in Texas elections, and the Fifteenth Amendment to the U.S. Constitution precluded women from voting in national elections. Although black men in Texas legally could vote by the turn of the twentieth century, white Texans in the latter nineteenth century reduced the participation of black male voters. Violence, intimidation, economic sanctions, and county white men's associations all prevented black male suffrage. As a result, especially in rural areas of the state, black Texans often did not vote. Early in the twentieth century the poll tax (1902) excluded additional black male voters. Three years later (1905) the Terrell Election Law provided that political parties must conduct primary elections (if they received over a certain number of votes the previous election) and the parties were allowed to set their own voting requirements for the primary election. Thus black Texans effectively found themselves precluded from Democratic primary elections and their political participation meant voting in Republican primaries, if at all. Exclusion from Democratic primaries meant no African American voice in the one-party state. African Americans subsequently were discouraged from voting in Republican primaries when black Republican leaders were forced out by "lily white" Republicans. White Texans opposed even this limited civic activity; in 1910 the state house of representatives urged modification of the Fourteenth and repeal of the Fifteenth amendments.[29]

A vast majority of white Texas males also opposed women's suffrage. Until 1918, no Texas woman could vote. Prior to that time, women, including black women, who participated politically in the Lone Star State did so in prohibition and women suffrage campaigns and in the woman's club movement. Beginning with the turn of the century, the Women's Christian Temperance Union's (WCTU) prohibition campaign offered an avenue of activity for some black women. The WCTU organized in Texas in the latter nineteenth century. Outside the South, the WCTU was a biracial group, but for southern black women the WCTU established a separate branch called the Thurman

WCTU after its first national president, Lucy Simpson Thurman. An early leader in the Thurman WCTU Texas campaign was Eliza E. Peterson, a music teacher from Texarkana. In 1898, Peterson became state president of the Thurman prohibitionists and membership grew rapidly. By 1909 Peterson's drive and energy was noticed beyond the state, and she was elected national superintendent. An indefatigable speaker and organizer, she held organization events throughout the state, including cities such as Houston and Waco. Peterson remained in a leadership role through the successful ratification of the Eighteenth Amendment in 1918 that prohibited the sale and manufacture of alcoholic beverages.[30]

In an ironic twist, whites encouraged African American efforts on behalf of prohibition, unable to see a relation to political activity, and white ministers and students spoke at black rallies. At the same time, one of the primary arguments by whites for prohibition was the unjust allegation that blacks were heavy consumers of alcoholic beverages. Even though accepting and encouraging black efforts for prohibition, whites used race as a means of supporting their position.

Other problems plagued black Texas society—segregation, poverty, illiteracy, discrimination, racism, and sexism. Afro-Texas women, as did national African American women, worked through the Woman's Club movement to challenge these features of Texas society. The Woman's Club movement started nationally as a biracial group. However, in 1900 the national organization excluded African American participation. Black Texas women continued working in the movement by organizing local clubs, and in 1905 established a statewide organization, the Texas Association of Colored Women's Clubs (TACWC). Mrs. M. E. Y. Moore of Fort Worth was elected as the first president, she urged Afro-Texas women to improve home, moral, and social existence in their communities. The following year the TACWC affiliated with the national association whose motto "Lifting As We Climb" also became Texas' standard. Black Texas women were not always sure where support or hindrance was coming from; in one annual report they declaimed that "our men have never given us the support and encouragement we so well deserve." The state association, together with numerous locals, remained active through the years by emphasizing civic and political goals as well as home and family concerns. Ethel Ransom served as president of the group in 1922, and from 1926 to 1930 Amelia Soders Johnson was the state president. Johnson, from Marlin,

earned a B.A. and an M.A. from Prairie View; she taught school and
served as a librarian in Marlin in addition to her many labors on behalf
of black women in Texas.[31]

During World War I black Texas women (as did black men) supported the war effort despite continuing antiblack actions during wartime. Black women purchased and sold Liberty Bonds, saved materials
needed for the military, provided supplies for soldiers, planted victory
gardens, aided the Red Cross, and overall contributed to the U.S. effort. To show their citizenship, black Texas women also participated
in patriotic events of World War I. They developed and operated recreational facilities for soldiers around the state. Galveston women prepared "comfort bags for our soldier boys who expect to leave."[32]

The support for the war effort did not mask the ugly face of antiblack sentiment in the state. During the war a black family was
lynched. When Sarah Cabiness's son refused to enlist, he was brutally
killed; Sarah Cabiness and her remaining six children were then shot.
As usual, no one was arrested for the brutal killings. Black women also
discovered that their sons were called into duty at a higher percentage than white males. Such sacrifices convinced some black women
to question the war's impact on black citizens. San Antonio leader
Mrs. W. E. Thompson doubted whether the war helped African Americans.[33] The racist discrimination by whites of African Americans led
black El Paso poet Bernice Love Wiggins to ask whether black women
mistakenly sent their sons to war; in her poem "Ethiopia Speaks" she
asked:

> *Why not take it back?*
> *Until in the South, the "Land of the Free,"*
> *They stop hanging my sons to the branch of a tree,*
> *Take it back till they cease to burn them alive,*
> *Take it back till the white man shall cease to deprive*
> *My sons, yea, my black sons, of rights justly won,*
> *'Til tortures are done?*[34]

If anything, the war strengthened the objective of black Texas women
to acquire the power of the ballot. Black women fought for the right to
vote along with white women, but inequities within the women's suffrage movement became a clear indicator of the precarious position of
black Texas women as they fought for the vote and against discrimination in white Texas society.

On the national level, though the woman's suffrage struggle began in 1848, a renewed effort occurred in 1913 when the National American Woman Suffrage Association (NAWSA) began a new campaign. In Texas, the woman suffrage movement reorganized in San Antonio in 1912, and created the all-white Texas Equal Suffrage Association (TESA). Excluded from the movement, black Texas women ardently supported the suffrage effort and formed their own organized suffrage movement. In Galveston in 1917, African American women clamoring for the right to vote established the Negro Women Voter's League of Galveston. The same year, the Texas Federation of Colored Women's Clubs endorsed the struggle for the right to vote. The succeeding year, Mrs. R. C. Andrews of Houston went to Denver for a meeting of the National Association of Colored Women where delegates called for passage of the Nineteenth Amendment to the U.S. Constitution. Christia Adair, in Kingsville, organized black women for the suffrage campaign, and when it was successful, registered to vote.[35]

Black women in El Paso worked with their white counterparts for suffrage, and since TESA would not allow them into membership, they petitioned the national organization (NAWSA) for auxiliary membership, thereby offending the all-white TESA. Orchestrated by Mrs. E. P. Sampson, the El Paso effort, though supported by their white counterparts in El Paso, did not succeed in gaining support from the national association. The white suffragists worried that black membership would affront white males as well as some of their own members.[36]

Black women suffered the political lash for both race and gender in Texas, and it was not always easy to determine which characteristic was more invidious. Former governor Oscar Colquitt argued against women's suffrage because "when you give the ballot to women, you give it to all women, regardless of color." A Texas legislator asserted that if women acquired the right to vote, "negroes and whites would intermarry and children of all colors would sit together in the public schools." Pauline Wells of Brownsville, the wife of political leader James B. Wells, and president of the Texas Association Opposed to Woman Suffrage, affirmed that only two types of women would vote, "the Socialists and the negro women. The Socialists will vote because they are interested, the negroes because they enjoy it."[37] Apparently Mrs. Wells was not the type of woman who would vote.

In the spring of 1918, the Texas legislature passed a law providing women with the right to vote in the primary election of 1918, the first instance of suffrage for women in Texas. Over 386,000 women registered to vote, including a number of black women. Black women quickly discovered that most election officials ignored that right and few voted in the primary election of 1918. Black registered voters such as Christia Daniels Adair and her friends were not allowed to vote. The legislature also passed a bill to amend the Texas Constitution to give women full suffrage, but that measure was defeated in a special election in which women were barred from voting. Nevertheless, the overall suffrage effort bore a fruitful conclusion; Texas became the ninth state in the nation to ratify the Nineteenth Amendment to the Constitution, which went into effect in 1920.[38]

Black women were "citizens at last," and they registered to vote, ran for office, and campaigned for their candidates. Three women in Houston ran for offices as members of the Black and Tan faction of the Republican party of 1920. During the primary election, black women voted in considerable numbers—the candidate for Harris County clerk (Mrs. F. L. Long) received nearly 4,800 votes, 19 percent of the ballots cast. In the first general election in which black women could vote they had done so in large numbers, generally surpassing the turnout of black men despite intimidation by white men loitering outside the voting places or, later in the 1920s, by members of the Ku Klux Klan.[39]

Even armed with the right to vote, black women found candidates unresponsive to their community. In the 1920 presidential campaign Republican presidential candidate Warren G. Harding visited Texas, and Christia Adair took Kingsville school children to see the candidate. Harding reached over the heads of the black children to shake hands with white children. This angered Adair so much that she switched her allegiance from the Republican to the Democratic Party although Texas Democrats of the day offered little to black women or black men.[40]

Racist voting restrictions increased during the 1920s. The state moved in 1923 to formalize black exclusion in the Democratic primary by legislation. Lawrence A. Nixon, a Wiley College graduate and physician from El Paso, challenged the law in *Nixon v. Herndon* (1927). The U.S. Supreme Court ruled that all-white primaries violated the Fourteenth Amendment. The next year the state defined political parties as private organizations not subject to legal restrictions, which therefore could select their own qualified voters. The court concurred.

Until 1944 most black Texans were barred from voting in the Democratic primaries and thereby effectively deprived of a vote at all in the one-party state.[41]

Even though black women generally were unable to vote during these three decades, they involved themselves in other political organizations that gave them a platform to protest racism and discrimination and to seek better circumstances for themselves and their children. The organization most influential in black Texas opposition to suffrage restrictions was the National Association for the Advancement of Colored People (NAACP). Black Texas women played an important role in its growth in the Lone Star State, and by 1919 Texas totaled the largest state membership in the nation. Women helped organize the branches in both Dallas and Houston, as well as many other locals throughout the state. By 1919, thirty-one branches existed in Texas. However, vicious opposition from the Ku Klux Klan during the 1920s reduced the number to a few.[42]

Black women also fought against the Ku Klux Klan and its political adherents, and participated in the fight for federal antilynching legislation. Such legislation was especially crucial for black Texans; in 1920 Texas led all states in the number of African Americans lynched. By 1930, although it ranked third overall in the total number of African Americans lynched, Texas ranked second in the total number of black women lynched. Among the organizations that stepped forward in Texas to oppose lynching and to seek national and state legislation was the National Anti-Lynching Crusaders; Ethel Ransom, a Fort Worth nurse and club leader, led the Texas affiliation as Texas state director. The Crusaders, started in 1922, sought to recruit "One Million Women United to Suppress Lynching." They worked to see the Dyer Anti-Lynching Bill passed by Congress, and to halt lynching and mob violence in general. Other groups of importance in the antilynching campaign were the Texas Association of Colored Women, the YWCA, the NAACP, and the League of Republican Colored Women. Ironically, the organization often credited with bringing about the decline of lynching, The Association of Southern Women for the Prevention of Lynching, did not allow African American participation, despite their years of antilynching protest. Jessie Daniel Ames, a white Texas woman, started The Association of Southern Women in 1930.[43] Lauretta Holman Gooden, from Dallas, best expressed the views of black

Texas women about white mob violence in her poem, "Question to a Mob":

> O, *cruel mob—destroying crew,*
> *Who gave the life of man to you?*
> *Why have you gathered, small and great,*
> *To murder, more through sport than hate?*[44]

Lynching was the epitome of white hatred, as well as the degradation of black Texans; that it continued illustrated the extent of white racism in the Lone Star State.

A biracial organization of importance in the struggle against lynching, discrimination, and prejudice was the Texas Commission on Inter-Racial Cooperation (TCIC). The Commission, founded in 1920, was composed of one hundred members, fifty white and fifty black, half men and half women. Two early leaders of the Negro Women's Division were Mrs. D. M. Mason of Dallas and Jennie Belle Covington of Houston. Born in DeWitt County, Covington attended Guadalupe College in Seguin, and with her husband, Dr. B. J. Covington, moved to Houston. She chaired the TCIC for a decade. Despite the efforts of the TCIC, the segregated society was too firmly entrenched for substantial victories. Together with local efforts, the TCIC improved the condition of streets by paving roads; provided a kindergarten and free lunches, teacher training, employment bureau, room registry; and the members sought to institute courses on race relations in Texas schools. More importantly, perhaps, the TCIC persuaded black and white men and women to sit down and discuss common problems and aspirations.[45]

Overall, the accomplishments of the Inter-Racial Commission, as well as the numerous other protests and improvements wrought by black Texas women in the years from 1900 to 1930, meant improved conditions for African Americans in Texas. Despite those accomplishments, segregation continued through the early twentieth century, a vicious lynching took place in Sherman as late as 1930, and few black women were able to vote for most of the first half of the century. But throughout that time black women used less-structured political venues to improve conditions in Texas. They also used the power of the pen and the voice to make themselves heard and appreciated in Texas.

At first glance the work-burdened lives of black Texas women appears to militate against cultural activities, but black Texas women persevered and succeeded in the cultural realm as well during the years from 1900 to 1930. Changing circumstances for black Texans—better educational opportunities; increasing numbers in the middle and upper classes; greater economic means; their political understanding; the growth of cities; and, by the 1920s, the influence of the Harlem Renaissance led to an expanded output and participation in cultural activities for black women. Their efforts were seen in writing, in music, and to a limited extent, in theater and in painting.

Black women wrote, and published their literary efforts, prose, poetry, and to a lesser degree, fiction. The first known books published by black Texas women appeared in 1905, two books published by Josie Briggs Hall of Mexia, Texas, an African American schoolteacher and writer. Born in Waxahachie, in 1905 Hall published one self-help book and one book of poetry (the manuscript of an earlier effort by Hall was lost in an 1898 fire). Hall's self-help book, espousing the accommodation ideas and philosophy of Booker T. Washington, was titled *Moral and Mental Capsule for the Economic and Domestic Life of the Negro, As a Solution of the Race Problem.* In this work, Hall argued that the time had "not arrived for the solution of the Negro problem," citing three reasons why conditions were not ready for improved black/white relations: a lack of moral status, a need for greater intellectual strength, and limited financial means. Hall's goal was to proscribe behavior patterns for Afro-Texans to improve black conditions, while at the same time avoiding behavior patterns that could inflame white retribution.[46]

Black Texas women published additional works of prose during these years. Maud Cuney-Hare, the daughter of late nineteenth-century Texas political leader Norris Wright Cuney, left Texas to study and became a prominent concert and lecture pianist. She returned to Texas and taught at the Deaf, Dumb, and Blind Institute as well as Prairie View State College. In 1906, Cuney-Hare returned to Boston and ultimately published a biography of her father, *Norris Wright Cuney: A Tribune of the Black People.* Later she wrote a book that emphasized black folk music, *Negro Musicians and Their Music,* a publication influenced by her studies, her work, and by the Harlem Renaissance. Cuney-Hare also wrote a number of articles, including some for her friend W. E. B. Du Bois' *Crisis,* and two for Nancy Cunard's magnum opus, *Negro: An Anthology.*[47] Manet Harrison Fowler published an article of historical importance, "History of the Texas Association of

Negro Musicians." Annie Maie Mathis wrote about another vital group of African Americans in "Negro Public Health Nursing in Texas."[48]

It was in the field of poetry that black Texas women found their chief medium of expression, and in which they exerted the greatest energy and influence. The poems of the period reflect an articulate group of poets, most of whom came from middle-class, college-educated backgrounds. The works of many of these poets are available through the efforts of J. Mason Brewer, who collected the black Texas poetry of the early twentieth century in a 1936 anthology, *Heralding Dawn: An Anthology of Verse*. The anthology included poetry by Josie Briggs Hall, whose other 1905 work was a book of poetry titled *A Scroll of Facts and Advice* with titles such as "Politics," and "Women's Rights" in which she urged black women not to engage in politics and to remain home as housewives, although Hall's own life seemed to contravene her published strictures. She taught, she wrote at least three books. Hall also attempted to start a junior college in Limestone County, and ran the Homemaker's Industrial and Trade School in Dallas from 1916 to 1928.[49]

Other women poets took a more activist view. Lauretta Holman Gooden, born in Sulphur Springs and raised in Texarkana, resided in Dallas where she and her husband operated a grocery store. In "Questions to a Mob" she cried out against lynching. Her spirit can be discovered in "A Dream of Revenge," a poem in which she plucked passionate tenderness from her heart. Some poets expressed their personal reactions and longings. Educator and poet Maurine Lawrence Jeffrey was born in Longview in 1900 and graduated from Prairie View College. She first published a poem in 1924; two of her sentimental, descriptive poems are "My Rainy Day" and "Pappy's Last Song." Jeffrey's father wanted his last song to be an African American spiritual. Lillian Tucker Lewis, born in Corsicana, was referred to by Brewer in his 1936 anthology as "among the most mature in thought of the Negro writers in Texas today," and he included her poem "Longing" in his collection. In "Longing" she expresses the ephemeral nature of unfulfilled aspirations. "Night," a revealing poem by Beaumont-born Birdelle Wycoff Ransom also indicated the strength of black Texas poetesses. She, according to Brewer, "speaks in terms of race without mentioning race." Gwendolyn Bennett, born in Giddings, Texas, in 1902, left the state at an early age and became a versatile artist and a significant figure in Harlem during the renaissance; she wrote well-received poems such as

"On a Birthday," "Heritage," "To Usward," and "Song" that were pub-
lished in prominent anthologies and magazines of the 1920s.[50]
The most celebrated of the black women poets undoubtedly was
Bernice Love Wiggins, whose father J. Austin Love was also a well-
known poet. Wiggins's delightfully sarcastic poem "Church Folks" was
included in Brewer's collection and originally was published in 1925 in
El Paso, in a volume of poetry that Wiggins published titled *Tuneful
Tales*. Her poetry appeared in a number of publications, including the
El Paso *Herald*, the Chicago *Defender*, and the Houston *Informer*. Born
in Austin in 1897, Wiggins was reared in El Paso. Tragically, in 1936
she left for California, not to be heard of again. She dedicated a poem
to Paul Lawrence Dunbar, was referred to as Texas' Dunbar, and in
her poetry emphasized the ordinary black community.[51]
Few black Texas women engaged in writing fiction, or, if so, they
were not successful in having it published. The first published black
Texas woman novelist was Lillian B. Jones. Born Lillian B. Ackard in
1886, in 1916 Jones self-published her novel *Five Generations Hence*, a
fitting precursor to the emerging New Negro or Harlem Renaissance
movement in Texas and the nation during the 1920s. A strong propo-
nent of education, Jones attended Bishop College, Prairie View A&M,
and Simmons University (Kentucky), where in 1921–22 she served as
Dean of Women and received her bachelor's degree. Married in 1900
at the age of fourteen and divorced in 1919, Jones taught school in Fort
Worth, worked for the Texas Commission on Inter-Racial Cooperation, maintained a diary, wrote and published a biography, completed,
but was not successful in publishing, another novel (*Annie Brown*), and
published articles for the *Eastern Star*. Espousing education and independence for African American women, and concerned with the lack
of freedom for blacks in the United States, Jones's protagonist in *Five
Generations Hence* was an Afro-Texas schoolteacher whose vision called
for blacks to go back to Africa "five generations hence." Jones undoubtedly was familiar with the efforts at this time of Chief Sam to send a
boatload of African Americans to Africa from Galveston. In the novel,
a black farmer befriended by the teacher moved to Africa to pursue
his dream of economic independence. In 1930, Jones married a man
named Horace, adopted her new name of Lillian B. Horace, and lived
until 1965.[52]
The author of the present chapter has been unable to locate a short
story published by a resident black Texas woman before 1930 (black

Texas men such as Melvin B. Tolson had similar difficulties in getting fiction published during those years). One or more stories may
yet be discovered in an African American newspaper, a college news-
letter/publication, or in a magazine of the era. However, Texas-born
and Harlem Renaissance writer Gwendolyn Bennett published a short
story, "Wedding Day," in 1926. The earliest known short story by a resident black Texas woman was published in the *Waco Messenger* in 1933,
"Doomed to Despair" by Jennie V. Mills, a Waco homemaker.[53]

Texas women musicians were more prominent and prevalent in
black artistic and cultural activities than women writers. The number
and growing concerns of black musicians coalesced in 1925 when they
organized the Texas Association of Negro Musicians. The Texas Association headquartered in Fort Worth, published a journal, *The Negro
Musician,* and in 1929 successfully sponsored the national convention
of Negro musicians in Fort Worth. The editor of *The Negro Musician,*
Manet Harrison Fowler, was the guiding hand behind the efforts of
the Texas Association. Fowler, born and educated in Fort Worth, was
a dramatic soprano who for a time operated a school in New York, the
Nawlimu School for the Development of African Music and Creative
Arts, before returning to her home state.[54]

African American women often received their music education
and training outside the state in the absence of training facilities and
teachers in Texas and often made their first appearances out of state.
During the 1920s contralto Roberta Dodd Crawford of Bonham studied at Fisk University and for six years at the University of Chicago;
she made her Chicago debut in 1926 to favorable reviews, and then
toured in the United States and Europe. Hearne native, Zelma Watson
George, graduated from the University of Chicago, studied pipe organ
at Northwestern, and then studied voice at the American Conservatory
of Music from 1925 to 1927, but for the ensuing twenty years worked in
education and community service rather than performance.[55]

While voice and the piano were the principal means of expression
in classical, blues, and gospel music, there were other outlets for Texas
women musicians as teachers and performers. Dallas teacher Priscilla
Tyler helped organize the Civic Music Guild to showcase touring black
artists. Portia Washington Pittman, Booker T. Washington's daughter,
taught private piano lessons and music at the Booker T. Washington
High School in Dallas from 1913 to the late 1920s. While in Texas Portia Washington married a prominent black architect, but when the

marriage soured she returned to Tuskegee in 1928. Black women in Houston also supported music. The Ladies Symphony Orchestra organized in Houston in 1915 when Jennie B. Covington initiated the Ladies Symphony. Conducted by Madame Corella Rochon, Covington and teenage daughter Ernestine Jessie performed with the group. Jessie later attended Oberlin Music Conservatory and Juilliard School of Music before becoming a concert pianist.[56]

The blues became the style of choice for women singers, especially by the 1920s. In Dallas's Central Tracks district (Deep Ellum), the prominent blues hub during the 1920s, Emma Wright, Jewell Nelson, Hociel Thomas, and Gertrude Perkins appeared at the Ella B. Moore Park Theater. The earliest Texas blues singer to be recorded was Fae Barnes of Hillsboro, who recorded under the name of Maggie Jones in New York City in 1923. Gainesville native Monete Moore, a pianist, recorded with the Choo Choo Jazzers in New York in 1924–25. Beulah "Sippie" Wallace of Houston perfected her stage and voice presence by working as a maid as she traveled the state singing the blues. Wallace gained a reputation as the "Texas Nightingale" and recorded scores of blues hits during the 1920s, including "I'm a Mighty Tight Woman" and "Women Be Wise." Bobbie Cadillac, in her recordings "Carbolic Acid Blues" (released in 1928), "I Can't Stand That," and "He Throws That Thing," sang of the violence and harshness of life on the street. Lillian Glinn, probably the most famous blues singer in Dallas, performed at Park Theater. Born about 1902 in a small town east of Dallas, Glinn was singing at a local church when Hattie Burleson (a respected though little-recorded Texas singer), persuaded her to sing blues and vaudeville songs. A contralto, Glinn's singing was direct and easy to understand; her first hit was "Doggin' Me"; another of her popular hits was "Cravin' a Man Blues."[57]

African American women sang gospel music, which was often an interplay between blues music and religious topics. Frequently these singers began as "holy roller women," singers who joined in with the preacher and started singing. The best known was Arizona Juanita Dranes, who performed in Fort Worth, Dallas, and Oklahoma City. Dranes's music was recorded by Chicago-based Okeh records in late 1920s, her hit songs included "He's the Lily of the Valley," "My Soul Is a Witness for the Lord," and "It's All Right Now." The earliest Texas woman gospel artist to earn widespread recognition, Dranes, born in Dallas, was a blind performer who sang with and was a member of the

Church of God in Christ. In 1928, she recorded music with the "Texas Jubilee Singers," a group of itinerant musicians who also were members of the Church of God in Christ. Dranes split with her recording company in a dispute over money; her last letter to them was sent from Oklahoma City in 1929. She apparently left Texas with the onset of the Depression.[58]

Although music and literature dominated artistic and cultural activities of black Texas women, some turned to drama and painting. Dallas African Americans organized the Dallas Negro Players and presented their first performance in December of 1928, yet San Antonio and Houston blacks did not establish Little Theater groups for potential black dramatists in their respective cities until 1931. Names of women actors or dramatists are largely unknown. Maud Cuney-Hare published at least one play, "Antar of Araby," which was performed in New York City. Black women painters were few, and almost none relied on their art for a livelihood. Rezolia C. Grissom Thrash taught art in the Dallas public schools beginning in the 1920s, and middle- and upper-class urban black women sponsored exhibits of women painters' art in the 1920s, such as at the Priscilla Art Club in Dallas and the Ethel Ransom Art and Literary Club of Houston. Few of their efforts have survived to the present day.[59] Nevertheless, efforts of African American women in artistic and cultural activities was impressive and provided a solid indication of the changes that transpired in African American life in Texas during the early twentieth century.

These changes reflected a maturing and advancing cadre of black Texas women intent on making community. More attended schools, some graduating from college, with a few earning doctoral degrees. As a result of migration, fewer earned wages with hard, physical toil in the fields, though most still did; other black women found employment as domestic servants in the urban centers. Politically black women united together for advancement, and achieved the right to vote in general elections. Although plagued by a discriminatory and segregated white-dominated society, African American women in Texas used their communities, networks, families, and friends to struggle and survive. Overall, these years became a time of transition for African American women in the Lone Star State. The succeeding decades proved equally as challenging and inspiring.

Notes

1. Bruce A. Glasrud, "Black Texans, 1900–1930: A History" (Ph.D. diss., Texas Tech University, 1969), 313–16; Alwyn Barr, *Black Texans: A History of African Americans in Texas, 1528–1995*, 2nd ed. (Norman: University of Oklahoma Press, 1996), 147–54, 164; Forest Garrett Hill, "The Negro in the Texas Labor Supply" (Master's thesis, University of Texas, 1946), 127.

2. Glasrud, "Black Texans," 100–102; Rose M. Brewer, "Black Women Workers: Yesterday and Today," in *Women in the Texas Workforce: Yesterday and Today*, ed. Richard Croxdale and Melissa Hield (Austin: People's History in Texas, 1979), 35–48; Ruth Allen, "The Negro Woman," in *The Labor of Women in the Production of Cotton* (Austin: University of Texas, 1931), 174–208; Rebecca Sharpless, *Fertile Ground, Narrow Choices: Women on Texas Cotton Farms, 1900–1940* (Chapel Hill: University of North Carolina Press, 1999), 159–87.

3. Thad Sitton and James H. Conrad, *Freedom Colonies: Independent Black Texans in the Time of Jim Crow* (Austin: University of Texas Press, 2005), 140–55; Sharpless, *Fertile Ground, Narrow Choices*, 189–93.

4. Glasrud, "Black Texans," 8–9, 133; Brewer, "Black Women Workers," 35–48.

5. Glasrud, "Black Texans," 133–34; Brewer, "Black Women Workers," 35–48; Ruthe Winegarten, *Black Texas Women: 150 Years of Trial and Triumph* (Austin: University of Texas Press, 1995), 175, 177.

6. Alan Govenar, "Them Deep Ellum Blues: A Street, a Sound, and a Time," *Legacies* 2 (Spring 1990): 4–9; Alan B. Govenar and Jay E. Brakefield, *Deep Ellum and Central Track: Where the Black and White Worlds of Dallas Converged* (Denton: University of North Texas Press, 1998), 27–35; Winegarten, *Black Texas Women: 150 Years of Trial and Triumph*, 166–71.

7. Johnnie M. Armstead, "Black Women and Texas History," in *Bricks without Straw: A Comprehensive History of African Americans in Texas*, ed. David A. Williams (Austin: Eakin Press, 1997), 114–24; *San Antonio Register*, January 17, 1964; Ruthe Winegarten, "Carrie Jane Sutton Brooks," in *Black Texas Women: A Sourcebook* (Austin: University of Texas Press, 1996), 240; Winegarten, *Black Texas Women: 150 Years of Trial and Triumph*, 158–59, 161; Foster Kidd, Jocelyn Kidd, and Cheryl Kidd, "The African American Dentist in Texas, 1890–1991," *Dallas Weekly*, February 20–26, 1992.

8. Winegarten, *Black Texas Women: 150 Years of Trial and Triumph*, 159–63; Annie Maie Mathis, "Negro Public Health Nursing in Texas," *Southern Workman* 56 (July 1927): 302–303.

9. Doris Rich, *Queen Bess: Daredevil Aviator* (Washington, D.C.: Smithsonian Institution Press, 1993); Elizabeth Hadley Freydberg, "Bessie Coleman," in *Black Women in America*, ed. Darlene Clark Hine (Brooklyn, N.Y.: Carlson Publishing, 1993), 1: 262–63; Roni Morales, "Coleman, Bessie," *The Handbook of Texas Online*, http://www.tsha.utexas.edu/handbook/online, henceforth,

all citations to the *Handbook* are available at this site; Ruthe Winegarten, "El-
lie Alma Walls Montgomery," *Black Texas Women: A Sourcebook,* 258–59; A. W.
Jackson, "Ellis Walls Montgomery," *A Sure Foundation and a Sketch of Negro
Life in Texas* (Houston: A. W. Jackson, 1940), 161–62; Sherilyn Brandenstein,
"Hunter, Mary Evelyn V. Edwards," *The Handbook of Texas Online.*

10. Alwyn Barr, *The African Texans* (College Station: Texas A&M University Press, 2004), 45–49; Glasrud, "Black Texans," 290–92.

11. Herbert G. Gutman, *The Black Family in Slavery and Freedom, 1759–
1925* (New York: Vintage Books, 1976); Jacqueline Jones, *Labor of Love, Labor
of Sorrow: Black Women, Work, and the Family, from Slavery to the Present* (New
York: Basic Books, 1985).

12. Allen, "The Negro Woman," *Labor of Women in the Production of Cotton,* 174–208; Sharpless, *Fertile Ground, Narrow Choices,* chaps. 1, 2, 4.

13. Bruce A. Glasrud, "Jim Crow's Emergence in Texas," *American Studies* 15 (1974): 47–60; Barry A. Crouch and L. J. Schultz, "Crisis in Color: Racial Separation in Texas during Reconstruction," *Civil War History* 16 (1970):
37–49; James M. Smallwood, "The Woodward Thesis Revisited: The Origins
of Social Segregation in Texas," *Negro History Bulletin* (1984): 6–9.

14. Glasrud, "Jim Crow's Emergence in Texas," 53–59; Barr, *Black Texans,*
140–42.

15. Winegarten, *Black Texas Women: 150 Years of Trial and Triumph,* 214;
Austin Statesman, April 10, 1906; Barr, *Black Texans,* 137; James M. SoRelle,
"Race Relations in 'Heavenly Houston,' 1919–1945," in *Black Dixie: Afro-Texan
History and Culture in Houston,* ed. Howard Beeth and Cary D. Wintz (Col-
lege Station: Texas A&M University Press, 1992), 177–78.

16. Glasrud, "Jim Crow's Emergence in Texas," 55–56; Barr, *Black Texans,*
141; Winegarten, *Black Texas Women: 150 Years of Trial and Triumph,* 195–96;
"A Brief History of the Crockett State School for Girls," in Winegarten, *Black
Texas Women: A Sourcebook,* 141–44.

17. Sitton and Conrad, *Freedom Colonies;* Sharpless, *Fertile Ground, Narrow Choices,* chap. 5.

18. Glasrud, "Black Texans," 275–79; Barr, *Black Texans,* 167–68; Winegarten, *Black Texas Women: 150 Years of Trial and Triumph,* 127–29.

19. Glasrud, "Black Texans," 15–16, 207–59.

20. Winegarten, *Black Texas Women: 150 Years of Trial and Triumph,* 96.

21. Michael R. Heintze, *Private Black Colleges in Texas, 1865–1954* (College
Station: Texas A&M University Press, 1985), 21–43; Glasrud, "Black Texans,"
232–36; Barr, *Black Texans,* 160–63.

22. Winegarten, *Black Texas Women: 150 Years of Trial and Triumph,* 114,
119; Jackson, "Fannie A. Robinson," *A Sure Foundation,* 162–63; Jo Eckerman,
"Artemesia Bowden: Dedicated Dreamer," *Texas Passages* 2 (Winter 1987):
1–2, 10; Winegarten, "Artemesia Bowden," *Black Texas Women: A Sourcebook,*
239; Winegarten, *Sourcebook,* 71.

23. John R. "Pete" Hendrick, "Mary Allen Junior College," *The Handbook
of Texas Online;* Heintze, *Private Black Colleges in Texas,* 33–34.

24. Glasrud, "Black Texans," 261–70; Barr, *Black Texans*, 165–67; Karen Kossie-Chernyshev, "Constructing Good Success: The Church of God in Christ and Social Uplift in East Texas, 1910–1935," *East Texas Historical Journal* 44, no. 1 (2006): 49–55.

25. William E. Montgomery, "Introduction: The Formation of African American Churches," in *Black Churches in Texas: A Guide to Historic Congregations,* by Clyde McQueen (College Station: Texas A&M University Press, 2000), 3–22; Kossie-Chernyshev, "Constructing Good Success," 49–55; Winegarten, *Black Texas Women: 150 Years of Trial and Triumph*, 132; Roxanne J. Evans, "Black Catholics," *The Handbook of Texas Online;* Ada Simond, "A History of African-American Catholicism in Texas," in *Bricks without Straw,* ed. Williams, 309–22.

26. Cheryl Townsend Gilkes, "Religion," in *Black Women in America: An Historical Encyclopedia,* vol. 2, ed. Darlene Clark Hine, Elsa Barkley Brown, and Rosalyn Terborg-Penn (Bloomington: Indiana University Press, 1993), 967–72; Winegarten, *Black Texas Women: 150 Years of Trial and Triumph,* 131–32; Algerene Akins Craig, "Fuller, Maud Anna Berry," *The Handbook of Texas Online;* Jackson, "M. A. B. Fuller," *A Sure Foundation,* 205–207; *African American*, November 4, 1922; Doris Hollis Pemberton, "Annie Buchanan," *Juneteenth at Comanche Crossing* (Austin: Eakin Press, 1983), 176–80; William A. Owens, "Seer of Corsicana," in *And Horns on the Toads,* ed. Mody C. Boatright (Dallas: Southern Methodist University Press, 1959): 14–31.

27. Glasrud, "Black Texans," 270–74; Winegarten, *Black Texas Women: 150 Years of Trial and Triumph,* 186–87.

28. Winegarten, *Black Texas Women: 150 Years of Trial and Triumph,* 115–17; Julia K. Gibson Jordan and Charlie Mae Brown Smith, *Beauty and the Best: Fredericka Chase Dodd, the Story of a Life of Love and Dedication* (Dallas: Delta Sigma Theta Sorority, 1985), 3–9.

29. Glasrud, "Black Texans," 53–60; Barr, *Black Texans,* 77–80, 113; A. Elizabeth Taylor, "The Woman Suffrage Movement in Texas," *Journal of Southern History* 27 (May 1951): 194–215.

30. Judith N. McArthur, "Woman's Christian Temperance Union," *The Handbook of Texas Online;* Winegarten, *Black Texas Women: 150 Years of Trial and Triumph,* 77–80; Winegarten, "Eliza E. Peterson," *Black Texas Women: A Sourcebook:* 262.

31. Ruthe Winegarten, "Texas Association of Women's Clubs," *The Handbook of Texas Online;* Winegarten, *Black Texas Women: 150 Years of Trial and Triumph,* 187–98; Jackson, *A Sure Foundation:* 291, 294–95; Deborah Gray White, *Too Heavy a Load: Black Women in Defense of Themselves, 1894–1994* (New York: W. W. Norton, 1999), 60; Winegarten, "Ethel Blanche Wilson Ransom," *Black Texas Women: A Sourcebook,* 264–65; Winegarten, "Amelia Elsenia Soders Johnson," *Black Texas Women: A Sourcebook,* 254.

32. Winegarten, *Black Texas Women: 150 Years of Trial and Triumph,* 207–208; Glasrud, "Black Texans," 69–70; Margaret Bouland Baker, "The Texas

Negro and the World War" (Master's thesis, University of Texas, 1938), 16–17, 63–65.

33. Glasrud, "Black Texans," 70–71; Winegarten, *Black Texas Women: 150 Years of Trial and Triumph*, 208; Baker, "Texas Negro and the World War," 63–66.

34. Bernice Love Wiggins, "Ethiopia Speaks," in *Tuneful Tales*, ed. Maceo C. Dailey Jr. and Ruthe Winegarten (1925; Lubbock: Texas Tech University Press, 2002), 38–39.

35. Janet G. Humphrey, "Texas Equal Suffrage Association," *The Handbook of Texas Online*; Taylor, "Woman Suffrage Movement in Texas," 194–215; A. Elizabeth Taylor, Ruthe Winegarten, and Judith N. McArthur, *Citizens at Last: The Woman Suffrage Movement in Texas* (Austin: Ellen C. Temple, 1987), 127–30, 153–55; Winegarten, *Black Texas Women: 150 Years of Trial and Triumph*, 209; Nancy Baker Jones, "Adair, Christia V. Daniels," *The Handbook of Texas Online*; Jackson, "Federation of Women's Clubs," *A Sure Foundation*: 291–92.

36. Winegarten, *Black Texas Women: 150 Years of Trial and Triumph*, 209; Winegarten, *Black Texas Women: A Sourcebook*, 187–89.

37. Debbie Mauldin Cottrell, "Texas Association Opposed to Woman Suffrage," *The Handbook of Texas Online*; Taylor, Winegarten, and McArthur, *Citizens at Last*, 181–82; Winegarten, *Black Texas Women: 150 Years of Trial and Triumph*, 208–209.

38. Taylor, "Woman Suffrage Movement in Texas," 209–14; Jane Y. McCallum, "Activities of Women in Texas Politics," in *Texas Democracy: A Centennial History of Politics and Personalities of the Democratic Party, 1836–1936*, ed. Frank Adams (Austin: Democratic Historical Association, 1937), 467–87; Winegarten, *Black Texas Women: 150 Years of Trial and Triumph*, 210–11; Winegarten, *Black Texas Women: A Sourcebook*, 189–90.

39. Glasrud, "Black Texans," 79; Winegarten, *Black Texas Women: 150 Years of Trial and Triumph*, 211–12; *Houston Post*, November 4, 5, 1920; Doris T. Asbury, "Negro Participation in the Primary and General Elections in Texas" (Master's thesis, Boston University, 1951), 71.

40. Jones, "Adair, Christia V. Daniels"; Alecia Davis, "Christia V. Adair: Servant of Humanity," *Texas Historian* (September 1977); Winegarten, "Christia Daniels Adair," *Black Texas Women: A Sourcebook*, 191–92, 236–37.

41. Bruce A. Glasrud, "Blacks and Texas Politics during the Twenties," *Red River Valley Historical Review* 7 (Spring 1982): 39–53; Darlene Clark Hine, *Black Victory: The Rise and Fall of the White Primary in Texas* (Millwood, N.Y.: KTO Press, 1979).

42. Michael L. Gillette, "National Association for the Advancement of Colored People," *The Handbook of Texas Online*; Barr, *Black Texans*, 144; Winegarten, *Black Texas Women: 150 Years of Trial and Triumph*, 215.

43. Winegarten, *Black Texas Women: 150 Years of Trial and Triumph*, 217–20; John R. Ross, "Lynching," *The Handbook of Texas Online;* Winegarten, "Ethel Ransom," *Black Texas Women: A Sourcebook*, 264–65; Jackson,

"Mrs. R. A. Ransom," *A Sure Foundation*, 293; Nancy Baker Jones, "Association of Southern Women for the Prevention of Lynching," *The Handbook of Texas Online.*

44. Lauretta Holman Gooden, "Question to a Mob," in *Heralding Dawn: An Anthology of Verse*, ed. J. Mason Brewer (Dallas: privately printed, 1936), 16.

45. Winegarten, *Black Texas Women: 150 Years of Trial and Triumph*, 215–17; Mary M. Standifer, "Covington, Jennie Belle Murphy," *The Handbook of Texas Online*; Winegarten, "Jennie Belle Murphy Covington," *Black Texas Women: A Sourcebook*, 243–44; Winegarten, *Black Texas Women: A Sourcebook*, 195–96.

46. Josie Briggs Hall, *Hall's Moral and Mental Capsule for the Economic and Domestic Life of the Negro, as a Solution of the Race Problem* (Dallas: F. S. Jenkins, 1905).

47. Douglas Hales, "Maud Cuney" and "Maud Cuney-Hare," in *A Southern Family in White and Black: The Cuneys of Texas* (College Station: Texas A&M University Press, 2003), chaps. 6, 7; Maud Cuney-Hare, *Norris Wright Cuney: A Tribune of the Black People* (Washington, D.C.: Associated Publishers, 1913); Maud Cuney-Hare, *Negro Musicians and Their Music* (Washington, D.C. Associated Publishers, 1936).

48. Manet Harrison Fowler, "History of the Texas Association of Negro Musicians," *Negro Musician* (August 1929): 114–16; Annie Maie Mathis, "Negro Public Health Nursing in Texas," *Southern Workman* 56 (July 1927): 302–303.

49. Josie Briggs Hall, *A Scroll of Facts and Advice* (Mexia, Tex.: Houx's Printery, 1905); Doris Hollis Pemberton, "Josie Hall," in *Juneteenth at Comanche Crossing* (Austin: Eakin Press, 1983): 138–40; Winegarten, "Josie Briggs Hall," *Black Texas Women: A Sourcebook*: 151–52; Paul M. Lucko, "Hall, Josie Briggs ," *The Handbook of Texas Online.*

50. J. Mason Brewer, *Heralding Dawn: An Anthology of Verse by Texas Negroes* (Dallas: June Thomason Printing, 1936); Lorraine Elena Roses and Ruth Elizabeth Randolph, "Lauretta Holman Gooden," in *Harlem Renaissance and Beyond* (Houston: G. K. Hall, 1990), 126–27; Winegarten, "Lauretta Holman Gooden," *Black Texas Women: A Sourcebook*, 111–12, 250; Roses and Randolph, "Maurine L. Jeffrey," in *Harlem Renaissance and Beyond*, 193–194; Roses and Randolph, "Lillian Tucker Lewis," in *Harlem Renaissance and Beyond*, 221–22; Roses and Randolph, "Birdelle Wycoff Ranson," in *Harlem Renaissance and Beyond*, 277–78; Sandra Y. Govan, "Gwendolyn Bennett," in *The Oxford Companion to African American Literature*, ed. William L. Andrews, Frances Smith Foster, and Trudier Harris (New York: Oxford University Press, 1997), 57.

51. Wiggins, *Tuneful Tales;* Maceo C. Dailey Jr., "Introduction," in *Tuneful Tales*, vii–xvi; Winegarten, "Bernice Love Wiggins," *Black Texas Women: A Sourcebook*, 270–71; Roses and Randolph, "Bernice Love Wiggins," in *Harlem Renaissance and Beyond*, 347–48.

52. Karen Kossie-Chernyshev, "The Juneteenth Reflections of Lillian B. Horace (1866–1965): Freedom a Fantasy (?) . . . Why?" *Houston Sun*, June 20, 2005; Karen Kossie-Chernyshev, "Reclaiming the Writings of Lillian B.

Horace (1886–1965): Texas' Earliest Known African-American Novelist and Biographer," *TSU Times*, November, 2004; Karen Kossie-Chernyshev, "Horace, Lillian B.," in *African American National Biography* (New York: Oxford University Press, 2008), forthcoming; Lillian B. Jones, *Five Generations Hence* (Fort Worth: privately printed, 1916).

53. Gwendolyn Bennett, "Wedding Day," *Fire!* (November 1926): 26–28; Roses and Randolph, "Gwendolyn B. Bennett," in *Harlem Renaissance and Beyond*, 11–15; Neil Sapper, "Black Culture in Urban Texas: A Lone Star Renaissance," *Red River Valley Historical Review* 6 (Spring 1981): 72; Jennie V. Mills, "Doomed to Despair," *Waco Messenger*, September 29, 1933.

54. Fowler, "Texas Association of Negro Musicians," 114–16; Bruce A. Glasrud, "From Griggs to Brewer: A Review of Black Texas Culture, 1899–1940," *Journal of Big Bend Studies* 15 (2003): 200–201.

55. Winegarten, *Black Texas Women: A Sourcebook*, 140, 213, 249–50; Nancy Baker Jones, "Roberta Dodd Crawford," *The Handbook of Texas Online*; Paul M. Lucko, "Zelma Watson George," *The Handbook of Texas Online*. George later earned a Ph.D. in Sociology from New York University; her doctoral dissertation is titled "A Guide to Negro Music: Toward a Sociology of Negro Music."

56. Winegarten, "Priscilla Tyler," *Black Texas Women: A Sourcebook*, 267; Winegarten, "Portia Washington Pittman," *Black Texas Women: A Sourcebook*, 263; Ruth Ann Stewart, *Portia: The Life of Portia Washington Pittman, the Daughter of Booker T. Washington* (New York: Doubleday, 1977); Winegarten, "Jennie Belle Murphy Covington," *Black Texas Women: A Sourcebook*, 243–44.

57. Govenar and Brakefield, *Deep Ellum and Central Track*, 56–79; Dave Oliphant, "Texan Jazz," in *The Roots of Texas Music*, ed. Lawrence Clayton and Joe W. Specht (College Station: Texas A&M University Press, 2003), 38; Winegarten, *Black Texas Women: 150 Years of Trial and Triumph*, 135; Winegarten, "Beulah Thomas (Sippie) Wallace," *Black Texas Women: A Sourcebook*, 267–68; Daphne Duval Harrison, "Sippie Wallace," in *Black Women in America: An Historical Encyclopedia*, ed. Darlene Clark Hine, Elsa Barkley Brown, and Rosalyn Terborg-Penn (Brooklyn: Carlson Publishing, 1993), 1220–23).

58. Govenar and Brakefield, *Deep Ellum and Central Track*, 100–107; N. H. Goodall, "Arizona Juanita Dranes," in *Black Women in America*, ed. Hine, Brown, and Terborg-Penn, 355–56.

59. Glasrud, "From Griggs to Brewer," 198; Maud Cuney-Hare, "Antar of Araby," in *Plays and Pageants from the Life of the Negro*, ed. Willis Richardson (Washington, D.C.: Associated Publishers, 1930), 27–74; Winegarten, *Black Texas Women: 150 Years of Trial and Triumph*, 146–48.

MERLINE PITRE

5. At the Crossroads

BLACK TEXAS WOMEN, 1930–1954

Set in motion by the stock market crash of 1929, the Great Depression was one of the most catastrophic periods in U.S. history. All Americans suffered measures of economic dislocation, but none more than the African American female. At the beginning of the Depression, 40 percent of African American women were in the work force. By 1931 one-quarter of these women had lost their jobs. For the great majority of these women lodged in domestic servant occupations, the powerful combination of racial discrimination and sexual stratification of labor imprisoned them at the bottom of the economic ladder. Also, the triple responsibilities of black women—earning cash through paid employment; caring for their families with meager resources derived from unwaged labor; and building community and social change with voluntary labor in churches, clubs, and political organizations—increased as they fought off the ravages of the worst economic crisis of the twentieth century.

Throughout the 1930s, black women tolerated a higher rate of unemployment than white women. The unemployment rate among African American women was the highest of all workers, for obvious reasons. When in competition with a white person, the black female was the first to be laid off, and the first to be subjected to shorter shifts and fewer days of work. If she lost her job, she could move from being a schoolteacher to a file clerk, to a waitress, to a house cleaning lady. In a word, she was downwardly mobile. To make matters worse, when President Franklin D. Roosevelt unveiled his New Deal program designed to inflate the depressed economy via relief and work programs, many facets of it discriminated against black women. So, the Depression era was one of irony for the black female—one of suffering and want, assistance and discrimination, ingenuity and determination. It was a period that can be described as one of self-help, relief, recovery and reform as blacks made it through hard times.

The Lean Years

The condition of black females in Texas mirrored that of the larger society. When the economic crash came in October 1929, many black Texans were already suffering from economic privation. This traumatic event caused a large number of them to lose their jobs in the cities, and many in the rural areas were doomed to starvation. At the outset of the Depression, the majority of black Texans were living in rural areas of the state. In 1930, 189 counties in Texas reported the presence of 85,940 black farmers. Eighteen and one-half percent of them owned their land, while 48.2 percent were sharecroppers and 39.3 percent represented some other form of tenant farming. The economic condition for black farmers was unpromising. Most farmers made no more than ten bales of cotton a year, and had an unwaged wife and an average of ten children. The average female worked ten hours per day on the farm picking cotton and was paid $1.25 per 100 pounds. Others like Emma got even less. "Me and my husband were sharecroppers," said Emma. "We made a crop [one] that year and the owner took all the crop. We weren't getting but 35 cents a hundred (pound) but I was able to make it, cause I also worked in people's home[s] where they give you old clothes and shoes."[1]

As the Great Depression deepened, the number of unemployed black people increased. There were 75,535 unemployed blacks in Texas by 1933. This represented 8.5 percent of the total black population in Texas and a large segment of the black female population, and mostly the unemployed resided in rural areas of the state. By 1935, the number of unemployed black persons in the state had decreased to 63,826, but the inescapable conclusion remained—unskilled black female workers on the farms bore the brunt of the burden.[2]

The traditional immobility of many black women living in East Texas was overcome during the Great Depression by migration. Exacerbated by falling prices for agricultural produce and the boll weevil plague, many black families left the countryside for the uncertainty of urban life in the Lone Star State. Consequently, by the mid 1930s, the black rural population was reduced by 13.5 percent. Similarly, the black urban population of the state increased from 239,929 in 1930 to 420,110 in 1940. As black females relocated between 1930 and 1940 to urban areas, the number of African American female domestic servants and semiskilled workers increased significantly while the number of blue-collar jobs increased only slightly. The 1930 census revealed that black women were concentrated in a handful of white-collar jobs with teachers comprising a majority of all black female professionals, and boardinghouse keepers constituting more than one-half of the black women of the proprietary class. Of the black women engaged in semiskilled occupations, over 40 percent were dressmakers and laundry operators. A total of 69 percent of black female workers were engaged in domestic occupations.[3]

Black Female Professional Workers in Texas, 1900–1950

Moving from rural to urban areas did not significantly alter the economic plight of the black female. Unemployment and underemployment hit black women hard and fast, more harshly than either black men or white women. Gender employment, fierce competition, and

	1900	1910	1920	1930	1940	1950
Accountants	NA	NA	0	NA	NA	9
Artists, Art Teachers	7	3	NA	6	8	27
Authors, Eds., Reporters	NA	NA	NA	3	5	10
Dietitians, Nutritionists	NA	NA	NA	NA	NA	55
Lawyers, Judges	NA	NA	NA	NA	1	2
Librarians	NA	NA	NA	13	36	104
Musicians, Music Teachers	69	150	130	188	175	316
Nurses, Professional (includes midwives)	676	64	84	158	228	440
Physicians, Surgeons	NA	NA	NA	NA	NA	9
Social, Welfare Workers	NA	NA	48	26	33	75
Teachers	1,097	1,846	2,909	4,284	4,928	6,186
Technicians, Med. & Dent.	NA	NA	NA	NA	NA	74
TOTAL	1,849	2,063	3,171	4,678	5,414	7,307

Source: William Brophy, "The Black Texan, 1900–1950: A Quantitative History" (Ph.D. diss., Vanderbilt, 1974), 51.

racial preference all contributed to job loss for black women. Women
from every occupation with or without experience competed for the
same jobs, as it was assumed that everyone could do housework. De-
pending on the nature of the work, black men also competed with
black women for domestic work, which paid an average of nine dollars
a week. To make matters worse, as white businesses folded and middle-
and upper-class white families began to feel the financial strain of the
Great Depression, they cut domestic and household workers, often
forcing many black families out of employment completely.

During the first month of President Franklin D. Roosevelt's administration, blacks had little more than their hopes to sustain them.
But their optimism rested on the bold new initiatives that became
known as the New Deal. With little resistance, Congress passed laws
aimed at overhauling the nation's financial, agricultural, and industrial
systems. Although these acts were intended to bring relief, recovery,
and reform to all Americans, they sometimes did so at the expense of
black men and women. In Texas, as elsewhere in the country, the New
Deal's recognition of public responsibility for economic well-being
produced mixed results for blacks. Not only did blacks find it more difficult than whites to get on relief rolls, but blacks also received less pay,
usually, for doing the same job. Although several policies of the New
Deal prohibited discrimination based on race, color, or creed, loopholes
were found to get around them. While local or state agencies did not
overtly disregard the federal law, discrimination often came disguised
as geographic wage differential and occupational classification.[4]

In Texas as unemployment doubled and wages fell, black women
found it increasingly difficult to receive relief. Black recipients received
lower allotments than their white counterparts although they paid the
same prices for food, goods, and services. Moreover, it was not always
easy for a black female to apply for assistance. Seeking relief was often
embarrassing and humiliating. Many black females had to endure racist judgment and comments from white social workers about their morality and their mental and physical health. But more than this, they
had to continue to prove to these social workers that they needed relief
despite the fact that as a black female in the Depression era, they were
in the "worse fix of all."[5]

There were some New Deal programs—the Works Progress Administration (WPA, later the Work Projects Administration) and the
National Youth Administration (NYA)—that could be considered bit-

tersweet for black females. The WPA administered large-scale public work programs for the jobless that paid higher wages and put blacks in positions where previously they had not had access. Yet, racist and sexist presumptions and also discrimination abounded in this agency. The Women's and Professional Division of the WPA in Texas employed 4,993 black women by 1936, but that number was only 3 percent of the total WPA workers in the state. And over half of that 3 percent was involved in sewing projects where discrimination was rampant, prompting B. E. Bone and I. M. Howard of San Antonio to report, "They treated us very bad at the WPA office." Besides sewing, the Women's and Professional Division of the WPA employed black women in food canning, recreational supervision, home demonstration, as teachers of music and hygiene, and in library work. Four hundred and sixty of the 4,493 females were hired as adult educators and taught approximately 35,415 students in 1933. Black women also provided assistance in the circulatory library project in Austin in 1936. Through this project, 5,000 books were made available to the public on a monthly basis. In rural and urban areas where emphasis was placed on homemaking, the WPA project was complemented by the Prairie View Extension Service and training schools.[6]

Designed to provide relief, but at the same time to keep black females in "their place," training schools for "colored" domestics became popular in Texas during the Great Depression. Emphasizing such subjects as table service and etiquette, breads and cakes, meat cookery, and vegetables and salads, the Dallas Gas Company offered a four-week course for black women aspiring to domestic service in 1934. Prairie View sponsored a similar three-month course that covered such subjects as health and personal hygiene, meals in the home, household management, care of children, and employer-employee relationships. Interestingly, the Houston Training School Program employed the same content and tactic. It sought to train not only housemaids, nursemaids, launderers, and cooks but also "happy and contented workers doing superior jobs for satisfied employers." This training, done in the home of a white director, was designed to give the student real-life experience. Upon completion of the course, a diploma certified the student's competency, but the diploma was withheld until the student successfully completed one year of employment as a domestic worker.[7]

The National Youth Administration, noted for its popularity in the black community, provided relief work and assistance to black youths between the ages of sixteen and twenty. It trained young black females in domestic work and sought the assistance of the Texas State Employment Service in obtaining jobs for them. The agency also provided part-time jobs and vocational training for needy high school and college students. In the words of an editorial in the *Houston Informer,* "The National Youth Administration not only helped young blacks to learn skill trades, it assisted blacks in acquiring a college education." This program was strengthened in Texas because its director, Lyndon Baines Johnson, allowed for race and gender involvement in it. Mary E. Branch, president of Tillotson College, devoted a great deal of her time working with the NYA in Texas. She, along with the members of the NYA Negro Advisory Board, established a Freshman College Center Program—a tutorial and enhancement program designed to help students make the social and academic transition from high school to college. During the Depression, fifteen of those centers were established throughout the state and served 440 black youths annually.[8]

Unlike the NYA, some New Deal agencies—the National Recovery Administration (NRA) and the Social Security Administration—had a mixed impact on black females. The NRA sought to stimulate industry, established codes of fair competition, provided a minimum scale of $10 to $12 for a forty-hour week, and allowed for wage differentials by regions. The NRA permitted the South to pay the lowest wages in the country and also to black females. When wages were raised in compliance with the codes, employers frequently dismissed black workers or paid whites higher wages. More often than not the codes did not benefit black Texan women. For example, two black women took Carter Wesley, editor of the *Houston Informer,* to court for working them in excess of eight hours a day on three separate occasions. Wesley was acquitted, in part because his lawyer, Percy Foremen, convinced a jury of six white men that Wesley had adequately compensated these women, despite the stipulations in the codes. "Could you be prejudice against a man who paid a colored woman $20 for approximately three days of work," said Foreman to the jury.[9]

No group needed social security more that the black female, and none got less of it. The landmark Social Security Act of 1935 provided for old-age pension and unemployment insurance. A payroll tax on workers and their employers created a fund from which retirees received a monthly pension after age sixty-five. Social security did not apply, however, to the masses of black workers locked into agriculture and domestic occupations. The latter contained more than half of the black female workers in Texas.

During the Great Depression the family was necessary for survival and support for black women. Although marriage and birth rates declined in the 1930s, the family increased as kin and older siblings moved back into the house to share meager resources. Also, many black females, especially black domestic workers who resided in California or some other state, often sent their children to live with grandmothers, sisters, and aunts. In each case, black women provided emotional and practical needs of the ever-changing household.

As familial cooperation increased in the 1930s, so did familial conflict and the black woman's role in it. For some women, as poverty and unemployment came into the door, love went out the door. Some women blamed men for their unemployment and vice versa. In the family, a loss of income on either the part of the husband or wife meant a difference between survival and eviction. Family conflict was not confined to marriage. Older women could not always depend on their children for assistance. While there was tension between the mother and children, the emotional stress was not as great as it was for black women living outside the family. For these women, the only alternative was living on relief.

The strain of the Great Depression allowed only a few women time to be creative in the cultural arts. Still, there were those who prevailed in drama and dance, and as writers and visual artists. For example, Myra Hemmings and Mary E. Ben Isaacs launched community theaters in San Antonio and Houston respectively in 1931. Several women (Beatrice Gildersleeve, Betty D. Wilson, and Lily Hall Chase) attempted careers in creative writing, but it was Gwendolyn Bennett, a native of Giddings, Texas, who became the first woman to receive a Guggenheim Fellowship. She also published several poems in a Harlem Renaissance magazine. She is best known for her poem, "To a Dark Girl," which conveyed a sense of black pride. In visual art, Houston native Jewel Woodward Simon became a painter, sculptor, and printmaker. Subsequently, her art was exhibited in New York, Atlanta, Los Angeles, and Moscow. These and other women who engaged in cultural art gave voice to black females, voice that enriched their lives and those of their families, their communities, and the larger society.[10]

The Great Depression and the New Deal era brought continuity and change to the African American female. Race and gender guaranteed many commonalities among black women's experiences. During the Depression, widespread unemployment had relatively little impact on race and gender stratification in the labor market. Most employers did not substitute a cheaper female employee for a higher paid white male or female. Although the New Deal did improve the economic and social conditions of some African American women, society remained largely bound by sexist and racist traditional values. That is, black women on relief programs were restricted to "women's work." The WPA reinforced this traditional idea by training black women as maids, dishwashers, and cooks. During the lean years, however, black women met these challenges via ingenuity, culture, extended families, and coping mechanisms. Some held onto and even found jobs in sectors that already traditionally employed them. Others became small-scale entrepreneurs in both the countryside and the cities. Still others used the church not only as a cultural and religious haven but also to raise funds to care for the needy. Hope mounted even as the United States drew closer to becoming involved in World War II.

The War Years

For African Americans, World War II was a welcomed reprieve from the Great Depression, as it almost doubled the number of blacks in the workforce and reduced significantly their number on the unemployment list. The war years, 1939 to 1945, were especially important for blacks who benefited from the expanding labor force, changing racial values, a revitalized migration out of the rural South, and the attempted enforcement of equal employment under a presidential mandate. The war also marked an important break with the historic allocation of work by race and sex by dramatically accelerating the pace of economic change for black women. Millions of new jobs were created in the clerical and manufacturing fields, opening up opportunities for women to secure new and better employment. Black women had a new range of job possibilities, and, in some instances, new opportunities to move up the vocational ladder or at least off its bottom rung. But, to present only the improvement wrought during the War, however, is to understate the extent to which race and gender served as an impediment to black females' economic and social mobility. And nowhere was this better evidenced than in the Lone Star State.

Despite the hardships of the Great Depression, prosperity returned to Texas after 1939 and continued for more than a decade thereafter. By 1939 the growing threat of war in Europe and Asia signaled more to the United States than a threat to world peace. According to President Roosevelt, it meant U.S. involvement and the creation of stockpile material that might be important for America's defense. The result of this was the establishment of a wartime economy that, in turn, led to a level of prosperity in Texas that was unknown in previous decades.

To a large extent, Texas' prosperity rested on industrial plants' conversion to the production of wartime materials. In the drive to create defense industries in Texas, massive aircraft manufacturing plants were built in north-central Texas. Shipyards were established on the Gulf Coast in Baytown, Galveston, and Houston. Petrochemical industries were created near existing petroleum refineries and were located at various points in the state.

In 1942, the economic expansion and manpower shortage accompanying the Second World War created heretofore-unrealized employment opportunities for all the people of Texas. The question was, to what extent would black women share in that prosperity? Black females did not penetrate many industries, though they were employed in four major ones during the War—the meat packinghouses of Forth Worth, the garment factories in Dallas (where military uniforms were made), the railroad industries in Kingsville, and the Houston Shipyard. Dallas industries employed more females than any other city combined. There were 2,119 in food and tobacco, 129 in textile mills, and 623 in apparel manufacturing.[11]

As industrial plants began to convert for the purpose of producing war materials, black women, as well as blacks in general, found difficulty in securing employment, in part because of their lack of education. Between 1942 and 1945 a large number of black workers—male and female—received training in semiskilled and skilled defense work in Houston. Despite their defense training at Prairie View and elsewhere in the state, the skilled and semiskilled black workers quite often were not employed in Texas industries. Instead, they were transported to Chester, Pennsylvania, or Oakland, California, to work in shipyards, while the shipyards of Texas were experiencing a labor shortage. When black workers were employed in the state, the prevailing practice was to assign them to semiskilled work despite any previous training.[12]

Not only were black female workers "short-changed" in hiring practices, wages, and working conditions by the ship building industry, but also by other industries. In the packinghouses of Fort Worth, they processed meat cut from hogs, cattle, and sheep, while white women sliced bacon. They also worked in hide cellars stretching and drying hides, tasks formerly done by men. On average black women worked as janitors in the petrochemical, aircraft, metal product, and shipbuilding industries, while their male counterparts worked in areas that were hot and hazardous. Working conditions in the railroad industry were not much better as they cleaned boxcars and washed and steamed engines. In the garment industries, their jobs included that of pressers, sleeve makers, collar makers, and buttonhole setters.[13]

In the aforementioned industries, white women's reluctance to expand job opportunities for the black females focused not on the issue of promotion but rather on the desire to maintain social distance. White females frequently objected to working closely with black women or sharing facilities with them because they feared that blacks were dirty and diseased. A case in point was the Atlas Dress Company in Houston. There, Lulu B. White, executive director of the Houston Branch of the National Association for the Advancement of Colored People (NAACP) protested (to no avail) the fact that a partition was placed between white and black female workers, and that most blacks were relegated to a night shift, while whites to a day shift.[14]

Early insistence by some employers on segregated gender work arrangements and facilities served as a rationale for excluding black women altogether or limiting their number in certain plants. The major agency charged with enforcing equal opportunity in employment, the Fair Employment Practice Commission (FEPC), could not and did not do anything about the discrimination that was meted out to black female workers of Texas. The FEPC, an agency created in 1941 in response to a threatened march on Washington by civil rights groups protesting discriminatory policies by war industries, could recommend the removal of war contracts from employers who continued to discriminate, and the Manpower War Commission could restrict work permits, but the federal government was not inclined to hamper the production of essential war material in order to foster racial equity. So, many times when black females with defense training applied for appropriate work and made complaints to the FEPC, they were often referred to jobs outside the area. The persistence of discrimination, despite a federal commitment to eliminate it, hampered the ability of all blacks, male and female, to find industrial employment in the Lone Star State.[15]

Although black females experienced discrimination in the industrial workforce, they continued to push for better working conditions and higher pay. For this they turned increasingly toward labor unions. World War II and the rise of industrial jobs made black females more conscious of the benefits that could accrue from such affiliation. African American women's involvement in union activities began in Texas in the early 1930s when a chapter of the Women's Auxiliary of the Brotherhood of Sleeping Car Porters was established and Olivia Rawlston of Dallas was elected its president. During the war years three of the most powerful unions worked for the interest of black females. Although segregated, the International Ladies Garment Workers Union (ILGWU), the Women's Auxiliary of the Colored Trainmen Association, and the United Packinghouse Workers of America (UPWA) appeared to have been more liberal toward black women in terms of salary and working conditions. These unions provided maternity leave for female members, aided them with voter registration, participated in the United Way fund-raising campaign, and defended the right of the employee against the employer.[16]

Where unions were in place, black women felt a sense of security. But in areas where there were no unions, they were left without any recourse. That only a small percentage of black females were employed in clerical positions in the Lone Star State is neither uncommon nor unique; the same held true in public employment in government. Other than public education, the opportunity for public employment at the local, county, and municipal levels was extremely limited for black females. Almost without exception there were very few nurses in public hospitals, a few home demonstration agencies, and a few librarians. The State Highway Department in Houston employed 7,000 workers by 1949, and the sole black employee hired by that agency was a male in a janitorial position.[17]

Despite the discrimination they encountered daily, some black women decided to combine employment and patriotic support of the war effort by joining the armed services. Perhaps the most important development for black women after the United States entered World War II on December 7, 1941, was the creation of the Women's Army Auxiliary Corps (WAAC) in May of 1942. Designed and established to allow women to fill noncombatant jobs, the WAAC was incorporated into the U.S. Army in 1943 and was later changed to the Women's Army Corps (WAC) but remained part of the Army. Initially,

blacks of the South were reluctant to join the WAC because Houston's
Oveta Culp Hobby was named the director, and they feared that her
southern upbringing might inhibit fair treatment toward them. This
fear, however, was quickly alleviated when Mary McLeod Bethune
was named her assistant. Bethune worked hard to enlist black officers,
recruiting primarily among African American colleges. When the first
group of thirty-nine black female volunteers arrived in Des Moines,
Iowa, for training in 1943, four were from Houston, Texas, and all were
graduates of Prairie View A&M College. Annie Lois Brown-Wright,
Ruth L. Freeman, Geraldine Bright, and Alice Marie Jones graduated
from training with a rank equivalent to second lieutenant. They along
with six other Texans were among the first four hundred women in the
WAC who served in the war. Of the 343 black women who served in
the nation's Army Nurse Corps, two Texans made outstanding contributions, Estelle Massey Lidele Osborne, who served on the staff of
the National Nursing Council for War Service, and second lieutenant
Leola Green, who spent ten months in active duty in North Africa.[18]

According to the *Houston Informer,* "the Women's Army Auxiliary
Corps offered a splendid opportunity for colored women to help achieve
success in the war effort." Elizabeth "Tex" Williams of Houston distinguished herself as a laboratory technician and medical photographer.
Others became teachers of the culinary arts and some also became
nurses. Mary Bingham August Anderson taught blacks and whites,
males and females, how to become a good cook. Although barred from
combat and attending to white troops, black nurses accompanied the
troops into combat in Africa, Italy, and France, and treated men under
fire. In the words of Leola Green, "an injured soldier ceases to be black
or white in the fighting forces." There is no doubt that Texas women
served valiantly in the war. Still, their performance was hindered by
racial and gender segregation. They were separated from their white
counterparts in mess halls, barracks, and assignments. The experience
of these women showed how much they could accomplish under less
than pleasant circumstances.[19]

World War II came to an end in August 1945, and conversion to
a peacetime economy resulted in retrenchment and displacement of a
large number of female workers. Demobilization after World War II
affected black women more severely than white women; wartime jobs
were not immediately replaced by new jobs in industry or offices. In the
long run, the greatest benefits of wartime experience for black Texas

females derived from their movement in large numbers out of poverty in rural Texas to the possibilities provided by an urban industrialized economy. The extent to which those possibilities were realized in the decade of the 1940s can be overstated, however. Young women who migrated from rural to urban areas without a good education usually found semi- and unskilled work. For those who did have an education, they were usually restricted to gender-specific areas such as teaching. To be sure, in industrial and professional jobs, black women made some improvement, but still the better-paying jobs in almost all categories went to black men and white women. At war's end, the situation was even more gloomy for the masses of black women; 60 percent of them held service jobs either in private households or in restaurants. Statistically, the number of those who worked in private households was smaller in the Great Depression, but this did not diminish the number of those lodged in domestic occupations. Although many black women experienced upward mobility during the war, the relative position of the African American female within the American social and economic sphere remained unchanged by 1954.

Education, Migration, and Self-Help

During the decades of the 1930s, 1940s, and 1950s, African American women's education was shaped by poverty, war, peace, prosperity, and prejudice. Like the rest of the country, the Great Depression hurt education in Texas and worked a special hardship on education of African Americans. Construction of new school buildings was curtailed. And not only were white teachers paid more than blacks, but also the miserably low number and salaries of black teachers were reduced even further. Despite these setbacks, females continued to enroll in large numbers at the elementary, secondary, and postsecondary levels. According to the 1932 *Bulletin* of Prairie View, "Women [were] crowding men out of high schools as they [had] long since done in elementary schools."[20]

As the enrollment of black students increased at the elementary and secondary levels, the need for more trained teachers became paramount. At a time when other white-collar occupations were closed to black females, normal schools and teacher training institutions provided them an opportunity. The fact that most black men could not obtain employment commensurate with their educational training resulted in black families educating daughters disproportionately to men. Consequently, many unskilled black families made great sacrifices during the Depression to educate their daughters. Young women whose parents did not have the financial resources to pay their tuition often relied on subsidies from the National Youth Administration or on monies from part-time jobs they held on campus.

Those black females who entered a Texas college between 1930 and 1954 were more often than not steered into a gender specific career—teaching. They attended one of the eleven historically black colleges. When most of these colleges (Paul Quinn, Wiley, Bishop, Jarvis Christian, Mary Allen Butler, Tillotson, and St. Philip's) were established during Reconstruction, they had one purpose in mind—to train teachers and preachers. Their curriculum included liberal arts training, but emphasis was placed on agriculture and home economics. By 1940 many of these institutions began to deemphasize vocational education training in agriculture, but maintained courses in clothing, food preparation, home nursing, child care, home management, and consumer education. Interestingly, these courses also flourished at the two black public institutions, Prairie View College and Texas Southern University.[21]

Regardless of the institution these women attended from the 1930s through the 1950s, the education they received tended to be more practical than classical. These institutions had a bent toward domestic ideology and the private sphere, but also catered to certain activities in the public sphere—public service and teaching. Many black females favored this kind of education because it took into consideration the realities of the black female experience that included work outside the home.

It is an understatement to say that the majority of black females who graduated from college became teachers. Teaching provided them professional work, a skilled vocation, and a lucrative salary, albeit lower than white women and black men. But teaching was not without its problems. Following the lead in other states during the 1930s, many Texas school systems prohibited married women from teaching. In 1932, the San Antonio School Board voted to dismiss all married teachers whose husbands were earning $2,000. This edict placed some black families at a disadvantage because in many instances the black female teachers were the sole breadwinners. Using their ingenuity, however, many black women found ways around this dilemma by keeping their marriage secret. Others used the profession as a stepping-stone to something greater—to become a political activist, a principal, a social worker, or to enter graduate school. Still others became leaders within their community.[22]

Two black women were indeed change agents in their communities as well as at the institutions where they served as presidents; they were Artemisia Bowden and Mary Elizabeth Branch. As presidents, these women guided St. Philip's College and Tillotson College through the Great Depression, World War II, and the postwar era. These were indeed trying times for individuals and also institutions, but these two black women met the challenge. Born in Georgia and educated at a normal school in North Carolina, Bowden arrived at St. Philip's in San Antonio in 1902. When called upon by the Protestant Episcopal Church to lead the said college, Bowden had only two years experience in teaching, but she left confident that she could handle the job because St. Philip's was still an elementary school. Years later under her tutelage, St. Philip's grew from an elementary school to a normal department and in the 1920s became a junior college. In 1926, the board of trustees named Bowden chief executive officer of St. Philip's, making her the first black female of Texas to become head of a college. While at the helm of the institution, Bowden served as business manager, spokesperson, and chief fund-raiser until her departure in 1960.[23]

Mary Elizabeth Branch, the first black woman to serve as a four-year college president in Texas, participated in a long tradition of black women as leaders in community affairs, state and national education, and community affairs. Born in Farmville, Virginia, in May of 1881, Branch came to Tillotson College in 1929 armed with education and experience. She held bachelor's and master's degrees in English and had over thirty years of teaching experience at the college level. When called upon by the American Missionary Association to become President of Tillotson College, her mission was to rescue this small black college from the brink of collapse. She knew that it was a declining institution, but was surprised at what she saw on her first day. There were approximately six worn-out buildings surrounded by eight unkempt trees, 140 students, a library with fewer than one hundred books, and a college that was unaccredited. A less courageous person might have resigned on the spot, but Mary Branch met this challenge with a five-year plan to upgrade the physical plant, improve academics, and attract more students. As a result, new buildings were added and old ones renovated. Branch's effort to improve academics included expanding the library holdings from one hundred to 2,100 books in fourteen years, doubling the size of the faculty with master's degrees, and reorganizing Tillotson as a coeducational college. Because of these innovations, enrollment grew from 140 students in 1930 to 502 in 1944, and the college received an "A" rating by the Southern Association of Colleges and Schools. Coupled with this crowning achievement, Branch also generated a good working relationship with the surrounding community, as well as officials at the state and national levels.[24] Bowden and Branch are only two examples of noteworthy black women, but there were many others working to make a difference. A large number could be found in the women's club movement that was prominent in the state. As agents of reform and community uplift, black women, through volunteerism and fund-raising, combated the illiteracy, high mortality, unemployment, and inadequate health care that plagued African Americans. The simultaneous explosion of World War II, urbanization, industrialization, and immigration into the state exacerbated tension between blacks and whites. The mass migration of African Americans into the urban areas of Texas, the low educational level of blacks, and their restricted access to the franchises were sharp reminders to black women that their collective club activities had become indispensable to sustenance and viability of black life. No doubt, these reasons boosted their resolve to continue their work as the migration simultaneously transformed the state's black population in general and the female's in particular.[25]

Thousands of African American females migrated to Texas between 1930 and 1954. The black female population jumped from 473,400 in 1940 to 501,834 in 1950. Of the 501,834 black females, 320,666 lived in urban areas of the state. Most of these women were in the prime of their lives, ranging in age from eighteen to forty-four. As with men, nearly half of them took up residence in Dallas, Fort Worth, and Houston.[26]

From the outset, women migrants faced greater challenges than their male counterparts. Desperate for employment opportunities and better wages, they willingly distanced themselves from family and familiar surroundings. They traveled without physical or educational weapons. A lady traveling alone in Texas was not only taking a risk, she was also asking for trouble. She became easy prey for criminal, sexual, and economic exploitation and in all cases was at a greater risk than her male counterpart. In the words of Darlene Hine, "a man could and did, with less approbation and threat of bodily harm, spend nights outdoors . . . men were better suited to defend themselves against attackers. However given the low esteem in which the general society held black women, even the courts and law officials would have ridiculed and dismissed assault complaints from a female traveling alone, regardless of her social status." [27]

For those women moving from one area to another, life was not easy. They had difficulty in obtaining adequate housing and gainful employment. The majority continued to be in domestic service, with single women comprising the largest percentage of the group. In Houston alone, the number of single women employed outside the home increased by 100 percent. As more women joined the group of married couples, they were soon to discover that limited access to child care, educational institutions, and social services restricted not only their own lives but also opportunities for their children as well. [28]

As agents of uplift, clubwomen were especially cognizant of the difficulties brought by this large migration of African American females into the state. No doubt, migration coupled with ethnic problems presented a major challenge to the reform efforts of the clubwomen. But, like their white counterparts who worked to improve the condition of women, black clubwomen sought to uplift their race while at the same time improving the economic, social, and political status of women. Starting in the late nineteenth century and continuing through the mid-twentieth century, there was a proliferation of women's organizations in the Lone Star State. These included, but were not limited to, lodges; secret societies; and civic, literary, and political clubs. At the turn of the century these clubs were placed under an umbrella organization known as the Texas Federation of Women's Clubs (TFWC). Because of their exclusion from this group, in 1905 black women organized the Texas Association of Colored Women's Clubs (TACWC). The educated community leaders who formed this network were usually middle-class homemakers, married to professionals, or were owners of small businesses. While committed to improving the quality of life in the Texas communities, black clubwomen's most obvious stimulus during the pre– and post–World War II period was that of meeting the basic survival needs of blacks, fighting the rising tide of Jim Crow, and battling against lynching and verbal attacks on black women's characters. Concentrating their efforts on health, education, welfare, politics, the aged, and the young, black clubwomen adopted the motto of "Lifting As We Climb."[29]

Perhaps the most basic of the health problems addressed by club leaders was that of building health-care centers and hospitals. The fear of disease, especially a contagious one such as tuberculosis, was especially troubling to blacks of all classes. Blacks throughout the state had been lobbying politicians and other state officials to build a state TB hospital for blacks since the 1920, but it was not until the TFWC and TACWC joined forces that this idea came to fruition in 1934. Coupled with this endeavor was that of seven black women's federated clubs whose members organized a Community Welfare Association in Austin in 1927. This organization was established with a twofold purpose in mind: to establish both a community health center and a multipurpose center for club activities. Chartered under the leadership of Mattie E. Holman Durden in 1929, this organization shifted its focus to serving preschool children with a nursery program during the Great Depression. In 1935, the school was taken over by the WPA, and in 1951, it came under the auspices of the Austin Public Schools. The health center and multipurpose center continued to serve needy families and as a meeting place for many groups. This organization subsequently secured the services of a city nurse and campaigned to secure a branch of the Austin Public Library. Such actions of supporting the less able and improving health care meant providing services normally supported by local government through public taxes. Thus, these services rendered by these women pushed their activities beyond that of charity work into community development.[30]

Sharing the pursuit of an agenda that encompassed community action, self- improvement, and social and political reform were a number of individuals and organizations. For example, Anna Dupree, a beautician, real estate agent, and businesswoman, contributed more than $40,000 toward the construction of an orphanage for black children and the Eliza Johnson Home for Aged Negroes in Houston. Complementing her action was the Jack and Jill Club, whose main focus was improving the lives of black youths. Concerned with social and political reform were the National Council of Negro Women and the Links. During the 1940s and 1950s, the latter pushed for civil rights and spoke out against political brutality, while the former sponsored drug education workshops and voter registration seminars.[31]

The black clubwomen did not embrace a black nationalist or a separatist ideology in favor of interracial cooperation despite the discrimination they encountered. For example, although the Young Women's Christian Association (YWCA) was established with a segregated chapter in 1915, the colored branches worked cooperatively with the parent body even while pushing for integration. The TFWC barred black membership, but still the TACWC cooperated with it in fund-raising and in exchanging speakers for different occasions. Consequently, the two groups united in establishing a juvenile school for black females in 1930. While black women took the lead in this venture, the TFWC assisted them in purchasing 10 acres of land in San Antonio for a permanent site and in lobbying the legislature for $96,000 for the construction of the State School for Juvenile Negro Youths. The TACWC interacted with whites, both out of necessity and out of a genuine belief that collaboration between the races was important. Lacking economic clout, the TACWC enlisted the financial aid of white philanthropists in building a state tuberculosis hospital for blacks in 1934. Barring sufficient political influence, black clubwomen solicited and accepted the assistance of Jessie Daniel Ames, a white activist, in the campaign against lynching.[32]

These clubwomen succeeded in spite of the racism and sexism that shaped their life experiences. Through education and organization they achieved impressive results with meager resources. During the period under study, the focus of their clubs was that of service rather than cultural enrichment. Even the few cultural clubs that developed eventually added social service work to their mission. As a result, they opened kindergartens, day nurseries, homes for the elderly, recreation and juvenile homes for youths, and medical facilities for the infirmed. Although these black women did not have much power, they were not inarticulate. Always concerned with education, race advancement, and community uplift, black clubwomen became a center of information for social change.

Politics and Reform

Black women have historically been considered outsiders in Texas politics, barred from voting until near mid-twentieth century. Yet, as outsiders they often became involved in politics to gain access to the economic, political, and local institutions of the state. In their struggle to become first-class citizens, most of the traditional avenues for attaining equality—the vote, a quality education, and economic opportunity—were closed to them by legally prescribed and fiercely enforced segregation rules. In seeking emancipation from the bondage of white supremacy, black females as well as black males challenged the political system for admission, even as they hoped to transform it by their participation.

Although black female politicians did not emerge until the late twentieth century, a long political tradition of advocacy and activism predates their entrance into formal electoral politics. In 1917, prior to the ratification of the Nineteenth Amendment, Texas became the first southern state to allow women the right to vote. Black women not only supported this cause but also made a concerted effort to gain access to the ballot. Some women organized voter leagues in Galveston and Austin, while others were turned away from the polls in Orange, Austin, and Fort Worth. As soon as they arrived at the voting precincts in Orange in 1918 and were denied a ballot, they took their case to court, but the judge promptly dismissed it. A similar scenario took place in Fort Worth, when six well-dressed women were not allowed to register because they were told that the law only provided for white women.[33]

Black women along with black men worked untiringly to alter this situation by staging a twenty-two-year battle to retrieve the ballot. The first major assault to the black franchise began thirteen years prior to 1918 when the state legislature in 1905 enacted the Terrell Election Law, which regulated electoral primaries and restricted blacks' access to the ballot. It was not until 1921 that the state adopted a white Democratic primary statute that said that only whites could vote in the said primary. The full impact of that statute cannot be grasped unless it is understood that Texas, like the entire South, was a one-party state and winning in the Democratic primary was tantamount to winning in the general election. To be excluded from the Democratic primary was, in effect, to be disenfranchised. According to Darlene C. Hine, "The white primary was like an iron curtain, for even if blacks became literate, acquired property and paid poll taxes, they could not conceal or change the color of their skin." Thus, as long as the white primary existed, blacks could not become active participants in Texas' electoral process. The white primary, then, symbolized blacks' powerlessness, their second-class citizenship, and their castelike position in society.[34]

In 1921, black Texans began an all-out attack on the white Democratic primary statue. In a series of cases, which included but were not limited to *Love v. Griffin, Nixon v. Herndon, Grovey v. Townsend,* and *Smith v. Allwright,* they challenged the constitutionality of such a law. This assault on the ballot not only resulted in the mobilization of blacks, but it also fueled the modern civil rights movement in Texas, of which black women played an integral role. They were actively involved as leaders, organizers, and activists. As such, they served as presidents of organizations, plaintiffs in lawsuits, and organizers in helping to mobilize the black community to fight for the elimination of the white primary. They also fought to integrate libraries, schools, universities, and other public facilities. Most gave moral and/or financial support to the NAACP, one of the few national organizations that placed women in leadership positions.[35]

Four black women who played outstanding roles in the fight for civil rights were Thelma Paige, Lulu B. White, Christia Adair, and Juanita Craft. Thelma Paige, a black teacher, is noted primarily for her role as a plaintiff in Texas' first equalization of salary case. Throughout the South, the school system for African Americans was never equal to that of whites in terms of salaries, working conditions, and positions accorded women. Female jobs differed from those of males. Women mostly were teachers, while men were both principals and teachers. In all cases, despite the position held, the salaries of whites were higher than those of their black counterparts. This situation began to change in 1937 when the U.S. Supreme Court declared a Maryland law on salary differentials unconstitutional. Motivated to a certain degree by this case, black teachers in Dallas filed an equalization of salary case in 1943, with Thelma Paige as plaintiff. Paige's successful petition was re-enacted by black teachers in several cities throughout the state, and by 1945, equalization of salary for schoolteachers had become a fait accompli.[36]

Probably the most vocal activist female of the period under study was Lulu Belle Madison White. Born in 1900 in Elmo, Texas, to Henry Madison, a farmer, and Easter Madison, a domestic worker, Lulu White received her early education in the public schools of Elmo and Terrell, Texas. Following her high school graduation, she attended Butler College for one year before transferring to Prairie View College where she received a bachelor's degree in English in 1928. After her marriage to Julius White, and after teaching school for nine years, White resigned her post to devote full-time service to the NAACP.

Consequently, in 1937 she became Youth Council director and field-worker, and in 1939, acting president of the Houston branch of the NAACP. In 1943, she was elevated to full-time executive secretary of the Houston branch, making her the first woman of the South to hold such a post. Finally, in 1946 she was named NAACP director of state branches for Texas.[37]

When Lulu White assumed the post of executive secretary of the Houston chapter in 1943, her job description included managing the office, conducting branch activities, helping to organize other branches, and, most especially, directing membership and fund-raising drives. On a salary of $89 per month and gasoline money for her automobile (provided by her husband), White immediately set out to make the Houston branch one of the largest in the nation. Under her guidance, the Houston branch grew from 5,679 members in 1943 to 10,705 in 1944, and to 12,700 in 1945. Elated over Lulu White's performance, NAACP national membership chair, Daisy Lampkin, wrote to her, "Each day I marvel at what you are able to accomplish."[38]

In taking the helm of the Houston chapter of the NAACP in 1943, Lulu White placed herself squarely in the forefront of the movement for political equality, beginning with the elimination of Texas' white Democratic primary. Not only did she mobilize the black community around the issue of the vote and raised funds to defray the legal expenses, but she also mounted a "pay your poll tax" campaign two months prior to a favorable decision by the Supreme Court. When the high court declared the white primary unconstitutional in *Smith v. All-wright* (1944), White hailed the Court's decision as a second emancipation. With so many changes that could radiate from *Smith v. Allwright,* White felt that blacks could not remain passive. In her own words, "We cannot sit idly by and expect things to come to us. We must go out and get them."[39] Probably more than any other black Texan of her time, Lulu White argued that a strong black vote was needed to shape governmental policies at local and state levels in the 1940s and 1950s. To ensure black participation in the movement for social change, she urged blacks to assume greater roles in the political lives of their communities, to learn about political techniques and organizations, and to prepare for future leadership positions. She argued convincingly that those who understood the movement for social and political change must identify with it fully and must interpret it to others. Not only did White urge blacks to vote and to seek office, but also she conducted voter registration seminars, helped to select candidates, aided in drafting platforms, and used black churches to address public issues—all without actually campaigning for specific candidates. Engaging in the politics of reform, everywhere Lulu White went she took the vote with her. Whether she was speaking before Franklin Beauty School graduates, a civic club, or people on the street, her message was the same, "Pay your poll tax and go out to vote."[40]

Just as White viewed the vote as a necessary ingredient to reform and full citizenship, she believed that if blacks were to enter the mainstream of American life it was necessary to expand the general basic concept of equality through equal economic opportunities. Consequently, White pressured white businesses to employ blacks, campaigned for the authorization of a permanent Fair Employment Practice Commission (FEPC), and established a coalition with labor unions to achieve the desired results. White encouraged her allies to seek employment at white establishments, and she supported their efforts personally. She led boycotts and protest demonstrations, and initiated letter-writing campaigns. For example, after trying unsuccessfully to get blacks employed at Southwestern Bell, White challenged the telephone company to honor its advertisement in the newspaper, which read "Wanted: To Train and Hire Operators." The manager's response was that the company did not hire "Negroes," to which White replied, "the advertisement said to train and hire operators, that's what I am interested in." When no positive action was taken, White started a letter-writing campaign against the company. Likewise, in pushing for a permanent Fair Employment Practice Commission, White sent a telegram to the White House asking President Truman "to use [his] influence to see to it that FEPC [is] made part of our own government." When the permanency of the FEPC was not forthcoming, White joined forces with labor unions, encouraging people to join them, supporting their political candidates, and opposing the Taft-Hartley Act in order to gain entry into the economic system.[41]

Lulu White also played an important role in the integration of the University of Texas. At the time that the NAACP decided to tackle the issue of segregation in higher education in 1946, there was only one black state-supported institution in Texas—Prairie View A&M College, and it did not offer any professional degree training. Because of the prevailing Jim Crow laws, it was necessary for African Americans who wanted to attain such a degree to attend a university outside the South. As the NAACP opined, this situation could only be altered by a change in the law. So, Lulu White, now director of state branches for the NAACP, persuaded Heman Marion Sweatt, a black mail carrier in Houston, to act as the plaintiff in the case against the University of Texas. This case, which became *Sweatt v. Painter*, commenced shortly after Heman Sweatt applied for admission to the law school, February 26, 1946. Denied because of race, Sweatt took his case to court. As in previous cases, White coordinated most of the activities among the local, state, and national headquarters of the NAACP, and played a major role in raising funds to defray Sweatt's legal expenses. Moreover, she supported and encouraged Sweatt's rejection of offers made to him by the state in lieu of integration. The offer that was most controversial was the one to establish a black university in Houston with a law school—Texas State University, later named Texas Southern University. Many blacks, including Carter Wesley of the *Houston Informer*, believed that Sweatt should continue to pursue his case to get into the University of Texas, but that blacks still needed a university of their own. Lulu White opposed a separate black university. Arguing that it only perpetuated Jim Crow schools and that she could see no equality in segregation, White griped, "I hope I die just that dumb." Meanwhile, Sweatt pursued his case in the court and was victorious in June 1951, when the Supreme Court ordered the University of Texas to admit him.[42]

The struggle to desegregate the University of Texas led by White and the NAACP not only resulted in a Supreme Court decision requiring admission of blacks to graduate and professional schools in the state but also established a precedent for *Brown v. Board of Education*. In the Sweatt case, the Court implied that the doctrine of "separate but equal" was unconstitutional. In *Brown v. Board of Education*, the doctrine was declared null and void. Striking a major blow at the "separate but equal" doctrine, the Sweatt case had far-ranging implications for Lulu White, the NAACP, and the state of Texas. For the state of Texas, it meant that de jure Jim Crow was on the decline and that segregation not only was costly but also would become increasingly so over the years. The case strengthened the NAACP's efforts to dissolve the color line on all fronts, especially in education. Similarly, *Sweatt v. Painter* affirmed Lulu White's belief of the impossibility of true equality with separation.

By the time the Sweatt case reached the Supreme Court in 1950,

White had tendered her resignation from the Houston chapter of the NAACP, but she remained director of state branches, and formed another women's club, The Chat-An-Hour Coffee Club. While the women of this club were responsible to community, individual, and cultural programs, White's underlying purpose for starting this women's club was to form a Political Action Committee (PAC) to elect more blacks to political office and to decide who was best suited to represent the black community. This club, however, gave White and her members an opportunity to design and implement reform programs within the context of their African American culture and to work toward improving the general standard of living in the ever-broadening communities of which they were a part.[43]

Working with Lulu White in seeking these changes were two other black women, Christia V. Adair and Juanita Craft. Born in Victoria, Texas, in 1897, Christia V. Adair was a graduate of Prairie View College. Her involvement with the NAACP began in 1925, when she became recording secretary of the Houston branch. Adair left the branch in 1939, when an investigation by the national office resulted in charges of financial improprieties. In 1946, Lulu White hired Adair as her administrative assistant. According to oral sources, White started grooming Adair to become her successor, but the two parted company after a few years because of personality conflicts and political and philosophical differences. Adair, a shy, introverted widow, was quite the opposite of the bold, gregarious Lulu White. To many it seemed that Christia Adair lacked the skills and personality needed to lead the Houston chapter in 1949 when Lulu White tendered her resignation. Despite this observation, Adair was elected executive secretary of the Houston chapter of the NAACP and served in that capacity until 1957. In that post, she pushed for the integration of public facilities, which included Houston's city hall cafeteria, airport, and golf courses. For those who doubted her ability to lead the Houston chapter, Adair scored high points with blacks in 1956 and regained some respect from the NAACP's national staff when Texas attorney general, John Ben Shepperd, made a concerted effort to drive the NAACP out of Texas by suing the association, intimidating its leaders, and confiscating its records and membership lists. In the case known as *State of Texas v. NAACP*, Adair was grilled on the witness stand for seventeen days, but still she refused to divulge a single name.[44]

Juanita Craft was one of Lulu White's foot soldiers, and she also was a mentee in building and selling the NAACP and in helping to destroy the apartheid system in Texas. Craft was a graduate of Prairie View with a certificate in dressmaking and millinery. She arrived in Dallas in 1925 after teaching school for one year, and worked at the Adolphus Hotel for ten more. Craft joined the NAACP in 1933 after the Tuberculosis State Hospital refused to admit her terminally ill mother. Almost immediately she became involved in the Dallas chapter's membership drive. After several years of hearing and reading about Lulu White's work with the NAACP, Craft came to Houston to meet and consult with her on how to increase the membership of the Dallas branch. The two quickly became allies and set out on a mission to expand and strengthen the state organization of the NAACP. They often traveled together from town to town in White's car, recruiting new members. Because of the quality of their efforts in 1946, Lulu White was appointed state director of branches and Juanita Craft was named state organizer. In that same year, Craft became the first black female deputized to sell poll taxes.[45]

Black women contributed their blood, sweat, tears, time, and money to the civil rights struggle. There is no question that these women knew how to organize, and they felt a strong kinship with members of the community beyond their immediate families. Through the politics of reform they sought to gain first-class citizenship and to eradicate inequity between the races. As such they participated in boycotts, demonstrations, acts of civil disobedience, and voter registration drives. They also worked with and inspired other women to get involved in politics. For example, Lulu White's last campaign for blacks to run for public office resulted in the November 1957 election of Hattie M. White to the Houston Independent School Board, making her the first black Texan to be elected to public office since Reconstruction. It was upon Lulu White's and Hattie White's shoulders that Barbara Jordan stood when she became the first black female elected to the Texas Legislature in 1966, and the first black female from the South to be elected to the U.S. Congress in 1972. Black women's entrance into politics simultaneously boosted both gender and racial consciousness, heightened awareness, and sensitized communities to race and gender issues, permanently changing the political landscape of Texas.

Notes

1. U.S. Bureau of the Census, *14th Census of the U.S., Population 1920*, vol. 3 (Washington, D.C., Government Printing Office, 1921); Lois Rita Helem-

bold, "The Depression," in *Black Women in America: An Historical Encyclo-pedia*, ed. Darlene Clark Hine, Elsa Barkley Brown, and Rosalyn Terborg-Penn (Bloomington: Indiana University Press, 1994), 323; Studs Terkel, *Hard Times: An Oral History of the Great Depression* (New York: Pantheon Books, 1986), 261–62, cited in Darlene Clark Hine and Kathleen Thompson, *A Shin-ing Thread of Hope: A History of Black Women in America* (New York: Broadway Books, 1998), 243. See also Rebecca Sharpless, *Fertile Ground, Narrow Choices: Women in Texas Cotton Farms, 1900–1940* (Chapel Hill: University of North Carolina Press, 1999); Donald W. Whisenhunt, ed., "Black Texans and the New Deal," in *The Depression in the Southwest* (Port Washington, N.Y.: Ken-nikat Press, 1980).

2. Neil Gary Sapper, "Survey of the History of Black People in Texas, 1930–1954" (Ph.D. diss., Texas Tech University, 1972), 232; see also William Brophy, "The Black Texan, 1900–1950: A Quantitative History" (Ph.D. diss., Vanderbilt University, 1974), 107.

3. U.S. Bureau of the Census, *14th Census of the U.S., Population 1920*, vol. 3 (Washington, D.C.: Government Printing Office, 1921); See also Judith W. Lanseley, "Main House, Carriage House: African American Domestic Em-ployees at Faddis House, Beaumont, Texas, 1900–1950," *Southwestern Histori-cal Quarterly* 102 (July 1999): 17–51; David Katzman, *Seven Days a Week: Women and Domestic Service in Industrializing America* (New York: Oxford University Press, 1975).

4. Sapper, "Survey of the History of Black People of Texas," 215–19.

5. Ibid.

6. Records of the Work Projects Administration, Record Group 69, Texas File 690, cited in Julia Kirk Blackwelder, *Women of the Depression, Class, Caste, and Culture in San Antonio, 1929–1939* (College Station: Texas A&M University Press, 1984), 68–69; see also Lucia Knott Rhone to District Direc-tor January 4, 1937, Rhone Family Box 36–171, Folder 2, Center for Ameri-can History, University of Texas at Austin; S. E. Boone and M. Howard to Eleanor Roosevelt, 69, State Series, Texas 693.0 National Archives; Ruthe Winegarten, *Black Texas Women: 150 Years of Trial and Triumph* (Austin: Uni-versity of Texas Press, 1995).

7. *Dallas Express,* October 27, 1934; "Prairie View Training for Domestic Service," Prairie View 1938, 9–11, passim, mimeographed. See also unidenti-fied newspaper clipping, January 1938, in Negro History Scrapbook, Hous-ton Metropolitan Resource Center; Lois Reynolds, "Sustenance Position of Texas Negro Domestic Servants in the Economy" (Master's thesis, Prairie View College, 1942), 51.

8. Administrative Report, "Texas, July–December 1935," National Ar-chives of the United States, Records of the National Youth Administra-tion, Record Group 119; Memorandum from Lyndon B. Johnson to Richard Browne, March 5, 1936, in Lyndon B. Johnson Library and Museum, Aus-tin, Texas; Mary E. Branch to Lyndon B. Johnson, March 11, 1936, clipping from *Dallas Gazette,* March 17, 1936; See also Christie L. Bourgeois, "Step-ping Over the Lines: Lyndon B. Johnson, Black Texans, and the National

Youth Administration, 1935–1937," *Southwestern Historical Quarterly* 91 (October 1987): 149–72.

9. *Negro Labor News,* August 14, 1937, 1; Editorial, *Waco Messenger,* September 22, 1933.

10. Winegarten, *Black Texas Women: 150 Years of Trial and Triumph,* 144–46. See also Julia K. Blackwelder, *Now Hiring: The Feminization of Work in the United States, 1900–1995* (College Station: Texas A&M University Press, 2003).

11. Winegarten, *Black Texas Women: 150 Years of Trial and Triumph,* 235. See Carolyn Cott Webber, "Negro in Texas Industrial Market, 1940–1947" (Master's thesis, University of Texas at Austin, 1948), 91; *Houston Informer,* December 26, 1942.

12. *Houston Informer,* December 26, 1942. See also Robert Eli Teel, "Discrimination against Negro Workers in Texas: Extent and Effect" (Master's thesis, University of Texas, 1947), 131.

13. Winegarten, *Black Texas Women: 150 Years of Trial and Triumph,* 235.

14. Merline Pitre, *In Struggle against Jim Crow: Lulu B. White and the NAACP, 1900–1957* (College Station: Texas A&M University Press, 1999), 36. See also NAACP, Houston Branch, Annual Report 1943, in NAACP Files, Manuscript Division, Library of Congress. Unless otherwise indicated, all letters to and from Lulu White come from the NAACP files.

15. Richard M. Dalfiume, "The Forgotten Years of the Negro Revolution," *Journal of American History* 55 (June 1968): 90–106.

16. Winegarten, *Black Texas Women: 150 Years of Trial and Triumph,* 235–40. See also Richard Croxdale and Melinda Heidl, eds., *Women in the Texas Workforce: Yesterday and Today* (Austin: People's History in Texas, 1979), 16–17.

17. Brophy, "The Black Texan, 1900–1950."

18. Winegarten, *Black Texas Women: 150 Years of Trial and Triumph,* 227–28.

19. *Houston Informer,* November 1943; *Brenham Banner Press,* December 30, 1981.

20. *Prairie View College Bulletin* (1937); see also S. J. Kleinberg, *Women in the United States, 1830–1945* (New Brunswick, N.J.: Rutgers University Press, 1999).

21. Michael Heintze, *Private Black Colleges in Texas, 1865–1954* (College Station: Texas A&M University Press, 1985), 73–76.

22. *San Antonio Register,* August 12, 1933.

23. Clarence W. Norris Jr., "St. Philip's College: A Case Study of a Historically Black Two-year College," (Ph.D. diss., University of Southern California, 1975), 68–70, 82, 166, 195, 210.

24. Olive Browne and Michael R. Heintze, "Mary E. Branch: Private College Educator," in Alwyn Barr and Robert Calvert, *Black Leaders: Texans for Their Times* (Austin: Texas State Historical Association, 1981), 114–27; Heintze, *Private Black Colleges in Texas 1865–1954,* 104–107.

25. Stephanie Shaw, "Black Club Women and the Creation of the Na-

tional Association for Colored Women," *Journal of Women's History* 2 (Fall 1991): 10–11.

26. U.S. Bureau of the Census, *14th Census of the U.S., Population 1920*, vol. 3 (Washington, D.C.: Government Printing Office, 1921), 368; ibid., *16th Census of the U.S., Population 1940* (Washington, D.C.: Government Printing Office, 1942–43); ibid., *17th Census of the U.S., Population 1950* (Washington, D.C.: Government Printing Office, 1952–57).

27. Darlene Clark Hine, "Black Migration in the Urban Midwest: The Gender Dimension, 1915–1945," in Joe William Trotter Jr., *The Great Migration in Historical Perspectives: New Dimensions of Race, Class, and Gender* (Bloomington: Indiana University Press, 1991), 132.

28. U.S. Bureau of the Census, *16th Census of the U.S.; 17th Census of the U.S., 1950.*

29. Winegarten, *Black Texas Women: 150 Years of Trial and Triumph*, 190–97; Carrie P. Hine, *The Surmounters* (Amarillo: Shepherd Printing, 1959), 131; Fannie C. Potter, *History of the Texas Federation of Women's Clubs, 1918–1983*, 3 vols. (Austin: Texas Federation of Women's Clubs, 1941).

30. Winegarten, *Black Texas Women: 150 Years of Trial and Triumph*, 200.

31. Yvette Jones "Seeds of Compassion," *Texas Historian* (November 1976): 16–21. See Anna Dupree Collection, in Houston Metropolitan Research Center; Collection of Black Women, History National Council of Negro Women Archives, Washington, D.C.; Houston Chapter of the Link, Inc., 6th Cotillion Souvenir Booklet.

32. "A Brief History of Crockett State School for Girls," undated typescript in George and Jeffie O. A. Conner Papers, Texas Collection, Baylor University, Waco; Andrew Webber Jackson, *A Sure Foundation: A Sketch of Negro Life* (Houston, 1938), 291–99; Jacqueline Dowd Hall, *Revolt against Chivalry: Jessie Daniel Ames and the Women's Campaign against Lynching* (New York: Columbia University Press, 1979), 111.

33. L. F. Beuchenstien to Minnie Fisher Cunningham, July 17–18, 1918, Minnie Fisher Cunningham Papers, Center for American History, University of Texas at Austin; *Dallas Morning News*, July 11, 1918; *Austin American Statesman*, June 29, 1919.

34. Darlene Clark Hine, *Black Victory, The Rise and Fall of the White Primary in Texas* (Millwood, N.Y.: KTO Press, 1979), 37–40.

35. *Love v. Griffin*, 266 U.S. (1924); *Nixon v. Herndon*, 273 U.S. 538, 47 Sup. Ct. 446 (1927); *Grovey v. Townsend*, 295 U.S. 45 (1935); *Smith v. Allwright*, 321 U.S. 657, 64, Sup. Ct. 757 (1944); Pitre, *In Struggle against Jim Crow*, 19–36; August Meier and John Bracey Jr., "The NAACP as a Reform Movement, 1909–1965: To Reach the Conscience of America," *Journal of Southern History* 59 (February 1933): 3–30.

36. W. Martin Dulaney, "Whatever Happened to the Civil Rights Movement in Dallas, Texas," in *Essays on the Civil Rights Movement*, ed. W. Marvin Dulaney and Kathleen Underwood (College Station: Texas A&M University Press, 1997), 26–27.

37. Pitre, *In Struggle against Jim Crow*, 3–53.

38. Daisey Lampkin to Lulu B. White, May 8, 1944. See also NAACP, Houston Branch, Annual Report 1944.

39. *Houston Informer*, January 24, September 14, November 2 and 30, 1946.

40. Ibid.

41. Lulu B. White to A. Maceo Smith, July 22, 1948; *Houston Informer*, January 27, 1946; *Houston Post*, February 25 and 26, 1946; Pitre, *In Struggle against Jim Crow*, 71.

42. Merline Pitre, "Black Houstonians and the Separate but Equal Doctrine: Carter Wesley v. Lulu B. White, *Houston Review* 12 (1990): 23–36; Pitre, *In Struggle against Jim Crow*, 92–104.

43. Minutes of the Chat-An-Hour Coffee Club, March 3 and December 8, 1949, in the Houston Metropolitan Resource Center.

44. Pitre, *In Struggle against Jim Crow*, 118–26. See Dorothy Robinson, "Interview with Christia Adair, April 25, 1977, in Oral History Project (Schlesinger Library at Radcliffe College, Cambridge, Mass.), and K. C. Saur Verlog 1: 62–67, 1: 89, 1: 46. See also Christia V. Adair Collection, Houston Metropolitan Resource Center; *Houston Informer*, February 9, 1946; Winegarten, *Black Texas Women: 150 Years of Trial and Triumph*, 244–45. Adair died in 1992 at the age of ninety-six.

45. Pitre, *In Struggle against Jim Crow*, 107; Juanita Craft, *A Child, the Earth, and a Tree of Many Seasons: The Voice of Juanita Craft* (Dallas: Halifax Publishing, 1982), 66; Juanita Craft Collection, Center of American History, University of Texas at Austin.

STEFANIE DECKER

6. African American Women in the Civil Rights Era, 1954–1974

On August 28, 1963, a crowd of more than 200,000 people of different races, ethnicities, and sexes gathered in front of the Lincoln Memorial in Washington, D.C. In what became a rally, a celebration, the peaceful assembly had gathered to protest the oppression of blacks in the United States. Dr. Martin Luther King Jr. eloquently addressed the crowd. He spoke of his dream for a new America, and many people viewed the moment as the great apex of the struggle for civil rights. While the March on Washington aided in the passage of the Civil Rights Act of 1964, it was the culmination of years of struggle at the state and local levels that had brought the civil rights movement into the national spotlight. As a segregated southern state, Texas experienced its own struggle with civil rights during the decades following the World War II era, and black women played an important part in the process.

Two monumental Supreme Court cases emerged out of the state of Texas in the years before the famous *Brown* decision. In *Smith v. Allwright,* the court ruled the all-white primary unconstitutional in 1944, thus opening the way for increased voting activity among African Americans. Six years later, in *Sweatt v. Painter,* the Supreme Court ordered the desegregation of the University of Texas Law School, offering one of the first challenges to *Plessy v. Ferguson.* Although the National Association for the Advancement of Colored People (NAACP) had been active in Texas since the 1920s, it was the *Brown v. Topeka Board of Education* ruling in 1954 that pushed civil rights activity into a new phase.

While many works have focused on the leadership of African American males in the civil rights battle in Texas, only recently are studies emerging that examine the role of African American women.[1] While Rosa Parks, Fannie Lou Hamer, and Daisy Bates are among those women who gained national recognition for their activism, hundreds of other women devoted themselves to securing rights for African Americans. To include women in the studies of the civil rights movement does more than acknowledge their roles or add their names to the list of heroes. According to sociologist Teresa Nance, it "adds to an understanding of Black women's collective experiences."[2] Thus, scholars of Texas history have turned their attention to the important role of women in the movement; yet, most works remain either a collection of short biographies or case studies.[3] Therefore, it is time that a synthesis of women's activities in the movement be written in order to fully comprehend their contribution to the struggle.

In the decades before the civil rights movement, African American women had been active in both church and civic activities—activities that prepared them for the role they would undertake in the movement. In fact, in the years before 1964, more women were involved in civil rights organizations than men.[4] Yet, rarely did African American women obtain center stage in the movement. According to historians Darlene Clark Hine and Kathleen Thompson, "while black women seldom spoke to the press or got their pictures in the paper, they were expert grassroots organizers."[5] Belinda Robnett identifies them as bridge builders—those activists who tied the formal leadership of the movement to the community.[6] Furthermore, Nance claims that African American women served three primary roles in the movement: mama, activist, and friend. Black women worked primarily behind the scenes and often helped organize and nurture the youth who would later serve as civil rights leaders.[7] In Texas, African American women undertook these roles with passion and dedication, helping to gain equality for blacks in the largest of the southern states and one of the largest in African American population.

One of the earliest leaders of the civil rights movement in Texas was Lulu B. White; historian Merline Pitre calls her the "Matriarch of the Civil Rights Movement."[8] A native of Houston, White graduated from Prairie View College with a degree in English in 1928. After teaching for almost ten years, White resigned her position as educator and became a more active member of the NAACP. In 1937, White was named the director of the Youth Council and was later appointed as the president of the Houston branch in 1939. Under her direction, membership in the Houston chapter more than doubled.[9] In the early 1950s, White returned to Houston and continued to help her local chapter with membership drives until her death in 1957. As Pitre states, "Lulu was the NAACP and the NAACP was Lulu."[10]

A close friend of Lulu White, Juanita Craft of Dallas also worked her way to a leadership position within the NAACP. In 1946, Juanita Craft assumed the role of state organizer, traveling with White across Texas to enlist members.[11] By 1958 Craft had organized 128 new NAACP chapters in the state and had worked diligently in voter registration drives. Craft was the first black woman to vote in Dallas County, as well as the first black woman deputized to sell poll taxes.[12]

Yet, the most important position Craft held in the NAACP was that of youth advisor beginning in 1947. She hoped to turn the Youth Councils into more than a social forum. She desired to educate the young people about the responsibilities of citizenship, as well as helping them organize their own civil rights struggle. In 1955, a year after the *Brown* decision, Craft and the Dallas Youth Council organized a protest of Negro Achievement Day at the Texas State Fair, a day traditionally set aside for blacks to attend the fair apart from whites. Although African Americans could attend the fair on any given day, a number of rides and eating establishments remained segregated. Thus, that year the Youth Council, under the direction of Craft, picketed the State Fair, drawing attention to its discriminatory practices. Although adults took over the picketing in subsequent years, leading to the desegregation of the fair by 1963, Juanita Craft and her Youth Council had initiated the first direct action protest in Dallas.[13]

Like many other black women in Texas, Craft continued her activism throughout the 1950s and 1960s. She was involved in the desegregation of both the University of Texas and North Texas State University. She also organized the Youth Council sit-in demonstrations at lunch counters and freedom walks at local theaters, as well as taking the Youth Council on cross-country trips. Encouraging hope, education, and peaceful demonstrations, Craft was one of the many African American leaders who helped keep Dallas peaceful during the turmoil that enveloped the civil rights movement during the late 1960s.[14]

The many awards that Craft received include the Linz Award, Dallas's oldest civic honor, the NAACP Golden Heritage Life Award, the

Eleanor Roosevelt Humanitarian Award, and four White House invitations (two from Kennedy, one from Johnson, and one from Nixon). In 1975, Craft made a successful bid for the Dallas City Council, becoming one of four African Americans, at the time, to ever sit on the council. After three more successful elections, Craft retired in 1980. When she died in 1985, at the age of eighty-three, Dallas mourned the loss of a great lady and civil rights leader.[15]

Another important figure in the NAACP was Christia Adair. After taking a group of black Sunday-school children to meet President Warren G. Harding, who ignored them because of their color, Adair was convinced to join the struggle for equality.[16] Adair's involvement with the organization began in 1925, working as the recording secretary for the Houston branch.[17] After World War II, Adair was hired as Lulu White's assistant, becoming executive director of the Houston branch of the NAACP by 1956. Adair and the NAACP successfully won the battle to end segregation in the Houston airports, as well as the public libraries.[18] Like White, Adair faced harassment by the House Committee on Un-American Activities and, in 1956, was subjected to seventeen days on the stand while Texas attorney general John Ben Shepperd attempted to force Adair to turn over her membership lists. Adair refused, and the NAACP won the case, reopening the Houston office that the state had earlier closed.[19]

The efforts of White, Craft, Adair, and other African American women, such as Dorothy Robinson, who worked for the NAACP and on voter registration drives, came to fruition. By 1964, black voter registration in Texas had increased to 57.7 percent, a big increase from the 18.5 percent of 1940.[20] Between 1955 and 1956, sixty-six school districts, including Austin, San Antonio, Corpus Christi, and El Paso had started "token" integration.[21] Yet, equality was far from obtained. African Americans throughout the state faced harsh resistance, police intimidation, and white backlash from their communities. It would take a number of arrests, violent confrontations, and a March on Austin to convince Texans that civil rights was inevitable. Intended to be a parallel demonstration to the March on Washington in 1963, black Texas leaders planned a March on Austin the same year. In 102-degree weather, nearly 1,000 blacks and fifty whites marched the 2-mile stretch through downtown Austin in the "March for Jobs and Freedom." While black men tended to be the primary leaders for the march, Erma LeRoy was also instrumental in gathering support. The majority of the protestors were high school and college students, many of whom were women.[22]

Although White, Craft, and Adair were pioneers in their leadership roles in the NAACP, many other black Texas women were also civil rights activists. In 1954, Texas had its own Rosa Parks in Ola Mae Lacy, who was arrested for sitting on a Dallas bus beside a white woman. A Dallas judge awarded Lacy $1,500 for the assault.[23] Lenora Rolla of Fort Worth was instrumental in organizing NAACP and Southern Christian Leadership Conference (SCLC) chapters. She later served as an administrative assistant to state senator Don Kennard. Erma LeRoy, who had run for state legislature in 1948, was appointed by President John F. Kennedy to the U.S. Civil Rights Commission.[24] Also, Mrs. Charles E. White (Hattie Mae) became the first African American woman to hold public office in Texas during the twentieth century when she won her bid for the Houston School Board in 1958. Despite white intimidation, such as having her car windshield shot out, she worked hard to speed up school desegregation in the 1960s.[25]

Black women also formed organizations to fight for civil rights. Ada Anderson and Bertha Means of Austin founded the Mother Action Committee (MAC) and fought to integrate a public ice skating rink in 1962. For a year, MAC picketed the Ice Palace, a skating rink opened in the African American community. By the end of the year, the skating rink desegregated. In 1961, Mable Chandler and Florence Phelps of Dallas organized Interested Women, a group of three hundred women who protested the segregation of local department stores. Cutting up their credit cards, closing their accounts, and refusing to buy clothes from segregated stores, Interested Women succeeded in getting department stores to allow African Americans to try on clothes.[26] Another civil rights organization led by black women was the Austin chapter of the National Welfare Rights Organization (NWRO). Led by president Velma Roberts, and supported by the University of Texas School of Social Work, the NWRO actively fought for decent housing, food, clothes, and child care for African Americans, as well as informing families who received federal aid that their children were eligible for free, or reduced-price, lunches.[27]

While women such as Lulu White and Juanita Craft worked within the NAACP, by the mid-1960s competing civil rights organizations attempted to gain support from the African American community. In the late 1960s, the Dallas chapter of the Student Non-Violent Coordinating

Committee (SNCC) was established, and Ernest McMillan, a Dallas native just returned from Morehouse College, became its leader. It was through her son's involvement that Eva "Mama Mac" McMillan became active in the civil rights struggle.[28]

SNCC's more radical rhetoric and grassroots organizing threatened some people in the Dallas community, both black and white, who hoped to keep the civil rights struggle peaceful. As SNCC met resistance from all sides, Eva McMillan decided to devote herself full time as the organization's advisor and community liaison. She saw SNCC through constant harassment by local police who would stake out SNCC meetings with rifles in hand. McMillan worked hard to get community support for SNCC, as well as trying to get the young people to tone down some of their more radical protests and rhetoric. Yet, her dedication was not enough to prevent Matthew Johnson and Eva McMillan's son, Ernest, from serving time for destruction done at the OK Supermarket during a protest. Although the reported damages totaled only $211, a court sentenced Ernie McMillan and Matthew Johnson to ten years for the destruction of private property. The trial proved to be the end of the Dallas chapter of SNCC, as its membership dropped to under thirty.[29]

For Eva McMillan, it was the beginning of a long fight for civil rights. McMillan took another approach by addressing the issue of prison reform, although she had been active in voter registration drives in the 1950s. With backing from Eddie Bernice Johnson, McMillan embarked on a prison reform campaign and became active in the People United for Justice of Prisoners (PUJP) and the Anti-Death Penalty Coalition. Yet, prison reform was only one area in which McMillan dedicated her time. She was active in the Black Women's United Front (BWUF), the Anti-Klan Coalition, the Anti-Apartheid movement, and sat on the board of the Southern Christian Educational Fund (SCEF) in Dallas. While McMillan's activism reached outside of the traditional civil rights organizations like the NAACP, those in her community recognize and are grateful for the work that "Mama Mac" did for African Americans.[30]

Not surprisingly, with the *Brown* decision of 1954, many black Texas women fought for school integration. Thanks to early pioneers, such as Thelma Paige, who won pay equalization for black teachers in *Paige v. Board of Education, City of Dallas* (1943), and Dr. Mary Branch who served as the second African American woman president of a

Texas college, Tillotson College (from 1930 to 1944), black women took advantage of the integration of public education as well as engaging in their own desegregation battles.[31] While Hattie Mae White was fighting for school desegregation in Houston, Yvonne Ewell waged her own battle in Dallas.

By the early 1960s, the desegregation order had made little impact in Dallas. It was not until 1961 that the Dallas Independent School District (DISD) adopted a "stair-step plan" to integrate Dallas schools.[32] Through the process of desegregation, Ewell was at the forefront. In the early 1960s, she became the first black female principal of Lincoln Elementary, later becoming the Elementary Education Consultant for the DISD. Throughout her term, she actively pushed for ethnic studies programs, inclusion, and bilingual education. She implemented and supervised the Affirmative Action Program, which, among other things, attempted to equalize school funding and allot $50 per student. In 1976, Ewell was appointed as assistant superintendent for East Oak Cliff, where she continued her struggle to obtain an equal education for blacks and other minorities, a fight that inspired her to run successfully for the Dallas School Board in 1987.[33]

As a result of the desegregation battles, many African American women took advantage of new opportunities to obtain higher education, many of them breaking new ground. At the University of Texas, Cora Eiland Hicks was hired as the first African American professor in the early 1960s. Hattie Briscoe, who graduated from the law school at St. Mary's University, was the first African American woman to receive a law degree in Texas. For twenty-seven years she was the only black woman attorney in the San Antonio region.[34] In 1966, Vivienne Malone-Mays became the first African American to obtain a doctorate in mathematics from the University of Texas. She later served as the first black professor at Baylor University.[35]

African American women continued to make great progress in professional fields from the 1950s to the 1970s, although it remained a tough climb to the top for many. In Houston, Margie A. Duty was the first African American woman to become a part of the police department in 1953.[36] In 1957, Azie B. Taylor became the first black secretary for the Texas AFL-CIO in Austin. She worked with the organization to test desegregation laws and to advance employment opportunities for African Americans. In 1977, President Jimmy Carter appointed Taylor the first black treasurer of the United States.[37] As the 1964 Civil

Rights Act banned discrimination in the workplace on both the basis of sex and color, black women during this era pioneered many "firsts" in Texas. Furthermore, Dr. Connie Yerwood Conner, who worked for the Texas Department of Health, was appointed the first black director of Maternal and Child Health Services in the 1960s. Finally, Iola Johnson emerged as one of the first female news anchors in Texas, working for WFAA TV in Dallas from 1973 to 1985.[38]

Although many African American women made strides in new professional spheres, the majority remained in the traditional roles of teachers and health care providers. Yet, black women proved their leadership ability in these areas, too. In 1950, Willie Lee Glass served as the first black consultant for home economics with the Texas Education Agency, and Vivian Bowser was elected to the executive committee of the National Education Association in 1967. From 1972 to 1984, Augustine Williams served as the first African American director of examinations for the Texas Cosmetology Commission.[39] Wilhelmina Delco became the first black elected to the board of the Austin Independent School District in 1968, working to speed school desegregation. Delco also helped found Austin Community College in 1973 and served on the board of trustees before beginning a career in politics.[40]

In addition to banning discrimination in the workplace, the Civil Rights Act of 1964 also resulted in increased voter participation by African Americans. Consequently, politics became a new arena in which black women demonstrated their ability and skills. From the 1960s onward, African American women entered politics at an unprecedented scale, and from 1971 to 1973, 50 percent of women in the Texas legislature were African American.[41] Leading the way for black female politicians was Barbara Jordan.

Barbara Jordan has been described as "the best politician of this century," "a hero," and "a cross between Lyndon Johnson and Mahatma Gandhi."[42] Born in the Fifth Ward in Houston in 1936, Jordan grew up the daughter of a minister who taught Jordan to excel at school and to set high goals for herself. Although her father wanted her to be a music teacher, Barbara Jordan graduated magna cum laude from Texas Southern University and attended Boston University Law School.[43] In the late 1950s, she returned to Texas and worked for the Kennedy/Johnson campaign in 1960, where her interest in politics began. Although a member of the NAACP, Jordan did not participate in sit-ins or demonstrations.[44] Instead, she focused her sight on political office.

She unsuccessfully ran for the Texas House of Representatives in 1962 and 1964; however, when the Civil Rights Act of 1964 opened the franchise for more African Americans, Jordan won an election to the state Senate in 1966. Jordan became the first African American to serve in the Texas Senate since Reconstruction. In 1972, her colleagues elected her Senate President Pro Tempore, and later that year she won a seat in the U.S. House of Representatives. Her election made her the first African American from Texas to serve in the U.S. Congress. Jordan continued her political career throughout the 1970s, returning to Texas in 1979 to take a position as a professor at the Lyndon Baines Johnson School of Public Affairs at the University of Texas at Austin. In 1994, Jordan was inducted into the National Women's Hall of Fame, and President Clinton awarded her the Presidential Medal of Freedom for her civil rights work.[45]

Throughout her political career, Jordan attempted to work within the system to secure rights for African Americans. Refusing to be identified either by race or sex, she supported cooperation among all nationalities and between the genders and worked to pass laws that would ensure equal rights for both minorities and women. The Texas legislature passed almost half of the 150 bills that Jordan introduced, most dealing with desegregation, the Equal Rights Amendment, the equalization of public school funding, and worker compensation laws. Although she never considered herself a feminist, she worked for the passage of the Equal Rights Amendment during her term in Congress. In 1978, Jordan claimed, "I am neither a black politician nor a female politician. Just a politician. A Professional politician."[46] For many black female politicians, Jordan paved their way through years of hard work and dedication.[47]

Following in Jordan's path, two other female Texans also began their political careers in the early 1970s. Eddie Bernice Johnson and Senfronia Paige Thompson were both elected to the Texas House of Representatives in 1973. A native of Waco, Johnson moved to Dallas after graduating from the University of Notre Dame. She later earned graduate degrees at Texas Christian University and Southern Methodist University. Although the majority of Johnson's political career took place in later years, her 1973 election marked the beginning of a long, successful career in politics.[48] Entering the Texas House the same year as Johnson, Senfronia Thompson began her political career in 1972 after teaching mathematics, biology, and physiology in the Houston public schools. Thompson's years in the Texas House, which lasted longer than any African American in the state, focused on issues related to women, minorities, children, labor, and the elderly. Because of Thompson's successful and enduring political career, many observers called her the "dean" of the Texas legislature.[49]

Other African American women have been appointed to important state or national positions. President Eisenhower appointed Dr. Zelma Watson George as a delegate to the United Nations. Her work was rewarded in 1961 with the Dag Hammarskjöld Award for Contributions to International Understanding.[50] In 1967, Governor John Connally was the first to appoint black women as heads of state boards and commissions. Connally put Jeffie Conner, a pioneer in health education, in charge of the Governor's Committee on Public School Education and made Ada Anderson head of the Governor's Committee on the Status of Women.[51] In later years, African American women became a permanent political force in the state of Texas, working for the improvement of minorities, women, education, and other challenges that they have encountered in their own struggles.

While a number of African American women vied for election to state offices, others successfully campaigned at the local level, or were appointed to state offices. In 1970, Joan Snell won a seat on the Lubbock City Council, while Lucy Patterson became the first black elected to the Dallas City Council in 1973. In 1974, Alice Bonner of Houston became a municipal court judge, and Kathlyn Gilliam was elected to the Dallas School Board.[52]

While African American women in Texas made strides in education, the professions, and politics during the civil rights era, they also made lasting contributions in the arts and to community organizations. Historically, black women have been active in social and cultural activities, and many organizations for them were founded before World War II. Organizations like the Jack and Jill Club and the National Council of Negro Women became very active in Texas during the civil rights era, working for the welfare of children, women, and the indigent, as well as promoting pride in African American history and culture. Through these organizations, black women found solidarity and sisterhood that enabled them to fight for equality and to find strength from one another.[53]

Black women have also been instrumental members of African American churches. The women have often been referred to as the "mothers of the church," indicating their active participation and their vital contributions to their congregations.[54] Honorific or elderly women are deemed "church mothers" and are often consulted by the pastors before making important decisions. "Church mothers" is a concept unknown to white congregations and is part of the historical tradition of the African American church. Yet, although women were essential to the survival of the institution, the roles of preachers and pastors are generally not open to women.[55]

While the influence of the black church became apparent during the civil rights movement, in the leadership of the SCLC and that of local ministers, women often worked behind the scenes. They organized philanthropic agencies, taught Sunday school, and organized social activities. Furthermore, youth groups also undertook these activities, training young women in leadership and organization. Much of the civil rights protests and activities started in the church, and it was through their congregations that many women first started to become active in the struggle for civil rights. Lulu White found support for the NAACP through the church, for "as an organizational tool in the struggle for civil rights, the church was second to none . . . the church gave blacks a sense of solidarity, self-identity, and self-respect."[56] Many civil rights activists turned to the church and its ministers to bring support to their cause. For women like Lulu White, close connections with local ministers was vital to the cause, as "the ministers were effective organizers because they knew their clients, knew how to motivate them, how to recognize local leadership, and how to put it out front."[57] Through education, women's conventions, and missionary work, many African American activists, such as Adair and Craft, began their activism as a direct result of their leadership positions within the church.[58]

As the civil rights movement gained momentum, African American women began to demand access to the role denied them—that of ministers. By 1948 the African Methodist Episcopal Church (AME) began to ordain women, while the Colored Methodist Episcopal Church (CME) extended the ministry to women in 1954. Black women found the struggle for ordination more difficult in the black Baptist congregations.[59] As a result, women separated from the traditional congregations, such as Baptist, to form Spiritual, Holiness, or Pentecostal churches. Eddie Mae Dupree from Marshall formed four congregations of Mount Zion Spiritual Churches from the 1930s to the 1970s.[60] In the 1950s, membership in traditionally white Protestant denominations like the Methodist churches, the United Church of Christ, and the Disciples of Christ began to increase among the African American community. In the era of both the civil rights struggle and the feminist movement, these denominations also began to ordain women. In 1957, Perry Joy Jackson was ordained as the first black woman itinerant minister in the Texas United Methodist Church.[61] In 1990, though, historians Eric Lincoln and Lawrence Mamiya estimated that African American women constituted less than 5 percent of the clergy in black denominations.[62] Despite the low percentage of female ministers, black women continue to contribute significantly to the vitality of African American churches.

The experiences of black women in the church resulted in a number of famous Texas vocalists. Virgie Carrington DeWitty, known as the "Diva Triumphant," began her singing career in the Ebenezer Baptist Church in Austin. A vocalist and pianist, DeWitty has spent her life singing, composing, and teaching, and she served as the music director of the National Baptist Convention of America for more than twenty years. Another diva, Beulah Agnes Curry Jones, also began her musical career in the Ebenezer church in Austin. Inspired and taught by DeWitty, Jones garnished a number of awards for her vocal talent and became the director of the music department at Huston-Tillotson College.[63]

Other world-renowned musicians and vocalists from Texas include Katie Webster, who toured with Otis Redding and James Brown; Viola Dixon-Cole, the first black musician to join a professional concert orchestra in Texas (the Dallas Symphony Orchestra); and opera diva Barbara Conrad. Conrad, forced to withdraw from the University of Texas opera in the 1950s because she was cast opposite a white male, moved to New York where she became a Metropolitan Opera diva.[64] In 1963, blues guitarist and songwriter Barbara Lynn of Port Arthur had a hit record, "If You Should Lose Me," while she was just a teenager.[65] Black women also made names for themselves in the world of jazz. Jewel Brown, a jazz artist, toured with Louis Armstrong in the 1950s and 1960s, and trumpeter Clora Bryant of Texas appeared on national television in the early 1950s with an African American woman's jazz ensemble.[66]

Black women also had success in literature and the visual arts. They had long been contributors to Texas culture and continued that tradition during the civil rights era. Texas writer Vivian Ayers's book of poetry, titled *Spice of Dawn,* was nominated for a Pulitzer Prize in the 1950s. Mother of actresses Debbie Allen and Phylicia Rashad, Ayers lived in Houston for almost forty years before moving to New York. Ayers also worked as a playwright, and her play *Bow Boly* was performed by an African American Houston theater in the 1950s.[67] Ada DeBlanc Simond of Austin became best known for her series of historical books, *Mae Dee and Her Family.* The books told the story of a black family living in Austin and were intended to inspire awareness and pride in the African American cultural heritage.[68] Writer J. E. Franklin of Houston produced the critically acclaimed play *Black Girl* in 1970. The play contains both autobiographical accounts of her own childhood and insights into African American folk culture, and was later adapted for the screen.[69] The Black Arts Movement of the 1960s revitalized an interest in African American folklore and tradition, a movement that would have an impact on the post–civil rights era artists such as writer Sunny Nash, storyteller Marian E. Barnes, and painter Naomi Howard Polk.[70]

By 1960, African American women faced job discrimination and low wages as well as segregation, violence, and other forms of discrimination. Only 2 percent of black women in Texas worked at professional jobs, while 42 percent were employed as domestics in private households. African American women also comprised 27 percent of female service workers.[71] Due to the limitations black women faced as both women and African Americans, occupational mobility proved limited and wages remained low. The median annual income of black women in 1960 was $750, compared to the median income of white women, $1,170. Not surprisingly, civil rights leaders denounced job discrimination and encouraged African Americans to enter professional careers.

In only a decade, African American women had made substantial gains in the workforce. By 1970, black women comprised 9.6 percent of professional workers. The majority of the professionals were nurses, clericals, and teachers, or employed in other "pink collar" jobs. However, black women's wages remained low. In 1970, the median income of black women was $3,411, more than one thousand dollars below that of white females. Contributing to the difference in pay was the fact that black women continued to dominate the service and domestic sectors (approximately 57 percent of the black female workforce).[72] Although black women were beginning to make their presence felt in the professional and political arena, many continued to face low wages and

limited job opportunities. The civil rights era opened new opportunities for African American women, and began, what Ruthe Winegarten
has termed, the "exodus from the domestic labor ghetto."[73]

African American women gained much support during the struggle for civil rights from their families. Many black women took issue
with the findings in Daniel Patrick Moynihan's report, "The Negro
Family: The Case for National Action." Moynihan's findings, published in 1965, argued that African Americans' problems were not the
cause of discrimination or racism, but were due to the nature of the
black family. Claiming that black women dominated their families and
established themselves as head, black men felt inept and often abandoned their children. Many black women denounced the report, arguing that the idea of the black matriarchal family was a myth. While
the divorce rate among African American women increased during the
1950s and 1960s, so, too, did the rate among white women. By 1970,
the percentage of black women heading households was actually less
than that of white women.[74] Despite Moynihan's findings, in Texas, the
black family remained relatively stable during the era of civil rights.

Regardless of the shortcomings of the civil rights movement, during the era 1954–1974, African American women were vital participants
in the struggle for equality. Not only did they organize and lead, they
also later came to the forefront of society, taking full advantage of the
rights they had worked so hard to acquire. Black Texas women during
this era demonstrated both determination and courage, paving the way
for future black leaders in education, politics, and professional occupations. Although the struggle was not over, African American women
in Texas proved that they could, and did, overcome.

Notes

    1. Some excellent studies of the civil rights movement in Texas include
Martin Herman Kuhlman, "The Civil Rights Movement in Texas: Desegre-
gation of Public Accommodations, 1950–1964" (Ph.D. diss., Texas Tech Uni-
versity, 1994); Robert Calvert, "The Civil Rights Movement in Texas," in *The
Texas Heritage*, ed. Ben Procter and Archie P. McDonald (St. Louis, Mo.:
Forum Press, 1980); Alwyn Barr, *Black Texans: A History of Negroes in Texas,
1528–1971* (Austin: Jenkins Publishing, 1973); Jim Schutze, *The Accommodation:
The Politics of Race in an American City* (Secaucus, N.J.: Citadel Press, 1986).

Absent from most of these studies is any in-depth examination of women in the movement.

2. Teresa A. Nance, "Hearing the Missing Voices," *Journal of Black Studies* 26 (May 1996): 544.

3. Few comprehensive works have been published on the history of African American women in Texas. For one of the best and most complete studies, see Ruthe Winegarten, *Black Texas Women: 150 Years of Trial and Triumph* (Austin: University of Texas Press, 1995). Also consult Ruthe Winegarten, *Black Texas Women: A Sourcebook: Documents, Biographies, Time Line* (Austin: University of Texas Press, 1996); Ruthe Winegarten and Sharon Kahn, *Brave Black Women: From Slavery to the Space Shuttle* (Austin: University of Texas Press, 1996).

4. Darlene Clark Hine and Kathleen Thompson, *A Shining Thread of Hope: The History of Black Women in America* (New York: Broadway Books, 1998), 267.

5. Hine and Thompson, *Shining Thread of Hope*, 268.

6. Belinda Robnett, "African-American Women in the Civil Rights Movement, 1954–1965: Gender, Leadership and Micromobilization," *American Journal of Sociology* 101 (May 1996): 1664.

7. Nance, "Missing Voices," 548.

8. Winegarten, *Black Texas Women: 150 Years of Trial and Triumph*, 242.

9. Merline Pitre, "Building and Selling the NAACP: Lulu B. White as an Organizer and Mobilizer," *East Texas Historical Journal* 39 (2001): 22–23. On White, see also Merline Pitre, *In Struggle against Jim Crow: Lulu B. White and the NAACP, 1900–1957* (College Station: Texas A&M University Press, 1999).

10. Pitre, "Building and Selling," 26–31.

11. Winegarten, *Black Texas Women: 150 Years of Trial and Triumph*, 243.

12. Stefanie Lee Gilliam (Decker), "Mama, Activist, and Friend: African-American Women in the Civil Rights Movement in Dallas, Texas, 1945–1998" (master's thesis, Oklahoma State University, 1998), 25; see also Stefanie (Gilliam) Decker, "Women in the Civil Rights Movement: Juanita Craft versus the Dallas Elite," *East Texas Historical Journal* 39 (2001): 33–42.

13. Gilliam, "Mama, Activist, and Friend," 29; Decker, "Women in the Civil Rights Movement," 33–42.

14. Gilliam, "Mama, Activist, and Friend," 29–33.

15. Decker, "Women in the Civil Rights Movement," 33–35; for more on Juanita Craft, see Rachel Northington Burrow, "Juanita Craft" (Master's thesis, Southern Methodist University, 1994); Juanita Craft, *A Child, the Earth, and a Tree of Many Seasons: The Voice of Juanita Craft* (Dallas: Halifax Publishing, 1982).

16. Johnnie M. Armstead, "Black Women and Texas History," in *Bricks without Straw: A Comprehensive History of African Americans in Texas,* ed. David A. Williams (Austin: Eakin Press, 1997), 120.

17. Ruthe Winegarten and Sharon Kahn, *Brave Black Women: From Slavery to the Space Shuttle* (Austin: University of Texas Press, 1997), 85.

18. Winegarten and Kahn, *Brave Black Women*, 85–86.

19. Winegarten, *Black Texas Women: 150 Years of Trial and Triumph*, 246; see also Alecia Davis, "Christia V. Adair: Servant of Humanity," *Texas Historian* 38 (1977): 1–7.

20. Barr, *Black Texans*, 178, 175.

21. Ibid., 206.

22. Kuhlman, "Civil Rights Movement," 243–54.

23. Ibid., 114–15.

24. Winegarten, *Black Texas Women: 150 Years of Trial and Triumph*, 247.

25. Ibid., 249, 256–58.

26. Winegarten and Kahn, *Brave Black Women*, 93–94.

27. Winegarten, *Black Texas Women: 150 Years of Trial and Triumph*, 259.

28. Gilliam, "Mama, Activist, and Friend," 41–44.

29. Ibid, 48–49.

30. Ibid., 41–56.

31. Winegarten, *Black Texas Women: 150 Years of Trial and Triumph*, 255; Marian E. Barnes, *Black Texans: They Overcame* (Austin: Eakin Press, 1996), 22. The first African American female president of a college was Artemisia Bowden.

32. Gilliam, "Mama, Activist, and Friend," 59; for a comprehensive study on the battle of the desegregation of Dallas schools, see Glenn M. Linden, *Desegregating Schools in Dallas: Four Decades in the Federal Courts* (Dallas: Three Forks Press, 1995).

33. Gilliam, "Mama, Activist, and Friend," 62–67.

34. Winegarten and Kahn, *Brave Black Women*, 90.

35. Winegarten, *Black Texas Women: 150 Years of Trial and Triumph*, 252–53.

36. Ibid., 261.

37. Armstead, "Black Women," 121; Winegarten, *Black Texas Women: 150 Years of Trial and Triumph*, 262.

38. Winegarten, *Black Texas Women: 150 Years of Trial and Triumph*, 261, 158–59, 183.

39. Ibid., 269–70.

40. Nancy Baker Jones and Ruthe Winegarten, "Wilhelmina Ruth Fitzgerald Delco," in *Capitol Women: Texas Female Legislators, 1923–1999* (Austin: University of Texas Press, 2000), 182–83.

41. Winegarten, *Black Texas Women: 150 Years of Trial and Triumph*, 275.

42. William Broyles, "The Making of Barbara Jordan," *Texas Monthly* 4 (1976): 127–28. A number of works have been produced on Barbara Jordan. For example, see Ira B. Bryant Jr., *Barbara Charline Jordan: From the Ghetto to the Capitol* (Houston: D. Armstrong, 1977); Jane P. Gooch, "Barbara C. Jordan: Her First Forty Years; A Rhetorical Analysis" (Master's thesis, Baylor University, 1977); Mary Beth Rogers, *Barbara Jordan: American Hero* (New

York: Bantam Books, 1998). Barbara Jordan coauthored her autobiography with Shelby Hearon, titled *Barbara Jordan: A Self Portrait* (Garden City, N.J.: Doubleday, 1979).

43. Broyles, "Making of Barbara Jordan," 127–29.

44. Ibid., 133.

45. Nancy Baker Jones and Ruthe Winegarten, "Barbara Charline Jordan," in *Capitol Women: Texas Female Legislators, 1923–1999* (Austin: University of Texas Press, 2000), 145–50.

46. Broyles, "Making of Barbara Jordan," 133.

47. Jones and Winegarten, "Barbara Charline Jordan," 146–48.

48. Nancy Baker Jones and Ruthe Winegarten, "Eddie Bernice Johnson," in *Capitol Women: Texas Female Legislators, 1923–1999* (Austin: University of Texas Press, 2000), 169–72.

49. Nancy Baker Jones and Ruthe Winegarten, "Senfronia Paige Thompson," in *Capitol Women: Texas Female Legislators, 1923–1999* (Austin: University of Texas Press, 2000), 176–79.

50. Winegarten and Kahn, *Brave Black Women*, 125–26.

51. Ibid., 279.

52. Winegarten, *Black Texas Women: 150 Years of Trial and Triumph*, 297–98.

53. Ibid., 203–205.

54. C. Eric Lincoln and Lawrence H. Mamiya, *The Black Church in the African American Experience* (Durham, N.C.: Duke University Press, 1990), 275.

55. Ibid.

56. Pitre, "Building and Selling the NAACP," 25.

57. Ibid.

58. Winegarten, *Black Texas Women: 150 Years of Trial and Triumph*, 131.

59. Lincoln and Mamiya, *Black Church*, 285–86.

60. Winegarten, *Black Texas Women: 150 Years of Trial and Triumph*, 132.

61. Ibid., 132–33.

62. Lincoln and Mamiya, *Black Church*, 289.

63. Barnes, *Black Texans*, 44–50.

64. Winegarten and Kahn, *Brave Black Women*, 102.

65. Ibid., 101.

66. Winegarten, *Black Texas Women: 150 Years of Trial and Triumph*, 138–40, 136.

67. Patricia R. Williams, "Literary Traditions in Works by African-American Playwrights," in *Texas Women Writers: A Tradition of Their Own*, ed. Sylvia Ann Grider and Lou Hasell Rodenberger (College Station: Texas A&M University Press, 1997), 253.

68. Barnes, *Black Texans*, 96–102; 7–12.

69. Williams, "Literary Traditions," 255.

70. Winegarten, *Black Texas Women: 150 Years of Trial and Triumph*, 142–48.

71. Bureau of the Census, *Characteristics of the Population, Volume I, Part 45: Texas,* prepared by the Bureau of the Census for the United States Department of Commerce (Washington, D.C., 1963), 341–44.

72. Bureau of the Census, *Characteristics of the Population, Volume I, Part 45: Texas,* prepared by the Bureau of the Census for the United States Department of Commerce (Washington, D.C., 1973), 1631.

73. Winegarten, *Black Texas Women: 150 Years of Trial and Triumph,* 262.

74. Ruth Rosen, *The World Split Open: How the Modern Women's Movement Changed America* (New York: Viking Press, 2000), 279; Bureau of the Census, *Characteristics of the Population, Volume I, Part 45: Texas,* prepared for the Bureau of the Census for the United States Department of Commerce (Washington, D.C., 1963), 72; Bureau of the Census, *Characteristics of the Population, Volume I, Part 45, Section I: Texas,* prepared for the Bureau of the Census for the United States Department of Commerce (Washington, D.C., 1973), 115, 116.

KENNETH W. HOWELL
and JAMES M. SMALLWOOD

7. *Expanded Opportunities*

BLACK WOMEN IN THE
MODERN ERA, 1974–2000

In 1974, the people of the United States experienced a great watershed in American history. Brought before the House of Representatives Judiciary Committee, President Richard Nixon stood accused of illegal activities connected to the Republican political cover-up of the 1972 Watergate break-in wherein Republican party operatives slipped into the Democratic national headquarters to photocopy important campaign documents and to tap the phone lines in the complex of offices. The judiciary committee included a Texan from Houston, Barbara Jordan, who became the first black Texan to go to Congress in the twentieth century. As the hearings progressed, Jordan became convinced that Nixon was guilty of "high crimes and misdemeanors" that undermined the authority of the U.S. Constitution. As a committee member she spoke eloquently to the nation, saying in part that her "faith in the Constitution is whole, it is complete, it is total. I am not going to sit here and be an idle spectator to the diminution, the subversion, the destruction of the Constitution."[1] The speech made her nationally famous and brought pride to the country's black community. Jordan's role in the impeachment hearings was concrete, but it was also symbolic.

African American women in Texas made significant contributions to the advancement of their race and gender during the 1960s and early 1970s. These women and the generation of reformers following them continued their crusades into the first decade of the twenty-first century. Many of the modern crusaders decided to fight their battles in the political arena, especially considering the monumental success of women such as Barbara Jordan, Zelma Watson George, and Juanita

Craft. Closely following in the footsteps of their political role models, the new generation of black women politicians addressed problems that continued to plague African Americans and women in general. Due to the efforts of these women, black Texans exerted more influence in politics, attended better schools, enjoyed more abundant economic opportunity, and gained greater access to health care facilities.[2]

While these black women achieved individual success in politics and improved their communities in the doing, others excelled in different fields, one being education. Yvonne Ewell, a former educator, in 1976 became the first female to hold the title of associate superintendent within a Texas public school. She served the Dallas Independent School District. Eleven years later, voters put her on the Dallas School Board; she became the vice president of that body. Throughout the 1990s, Ewell struggled to make sure that African American parents maintained an influential voice in educational decisions that affected their children, a crusade that has become complicated by the demographic changes taking place in the Dallas school district. As the Hispanic population in the city increased during the last decade of the twentieth century, white educational leaders aligned themselves with their Hispanic counterparts in an effort to seemingly erode the influence of the black community within the school system. Undoubtedly, this is an issue that will continue to plague the black community in the early decades of the twenty-first century.[3]

Black women in Texas also made their presence known in higher education. In 1994, Carol Surles became the first black president of Texas Woman's University (TWU), one of the nation's largest schools primarily for women. Before arriving at TWU, Surles had already achieved great heights. She earned her bachelor's degree in psychology from Fisk University in Nashville, Tennessee, a master's degree in counseling from Chapman College in Orange, California, and a doctorate in education from the University of Michigan in Ann Arbor. In addition, Surles held posts at universities in Florida, Mississippi, and in California. At the time of her appointment to TWU, she was serving as the vice president for administration and business affairs at California State University, Hayward, where she was a colleague of the coeditor of this volume, Bruce Glasrud. Surles's appointment at TWU clearly illustrated the changing nature of higher education in the southern states, marking the beginning of a new process of more cross-racial appointments to colleges and universities in the South. Her accomplishments will no doubt serve as an inspiration to other African American women interested in obtaining top administrative positions in southern colleges and universities. Franklyn Jenifer, president of the University of Texas–Dallas (1994–2003), summed it up best when he stated that "Surles and myself are just part of the first wave. There are others. Those of us who are doing exceptional jobs in the South have opened doors." Surles resigned from TWU in 1998 to become president of Eastern Illinois University.[4]

Earlier, in 1990, Marguerite R. Barnett became the first black president of the University of Houston, but her tenure was cut short by her unexpected death in 1992. Before arriving in Texas, Barnett achieved national acclaim as a successful educator. She earned her bachelor's degree from Antioch College and her master's and Ph.D. degrees from the University of Chicago. She taught political science at several prestigious universities, including the University of Chicago, Princeton, Howard, and Columbia, before becoming an administrator. Barnett served as a vice-chancellor for academic affairs at the City University of New York and chancellor for academic affairs at the University of Missouri–St. Louis before accepting the position in Houston. At the University of Houston, Barnett proved to be a real force for change; as well, she raised $150 million for her institution before her untimely death.[5]

Another prominent black educator is Merline Pitre, coeditor of this volume. Armed with a Ph.D. in history from Temple University, Pitre became a noted scholar and educator at Texas Southern University in Houston. As a specialist in African American history, she has published a number of articles in professional journals as well as influential books on black political leaders in the late nineteenth and early twentieth centuries. Her most significant books are *Through Many Dangers, Toils and Snares: The Black Leadership of Texas, 1868 to 1898* (Eakin Press, 1985) and *In Struggle against Jim Crow: Lulu B. White and the NAACP, 1900 to 1957* (Texas A&M University Press, 1999). Pitre's commitment to academic excellence not only earned her the rank of full professor but also led to her appointment as dean of the College of Liberal Arts and Behavioral Sciences at Texas Southern.

As well as in education, a number of black women in Texas have achieved distinction in the sciences. Judith Craven and Mae Jemison are two representatives of this group. In 1974, Judith Craven graduated from the Baylor University College of Medicine, after which she launched a successful career in the medical field, holding posts such as the chief of anesthesiology for Houston's Riverside General Hospital and the director of the Houston City Health Department. She achieved another personal milestone in 1992 when she became dean of the School of Allied Health Services in the University of Texas Health Science Center in Houston; she also served as vice president for multi-cultural affairs for the center. In 2001, Governor Rick Perry appointed Craven to the board of regents of the University of Texas at Dallas.[6]

Mae C. Jemison broke the color line in 1987 when she became the first black female astronaut. A science specialist, she participated in an eight-day space mission in 1992. A joint effort with Japan, the mission included allowing the first Japanese astronaut to float through space. Although she was not a native of the Lone Star State, after she joined Houston's NASA, Texans claimed her as one of their own.[7]

In the modern era, several black women from Texas became noted for their contributions to the arts and letters. Hermine Pinson's career illustrates the trend. After securing her academic degrees at Fisk University (B.A., 1975), Southern Methodist University (M.A., 1979), and Rice University (M.A. and Ph.D., 1991), the Beaumont native became a university professor at William and Mary College. In addition to teaching, she developed a career in letters, writing both short stories and poetry. Her work has appeared in such publications as *African American Review, Common Bonds, Mississippi Quarterly,* and *Sage.* Among her short fiction is "Kris/Crack/Kyle," a 1990s piece about a family of four's struggle with hard drugs. A male child named Kyle became addicted to crack and destroyed his life. Then he tried to use his family to feed his habit after his parents and his sister tried to help him by finding him and bringing him home. But the sister saw Kris (Kyle's real name) stealing what little jewelry his mother had. Kris's sister ran to a closet, grabbed the family's rifle, cocked it, and pointed it at Kris/Kyle. As his sister prepared to shoot him, Kris dropped the jewelry and left the room. In the coming days and months, the sister sometimes saw Kyle on the street begging for money to feed his continuing habit, but she refused to believe that he was Kris, for that was her brother's name before he began his downhill slide. Rather, she remembered her sweet brother Kris before he destroyed his life. Kyle was not known to her.

Talibah F. Modupe of the Dallas vicinity attended that area's community colleges before transferring to the University of North Texas, where she majored in political science. Yet her first love was writing about the black community, and she portrayed it with several short story collections, including *Talibah, Can We Talk?; Let's Be Frank, Okay!;* and *Transformed.* Her stories usually related to the workaday world and the experiences of other African Americans.

Like Pinson and Modupe, Sunny Nash—a Texas A&M University graduate and a Bryan native—has become a premier Texas writer. She became a journalist by trade, and, in addition to other assignments, wrote a syndicated column about Candy Hill, a black enclave in Bryan. She also devoted time to her short stories, many of which reflected her own experiences; others are pure fiction. She contributed stories to *Common Bonds,* an anthology; to the *Houston Post,* wherein one of her stories, "Sanko's World," won a literary prize given by the Houston Public Library. Her "Amen" appeared in *Southwestern American Literature*'s spring 1995 issue. The story featured a fake faith healer and a child's keen disappointment upon realizing the sham. Nash's first book came in 1996 when Texas A&M University Press published her *Bigmama Didn't Shop at Woolworth's,* a look at the dual societies created by segregation. Also a classy photographer, she arranged an exhibition titled "Shopping for Hope: A Photographic Study of Back Street Churches in America." The exhibition toured the United States in 1992.

J. California Cooper of East Texas won a national reputation with her short stories, novels, and plays. For her play *Strangers,* she won the 1978 competition for Best Black Playwright. Her 1991 novel *Family* also won national recognition. The epic chronicled the lives of a slave woman's descendants, which, after a fashion, followed Alex Haley's renowned *Roots.* Collections of her short stories include *A Piece of Mine* (1984) and *Homemade Love* (1987). The latter won the American Book Award in 1989. Many of Cooper's story plots include strong black women who struggle in life but who survive and find life worth living. In addition to other honors, Cooper has received the University of Massachusetts Woman of the Year Award (1990), the James Baldwin Award, and the American Library Association's Literary Lion Award.

Fort Worth's Rosalyn M. Story has multiple talents. She performed as a violinist for the Fort Worth Symphony Orchestra and in 1990 published *And So I Sing: African-American Divas of Opera and Concert,* a history of black opera singers. Then, she ventured into fiction. One of her stories, "Quiet As It's Kept" dealt with the shock that an African American career woman felt when she visited home after many years only to learn the secrets of her past. She finally realized that those secrets had made her the woman that she had become. The tale won the 1994 Betty Green Fiction Award for the best story to appear in *New Texas 94.*

Houston's Anita R. Buckley won acclaim with the historical novel *Emily: the Yellow Rose* (1989). Buckley tells the saga of Emily West, the mulatto who—according to Texan lore—kept Santa Anna occupied just before and during the opening phase of the Battle of San Jacinto, thereby guaranteeing that the Sam Houston–led revolutionary army would carry the day and win the independence of Texas. Buckley's 1994 novel, *Black Gold,* also won followers. It examines the lives of two African American families who discovered oil in Mexia and how their lives changed as a result.[8] Female playwrights, novelists, poets, short story writers—Texas' black community has them all. They are now legion, and they are at full sail.

While there were many "stars" in the Texas black community, the "rank-and-file" also experienced gains over time, especially in the workplace. According to census data, for example, female service workers, including private domestics, comprised 74 percent of the black female work force in 1950; whereas, by 1980 the percent had declined to 35.7 percent, including only 7 percent in private homes. That trend continues today. Conversely, in 1950 only 6 percent were in professional, technical, administrative, sales, and kindred jobs; by 1980 the figure stood at 14.6 percent, a figure more than double. Some of the gains could be explained by the changes in the overall economy of the country and the desire of all workers to improve their living standards, but the differences are more staggering for black women than for white women in part because civil rights laws helped create more equal opportunities. Over the years, more black women also became teachers at all levels, from elementary schools to universities. Given antidiscrimination laws, black women made 95 percent of the median income of white women by 1974.

Despite progress, in the 1970s glaring examples of discrimination still surfaced. One case involved Stephen F. Austin State University in Nacogdoches. As late as 1972, the school systematically discriminated against African Americans, with both women and men hired for menial labor only. Most of the women worked as housekeepers and cooks; the college administrators denied them merit pay raises, promotions, and/or transfers. Disgruntled black workers, using NAACP legal assistance, filed a suit, *Annie Mae Carpenter et al. v. Stephen F. Austin State University.* Upon winning the suit in 1975, area African Americans celebrated their victory, but it proved to be a hollow one. The university did not exhaust its appeals until 1979 and then refused to settle the issue of back pay. In 1983, the NAACP brought pressure by helping unionize the college's black workers. About 80 percent of the food servers (95 percent of them black women) became members of the Communications Workers of America. The university's regents and its administrators retaliated in 1985 by contracting out food services, thereby eliminating all benefits for union members even though the food service department as it had existed had made millions of dollars in profits for the university. The plot thickened when top administrators formed a private corporation and received the contract on food services with university money, even paying for the corporation's stationary.

Many observers saw ominous signs and cried foul as the crisis played itself out. If the university could privatize food services, all state institutions and agencies dealing with labor unions could do likewise, thereby delivering an agonizing blow to union members throughout Texas. Leaders of those institutions and agencies gave Stephen F. Austin University their full support, believing that a deathblow could be delivered to unions contracting with the state, leaving workers helpless before management. In addition, political conservatives beat the drums of privatization because such was part of their ideological agenda. On behalf of the workers, the NAACP filed another suit, but the controlling court refused to override the attempt to privatize; however, the presiding judge ruled that the workers who were willing to accept their new situation should be allowed to keep their jobs. Once in the private sector, those workers who remained with the university appealed to the National Labor Relations Board to recognize their union; whereupon, the university fired more than half of them. In early 1986 the workers began picketing the school and developed a campaign called "jobs for justice."

Three thousand people—including members of fifteen major unions in a four-state region—turned out for a climactic rally in December of 1987. Nacogdoches' finest did not exactly welcome their uninvited guests. They put pressure on the university regents to end the protests that brought so much negative attention to their corner of Texas,

especially after the national media began covering the crisis. The immediate problem was solved when the corporation handling the food
services agreed to a 75-cent-an-hour wage increase for workers and a
few standard benefits that included a sick leave plan. Given some on-
going complaints, the state attorney general, who had acted as the university's attorney, called a hearing less than a year later. At that juncture
the university agreed to provide $800,000 in back pay to the workers,
most of whom were black women. Although their struggle had taken
more than fifteen years, the women finally achieved a partial victory.

The Stephen F. Austin affair was but the tip of the "iceberg" regarding management-employee relations. Increasingly in the modern
era, employers have sought ways to limit benefits to employees, especially those nearest the bottom of the socioeconomic class structure,
beginning with resistance to any suggested rise in the minimum wage.
Other critical problems facing the American laborer included limited
access to affordable health care; employers increasing dependency on
part-time laborers (who received no benefits such as health plans and
pensions); and federal and state government's reduction in government programs designed to provide assistance to the poorest citizens
in American society. Millions of whites, as well as blacks, are trapped
by a "system" of aristocratic plutocracy that ignores their plight. In the
"pecking order" of who gets hurt the most, black women inhabit the
lowest rung. In many ways, the United States had entered a new era
of Social Darwinism. Some people seemed to believe that the strong
survive, obviously because of their inner strength, and the weak perish,
obviously because they are feeble and worthless. The lower economic
class exists only for the benefit of the upper and middle classes. Obviously, this "system" hurts the poor in general, but, by percent, it traps
far more black men and women than whites.

Still, most African Americans work within the unreformed "system"
because they must, and when opportunity exists, they seize their
chance at upward socioeconomic mobility. Increasingly, for example,
black women from Texas have opted for military careers. Equal opportunity policies in the military offered better training and better jobs for them than jobs in the civilian sector. As well, achievers
found themselves eligible for promotions throughout the ranks, although such advancement was not proportional to their number. By
1991, 20.6 percent of all active duty soldiers were African Americans,
and black women accounted for 30.9 percent of all women on active

duty. However, only 13.4 percent were in the officer ranks. But among these individuals there were personal accomplishments. In 1979, Houston's Stella Youngblood became the first black women to enter the U.S. Naval Academy after Congresswoman Jordan lobbied for and helped pass a new law that allowed women to enter all the service academies. In 1990, the Air Force's Marcelite Harris, also from Houston, became the first black woman to win promotion to the rank of brigadier general. In 1995, she was promoted to major general, another first for African American women. During General Harris's distinguished military career, she received the Legion of Merit, the Bronze Star, Meritorious Service Medal, and the Vietnam Service Medal. In addition, she was the first female aircraft maintenance officer, and the first female commander of a maintenance squadron in the Strategic Air Command of the USAF.[9]

Other black women in the modern era made their marks in business working beside men, working with other women, or working alone. For example, Annette and Bill Hamilton of Dallas founded Annette 2 Cosmetiques in 1982. By the early 1990s, they had developed a multi-million-dollar business. They employed three thousand people and grossed approximately $5 million annually.[10] Denise Armstrong and Shirley Bridgewater of Houston founded Amistad Bookplace. Like many black businesswomen, they had problems raising capital, such problems being a throwback to the old days before Congress passed the Equal Credit Opportunity Act of 1974. The Small Business Administration rejected Armstrong and Bridgewater's application for start-up funds. Some private lenders also turned them down because— according to one of the would-be lenders—"everyone" knows that black folks do not read. After all the failures, the two women hit the streets. They contacted their friends asking for a $5 loan from each; when they ran their total to $2,000, they opened their Amistad Bookplace and went on to develop it until they had a great success. Such success in small business came to many blacks. By 1990, only California ranked above Texas as the state having the most firms owned by female African Americans.

Many young black women achieved prominence in athletics, ranging from high school to college and professional sports. These athletes benefited from the Civil Rights Act of 1964 that forbade discrimination not only by race but also by gender. The 1972 Federal Educational Amendment's Title IX pointedly forbade discrimination by any educational facility that received federal funds. Responding to a civil rights suit, the University of Texas at Austin settled a lawsuit in 1993 by agreeing to spend almost 50 percent of its athletic budget on women's sports. Many other colleges took similar action rather than face legal action and/or the loss of federal funds.[11]

Results have been stupendous as women began to excel in basketball, soccer, track and field, softball, and other sports. At the university level, standouts emerged. One was Carol Lewis, a long jumper, who became the Southwest Conference Athlete of the Year for 1983–84. The sprinter Carlette Guidry-White received the same honor in 1990–91. The University of Texas' Clarissa Davis became an All-American in basketball. Several female black collegians won fame in various Olympic games. Benito Fitzgerald-Brown won the gold medal in 1984 in the 100-meter hurdles; in 1992 Sandra Farmer-Patrick won a silver medal; and Davis shared the bronze for the American basketball team. In 1991, gymnast Stephanie Woods won three golds in the Pan American Games in Havana; Woods was still in high school when she took the honors.[12]

The Women's National Basketball Association (WNBA) made its appearance in professional sports in the 1990s. The Houston Comets won the first four titles before giving way to the Los Angeles Sparks, which in turn gave way to other upcoming teams. With foresight, the WNBA executives schedule all WNBA games in the summer rather than in competition with the National Basketball Association (NBA). A number of the WNBA stars were born in the Lone Star State and/or attended colleges in Texas. During the last decade, the most dominant players on the Houston Comets have been Sheryl Swoopes, Tina Thompson, Cynthia Cooper, and Dawn Staley.[13]

Even though black women in Texas enjoyed measured success during the final decades of the twentieth century, leaders of the black feminist movement asserted that African American females remained the victims of gender biases. Such arguments led a number of black Texas women to actively support the feminist movement in the state. Generally, African Americans distanced themselves from the white feminists who were primarily involved in an elite middle-class movement that ignored the African American community. In the black movement, the women believed that they were already equal vis-à-vis black men, and, instead of endlessly debating that issue, African American women focused on issues that directly affected them, ranging from abortion and welfare reform to domestic violence and improving the diets of blacks. Leaders among the movement realized that African American women faced challenges unknown to middle-class white women. The dire problem for blacks was widespread poverty coupled with widespread unemployment. Thus, they could not divorce themselves from the larger problems of the entire African American community.

Between 1975 and 1985, organizations that focused on the needs of black women increased from about three hundred to one thousand nationwide. Most had chapters in the larger metropolitan areas of Texas such as Houston, Dallas, and San Antonio. A limited number of African American women from Texas served in leadership positions of international organizations that viewed the different conditions of black women from a global perspective. Due to the efforts of capable leaders such as Edith B. King, supervisor of employee development for Gulf Oil Corporation, and Judge Gabrielle K. McDonald, U.S. District Court of Southern Texas, the black feminist movement in Texas witnessed a steady increase in its number of supporters over the last three decades.[14] In response to the efforts of black feminists and pioneering women such as those already mentioned, African American women increasingly gained a place within the Texas economy. Their newfound economic status, however, has significantly altered the family life of black women, redefining their role within the black home.

While all classes of African American women are affected by the feminization of the economy, women in blue-collar families generally have found it more difficult to balance work schedules with their domestic duties. Living with husbands who often resisted changes occurring to the traditional family structure of the mid-twentieth century, black women in the workforce often experienced more stress within their marriages. In part, added stress accounts for the increase in divorce rates between 1974 and 1990.[15] Divorce followed by subsequent remarriage has also played a significant role in the lives of many black women. Often second marriages have been accompanied by the birth of more children, a fact that has made the stepfamily commonplace in the modern era. These women tend to have children further apart than do women who are married only once, thereby extending their childrearing years by as much as ten to fifteen years. For many black Texas women, divorce, remarriage, and the extended years of child rearing complicate the already difficult task of balancing their work life against domestic responsibilities.[16]

Unlike their mothers and grandmothers, African American women in the late twentieth century were more likely to head families. Although some scholars contend that numerous factors have combined to encourage matriarchy within black families, most agree that economic conditions shaped the structure of black families more so than cultural influences. Other scholars, such as Jacqueline Jones, resist the concept. As young African American males experienced limited economic opportunity, black women began to shoulder more of the financial burdens of their families. As African Americans increasingly accepted the new role of women in the black family, a changed family structure emerged. In the twenty-first century, the rising number of children born outside of wedlock to fathers who avoid the responsibilities of fatherhood has further entrenched the problems faced by young black women and their families within the black community. Jones, in *Labor of Love, Labor of Sorrow: Black Women, Work, and the Family, from Slavery to the Present*, noticed these forces, and worried about the results. As she argued, "clearly, only a new moral vision of community can guide the unorthodox and far-reaching social changes necessary to the well-being of black women as wives and as wage earners."[17]

As the twenty-first century dawned, African American women experienced new challenges that were unique to their generation. Based on statistics compiled by the Texas Department of State Health Services and the Texas State Data Center and Office of the State Demographer, monumental health problems have continued to threaten the lives of black females. Of these problems, the most serious has been the rise in the number of African American women infected with the HIV/AIDS virus. In 2000, officials at the Texas Department of Health reported 1,259 new cases of HIV among Texas females. African American women represented 60 percent of those infected (754 cases). Unfortunately, the percentage of infected black females remained constant between 1999 and 2003. According to the Texas Department of Health, the primary mode of exposure among all Texas women was through intravenous drug use and heterosexual contact. While government agencies are attempting to solve the problem of HIV/AIDS, it seems evident that the high rate of infection among African American women was closely associated to socioeconomic factors that deny urban blacks access to proper health care, which could potentially help in the early detection of and treatment of the disease in both males and females.[18]

Another major health issue confronting African American women at the turn of the century was an increase in the number of children born with low birth weight (premature births). In Texas, 7.7 percent of all children born in 2002 were low-birth-weight (less than 2,500 grams) infants. Of the children born to African Americans, 12.7 percent were born with low birth weights. In comparison, white and Hispanic infants were below the state average for low birth weight, 7.1 percent and 7.0 respectively. The high percentage of African American infants born with low birth weight seemed closely associated with socioeconomic factors. African American women living in low-income urban areas have limited access to prenatal care. In addition, a significant number of black females gave birth before the age of seventeen years. These young girls often lacked necessary medical insurance and lacked the financial resources to pay the rising cost associated with prenatal care. The lack of medical attention during the first trimester of pregnancy was also directly related to the total number of infant deaths occurring within the first twenty-four hours after birth. On average in 2002, African American neonatal death rates were 8.4 per 1,000 live births, compared to 3.3 deaths per 1,000 for whites and 3.5 per 1,000 for Hispanics.[19]

African American women continued to experience economic hardship in the twenty-first century. According to the Texas State Data Center and Office of the State Demographer, more than 20 percent of African American families lived below the poverty level. Of the 842,713 black families in the state, more than 18 percent earned less than $10,000 annually, a figure that is 10 percent higher than white families in the same income bracket. The hardship of living in low-income families undoubtedly contributed to the psychological and physical burdens that black women experienced in the first years of the new millennium.[20]

Despite the new problems of the twenty-first century, most of the Lone Star's black women have witnessed their circumstances improved as 1974 became 1984, as 1984 became 1994, and as 1994 gave way to a new century.[21]

Beginning with the historic civil rights acts of 1964, 1965, and 1968, African American women saw their opportunities growing in number—in all fields of academic education; in all athletic pursuits; in the field of politics and governance; in the health care field; in the military, even including space flight; in the sciences; and in a host of other fields as well. Black women fought hard for their post–civil rights era freedom and saw improvements come as the years swept by. They have come a long way since the mid-twentieth century, and evidence suggests that they will continue to make substantial, if halting, progress in the future decades.

Notes

1. Barbara Jordan and Shelby Hearon, *Barbara Jordan: A Self-Portrait* (Garden City, N.Y.: Doubleday, 1979), 187; Alwyn Barr, *Black Texans: A History of African Americans in Texas, 1528–1995*, 2nd ed. (Norman: University of Oklahoma Press, 1996), 231. See also Ira B. Bryant Jr., *Barbara Charline Jordan: From the Ghetto to the Capitol* (Houston: D. Armstrong, 1977) and Mary Beth Rogers, *Barbara Jordan: American Hero* (New York: Bantam Books, 1998). For a brief overview of Jordan's accomplishments, see Vista McCroskey, "Barbara Jordan," in *Profiles in Power: Twentieth-Century Texans in Washington,* ed. Kenneth E. Hendrickson Jr. and Michael L. Collins (Arlington Heights, Ill.: Harlan Davidson, 1993), 175–95.

2. The most influential of the modern politicians were Azie Morton, Eddie B. Johnson, Lanell Cofer, Sheila Jackson Lee, Wilhelmina Delco, Lou Nelle Callahan Sutton, Gabrielle McDonald, Senfronia Thompson, Karyne Conley, Yvonne Davis, Terri Hodge, and Ruth Jones McClendon. The role of black women in politics is covered extensively in chapters 6 and 8 of this volume. For more on these female politicians, see Barr, *Black Texans;* Nancy Baker Jones and Ruthe Winegarten, *Capitol Women: Texas Female Legislature, 1923–1999* (Austin: University of Texas Press, 2000); "The Woman Behind the Signature in America's Wallets," *New York Times,* January 3, 1978; "Obituary," *New York Times,* December 14, 2003; "Personalities," *Washington Post,* September 13, 1977; "Former U.S. Treasurer Named to Top Va. Post," *Washington Post,* May 1, 1982; Ann Fears Crawford and Crystal Sasse Ragsdale, *Texas Women: Frontier to Future* (Austin: State House Press, 1998); Texas House of Representative, s.v. "Representative Senfronia Thompson," at http://www. house.state.tx.us/members/dist141/bio/thompson.htm, accessed July 24, 2005 and April 21, 2007; Texas House of Representatives, s.v. "Representative Ruth Jones McClendon," at http://www.house.state.tx.us/memberes/dist120/bio/ mcclendon.htm, accessed August 8, 2005. Information on Yvonne Davis and Terri Hodge can also be found on the Texas House of Representative's Web site. The best single-volume reference book on black women in Texas currently available is Ruthe Winegarten's *Black Texas Women: A Sourcebook: Documents, Biographies, Time Line* (Austin: University of Texas Press, 1996). This study proved an invaluable resource to the authors. The best single-volume topical narrative on black women in Texas is Winegarten's *Black Texas Women: 150 Years of Trial and Triumph* (Austin: University of Texas Press, 1995). See also

Winegarten and Sharon Kahn's *Brave Black Women: From Slavery to the Space Shuttle* (Austin: University of Texas Press, 1997).

3. "Conflicts Growing between Blacks Latinos," *Morning Edition* (Washington, D.C.), June 1, 1992; "Race Issue Boils Over in Dallas," *New York Times,* June 27, 1996; "Blacks on Dallas School Board Boycott Superintendent Vote," *New York Times,* January 19, 1997; "Racial Power Struggle in Dallas School System Takes New Turn," *New York Times,* October 12, 1997; Winegarten, *Black Texas Women: A Sourcebook,* 311, 312, 315.

4. B. Denise Hawkins, "Being Presidential in Dixie: Black Academics Finding Fewer Barriers at Traditionally White Colleges," *Black Issues in Higher Education* 13 (February 8, 1996): 18; "Dr. Carol Surles Named First Black President of Texas Woman's University," 86 *Jet* (June 6, 1994): 24.

5. "Marguerite Ross Barnett, 49, Dies; Was Head of Houston University," *New York Times,* February 27, 1992; Winegarten, *Black Texas Women: A Sourcebook,* 238.

6. "Texas Governor Appoints First African American Woman to UT System Board of Regents," *Black Issues in Higher Education* 18 (May 10, 2001): 17; UTD Perspectives, s.v. "News From the Board of Regents," at http://ospa.utdallas.edu/UTDPerspectives/Fa112001/page9.htm, accessed July 24, 2005 and April 21, 2007.

7. "New Astronaut Candidates Include Program's First Black Woman," *Washington Post,* June 6, 1987; "NASA Names 5 Shuttle Crews," *New York Times,* October 1, 1989; "For a Black Woman, Space Isn't the Final Frontier," *New York Times,* March 3, 1993; "What Was Space Like?" *New York Times,* February 2, 2003; National Women's History Project, s.v. "Mae C. Jemison," at http://www.nwhp.org/tlp/biographies/jemison/jemison-bio.html, accessed July 25, 2005.

8. For more information about Pinson, Modupe, and other black writers, see Sherry McGuire and John R. Posey, eds., *KenteCloth: African American Voices in Texas* (Denton: Center for Texas Studies, University of North Texas, 1995); Silvia Ann Grider and Lou H. Rodenberger, eds., *Texas Women Writers: A Tradition of Their Own* (College Station: Texas A&M University Press, 1997); Jas. Mardis, ed., *KenteCloth: Southwest Voices of the African Diaspora* (Denton: University of North Texas Press, 1997).

9. Winegarten, *Black Texas Women: A Sourcebook,* 312; Mike Vogel, "Trendsetters: Marcelite Harris, Keeping the Shuttle on Track," *Florida Trend* 41 (April 1, 2000): 24; Roosevelt Wright Jr., "A Historical Perspective: Opportunities for African Americans in the Armed Forces," *Black Collegian* 27 (February 1997): 122–28; "Major General Marcelite Harris: A Trailblazer in the U.S. Air Force," *Jet* 91 (November 18, 1996): 16–18; Linda Rochelle Lane, "Marcelite Jordon Harris," in *Black Women in America: An Historical Encyclopedia,* ed. Darlene Clark Hine, 2nd ed. (New York: Oxford University Press, 2005), 27.

10. Roger Witherspoon, "Beauty in the Eye of the Hamiltons," *Black Enterprise* 18 (June 1988): 75.

11. For more on Title IX of the Federal Educational Amendments, see Welch Suggs, *A Place on the Team: The Triumph and Tragedy of Title IX* (Princeton, N.J.: Princeton University Press, 2005).

12. George Vecsey, "Sports of The Times: Carol Lewis, Herself," *New York Times*, February 24, 1984; W. Scott Bailey, "40 under 40: Clarissa Davis-Wrightsil," *San Antonio Business Journal* 15 (November 9, 2001): B11; Paul Harber, "Do You Know Her Name?: Top Women's Basketball Player Basks in Anonymity," *Boston Globe*, April 22, 1989; Karen Rosen, "Farmer-Patrick a Close Second," *Atlanta Constitution*, August 6, 1992; "World-Class Speed, Family Style," *Ebony* 45 (December 1989): 116–20; Merrell Noden, "A Pair of Aces," *Sports Illustrated* 71 (October 16, 1989): 64–68.

13. Melody Gutierrez, "WNBA Hangs 10: League Has Defied the Skeptics in Lasting 10 Seasons," *Knight Ridder Tribune Business News*, May 19, 2006.

14. For a comprehensive examination of African Americans' roles in the feminist movement, see Benita Roth, *Separate Roads to Feminism: Black, Chicana, and White Feminist Movement in America's Second Wave* (New York: Cambridge University Press, 2004); Nadine Brozan, "Coalition of Black Women Goes National," *New York Time*, October 26, 1981.

15. Julia Kirk Blackwelder, *Now Hiring: The Feminization of Work in the United States, 1900–1995* (College Station: Texas A&M University Press, 1997), 213–15.

16. Blackwelder, *Now Hiring*, 213–15.

17. Ibid., 215–17. Jacqueline Jones, *Labor of Love, Labor of Sorrow: Black Women, Work, and the Family, from Slavery to the Present* (New York: Basic Books, 1985), 322–30, quote on 330.

18. Texas Department of Health, *Annual Report 2000: HIV/STD Surveillance Report* (December 31, 2000); Texas Department of Health, *Annual Report 2003: HIV/STD Surveillance Report* (December 31, 2000), Austin, Texas.

19. Texas Department of Health, *Vital Statistics 2002 Annual Report* (April 5, 2005), Austin, Texas.

20. Texas State Data Center and Office of the State Demographer, s.v. "Table 24b: Number and Percentage of Black or African American Alone Households by Income Category for the State of Texas and Metropolitan Statistical Areas in Texas, 1999"; "Table 27b: Number and Percentage of Black or African American Alone Families Below Poverty Level for the State of Texas and Metropolitan Statistical Areas in Texas, 1999"; "Table 27: Number of Families Below Poverty Levels for the State of Texas and Metropolitan Statistical Areas in Texas, 1999"; "Table 52a: Number and Percentage of White Alone Families Below Poverty Levels for the State of Texas and Metropolitan Statistical Areas in Texas, 1999," at http://txsdc.utsa.edu, accessed July 24, 2005 and April 21, 2007. These tables are located under the heading of "subjects A to Z." This Web site is a comprehensive collection of statistical data for Texas. The statistics compiled for this site are based on data from the 2000 U.S. Census.

21. The best published bibliography of the black experience in Texas, one that includes many citations for black women, is Bruce A. Glasrud and Laurie Champion's *Exploring the Afro-Texas Experience: A Bibliography of Secondary Sources about Black Texans* (Alpine, Tex.: Sul Ross State University Center for Big Bend Studies, 2000).

JEWEL L. PRESTAGE
and FRANKLIN D. JONES

8. Contemporary Black Texas Women

POLITICAL AND EDUCATIONAL
LEADERSHIP, 1974–2000

> *A 1972 poll showed that 48 percent of women favored efforts to strengthen or change women's status in society while 36 percent opposed such efforts.... Many black women felt that neither the white women's movement nor the male dominated black movement addressed some of their basic concerns.*
>
> Barbara Deckard, *The Women's Movement*

As the American female population approached the last quarter of the twentieth century, it was for them a time of questioning and equivocation. As the epigraph heading this chapter demonstrates,[1] this was especially the case for African American women in Texas, a state that, in addition to experiencing the changes faced by the nation at large, was facing its own political and cultural metamorphosis.[2] By the year 2000, black Texas women changed traditional perceptions of their roles in society, especially in the realm of leadership, politically and educationally. The dismal statistics that follow explain the impediments that black women faced before emerging as new political leaders and change-agents in education. Confronting the reality of the dual minority status that defined their identity, black women in Texas moved in ways that would change the two arenas that might alter their disadvantaged socioeconomic conditions—politics and education.

In 1977, approximately 9.5 million black women lived and worked in America. Their life expectancy was sixty-nine years compared to seventy-six years for white women. While white women's fertility rate was 1.8, theirs was 2.4. That same year black women experienced a disadvantage in median income compared to the other three race/sex groups. The figures were: white men, $14,055; black men, $10,365; white women, $7,361; and black women, $4,465. Black women were also at the base of the heap in managerial positions, holding only 1.7 percent, just below white women, who held only 4.2 percent. In terms of educational status, statistics show that only 7.6 percent of black women were college graduates in 1974. Disadvantaged as family breadwinners and providers, black women heads of households had a median income of $4,595, while white women in similar status survived on $7,019. An estimated 45 percent of black female-headed households were below the poverty level. To compound this situation 51 percent of black females twenty-five to forty-five years old were without male spouses.[3] When women are viewed as a part of the state's population, there is no major dramatic shift in either relative numbers or characteristics in the period from 1974 to 2000.

The total population of Texas was 11,198,730 in 1970. African Americans numbered 1,399,055, constituting about 12.5 percent of the populace. Females comprised 726,104, or 51.8 percent, of the black population.[4] When the state's population rose to 14,229,190, in 1980, 12 percent, or roughly 1,710,175, were blacks, and women made up approximately 51.8 percent of these African American Texans. A decade later, the black population, 2,021,632, of 1990 was reported to constitute 11.9 percent of the state total of about 16,986,510. Black females numbered some 1,048,847, or 51.8 percent, of blacks in the state. The population of Texas reached 20,851,820 by 2000 and the 2,404,566 African Americans were 11.6 percent of the state's population, thus continuing a declining percentage trend that began at the beginning of the twentieth century. At the same time, the African American share of the national population reached 12.3 percent.[5] The total black female population of Texas in 2000 was 1,160,413. Of these, 875,017 were over the age of eighteen. In 1970, the black female population was 728,593, and those age twenty-one and above numbered 391,619. Overall there was a 41 percent growth in black female population of the state in thirty years.[6]

Population numbers, though obviously important, do not provide the entire picture of African Americans in Texas society in the modern era. Another important indicator is employment status; according to Steve Murdock and colleagues in *The Texas Challenge,* African Americans comprised 10.8 percent of the state labor force in the 1990s, a number near their percent of the total population. With minimal changes, that percent produced a labor force participation rate in 2000 of 62.2 percent for black females and 61.4 percent for black males.[7] During the quarter-century under study both black males and females were underrepresented in what traditionally were called white-collar or higher-paying jobs and were unemployed at disproportionately higher rates.

In the 1970s, black women's unemployment rates were consistently higher than their rate in the total population and the rates in other race/sex groups. As the decade opened, women's unemployment was at 7 percent while black male joblessness hovered around 5 percent.[8] The 1978 figures from the Bureau of Labor Statistics show that black male unemployment was at 8.4 percent, black female was 10.9, the Hispanic male rate was 6.3, Hispanic female 11.1, while the white male level was 3.1 and white women's workless rate was 5.7. Texas' basic pattern was not altered as the population eased toward the 1980s.[9] In 2000, unemployment rates for blacks were males, 6.5 percent and females, 6.3 percent. Alwyn Barr noted that between 1970 and 1995 black unemployment remained at about twice the white level.[10]

Despite the above statistics, "median earnings of black year round, full time workers increase as educational attainment increases," thus educational disadvantage has widespread spin-offs for black women and their families.[11] The table below shows the relative educational attainment status of Texas women by race in 2000 based on information compiled by the National Urban League. For black women, college attendance in Texas was concentrated heavily in the state's Historically Black Institutions, especially the two public universities, Prairie View A&M University and Texas Southern University. Prairie View's student enrollment from 1970 to 2000, as well as that of Texas Southern, revealed a general pattern of about 56 to 58 percent females each fall registration, with male enrollment hovering around the 42 to 44 percent range. Specific levels for Prairie View were fall enrollment female percentages, 1997–2000, 57.8, 58.3, 58.3, 58.7, and at Texas Southern the fall 2000 figure was 56 percent.[12] Overall college enrollment in Texas grew from 350,668 in 1970 to 1,999,047 in 1990.[13] In 2000, black collegiate enrollees numbered 97,671. An estimated 56 percent were females. Fall 2000 enrollment at the two Historically Black Colleges and Universities (HBCU) in Texas was 12,316 with Prairie View enrolling 5,893 and Texas Southern 6,423.

Black Texans' contributions and involvement during the contem-

EDUCATIONAL ATTAINMENT

	Total Female Population (%)	Black Female (%)	Hispanic Female (%)	White Female (%)
Less than High School	24.2	23.7	49.8	13.2
High School Graduate	26.0	28.5	22.4	27.6
Some College	23.0	25.7	15.3	26.2
Associate Degree	5.3	5.8	3.4	6.0
Bachelor's Degree	15.0	11.3	6.4	18.9
Master's Degree	4.9	—	—	—
Professional Degree	1.1	—	—	—
Doctorate	0.5	—	—	—
Graduate/ Professional	—	4.9	2.8	8.0

porary era can only be understood along with the other major population group in the state, Mexican Americans. In assessing the relative state of African American and Hispanic life in Texas in the 1990s, Dhananjaya Arekere and Mitchell Rice of the Race and Ethnic Studies Institute at Texas A&M University asserted that

> the status of African American Socio-Economic conditions also improved for the most part, but is not as widespread as that experienced by Hispanics. While improvements were seen in a majority of the counties and the major metropolitan regions, the well beings as measured by education attainment, income and poverty incidence worsened for a considerable portion of the African American population.[14]

The national political scene for the years under review presented an understandable backdrop for the conflicted nature of women's attitudes regarding their status in American society, as well as the overall political posture of African Americans, consequently of African American women.

With an eye on the executive, in 1976 former Georgia governor Jimmy Carter assembled a coalition that transcended race, gender, class, geography, and age. In this mix, probably "the newest players were black women" as a specific category. If there is any area that was new and different for black women in this period, it is the political arena. In no period in the history of this nation or state had black women been so actively involved in electoral politics as in 1976–2000. As a result, black women served as delegates to the 1976 Democratic National Convention, including from Texas Mrs. Robert Barbour, Juanita Craft, Myrtis Evans, Eddie Bernice Johnson, Harriett Murphy, and Dorothy Starling.[15] Harriet Murphy later served as a presidential elector in 1976, another first for Texas African American women. Despite a setback in the period of Republican control of the Oval Office by what Richard Scammon and Ben Wattenberg have labeled, "the unyoung, the unpoor, and the unblack," black women continued to pursue the political process.[16] In 1992 and 1996, Democrats, with Arkansas governor William Clinton as standard-bearer, won the presidency with support of young people, moderates, southerners, African Americans, and women. African American women of Texas were very active supporters.

Three national events with special significance for African American women, as women, in the 1970s and 80s included the 1977 National Conference in Observance of the International Women's Year held in Houston, Texas, with Texan Gloria Randle Scott as chair; a U.S. Department of Education national conference on women's equity issues at Texas Southern University, chaired by Hortense Dixon; and the 1985 meeting of the National Political Congress of Black Women in Atlanta, Georgia, with congresswoman Shirley Chisholm and Pennsylvania secretary of state C. Dolores Tucker as moving forces. Winsome Jean and Hazel Obey of Austin played key roles in state-level work for the latter in key cities in Texas.[17]

Political scientist Harold Lasswell wrote that politics is "who gets what, when and how." Passage of the 1965 Voting Rights Act and its implementation rendered the last quarter of the twentieth century the first period in which African American women would have the potential to experience the fullness of the American political experience as it had been enjoyed by the other race/sex groups for "at least some period" in the history of the Republic. In 1964, black voter registration in Texas was 375,000, or 57 percent of the black voting age population. In 1975, a decade after passage of the 1965 Voting Rights Act, it was 83 percent. There were twenty-nine black elected officials in Texas in 1970, four women; 158 officials in 1977, with "nineteen women"; and 260 officials with nineteen of them women by 1980. By 2000 some 471 officials were in office; 147 were women.[18]

Three black women have represented Texas in Congress since 1974, all in the House of Representatives: Barbara Charline Jordan, 1973–79; Eddie Bernice Johnson, 1992; and Shelia Jackson-Lee, 1994.

Jordan was born February 21, 1936, in Houston, Texas, and became an outstanding student at Phillis Wheatley High School in Houston as a star debater and member of the upper 5 percent of the 1952 graduating class. At Texas Southern University she majored in political science, joined the internationally prominent debate squad, graduated magna cum laude, and was admitted to Boston University Law School in the entering class of 1956. Upon graduation she accepted her first professional position as a political science teacher at Tuskegee Institute in Alabama for one academic year but returned to Houston to pursue a career in law that soon expanded into politics.

After federally mandated redistricting created a new state senate seat, Jordan was able to win the primary by 60 percent and the general election unopposed, to become the first African American woman in the Texas Legislature in 1966. She served until 1973. Free legal aid for the poor, increasing the minimum wage, and the benefits received by the sick and elderly were Jordan's legislative priorities. She was cast into the national spotlight when she called for the impeachment of President Richard M. Nixon during the Watergate hearings. A special mentor relationship with former President Lyndon B. Johnson enhanced her political career. At the 1976 Democratic National Convention, Jordan achieved another "first in history" as an African American woman keynote speaker. Because of a crippling medical disorder, in 1978 she declined to seek reelection and joined the faculty of the Lyndon B. Johnson School of Public Affairs at the University of Texas at Austin, where she remained until death, at age fifty-nine, on January 17, 1996, in Austin.[19]

Eddie Bernice Johnson, a Democrat from Dallas, was the first woman to represent Dallas in both the Texas House, in 1972–76, and in the Texas Senate, in 1986–92. In the Texas House she chaired the Labor Committee; she was the first black female chair of a major committee. Between 1976 and 1986, she served some time in the Carter administration as regional director in the Department of Health, Education, and Welfare. A nurse, Johnson holds a bachelor's degree from Texas Christian University, a master's degree in public administration from Southern Methodist University, and was once chief psychiatric nurse at a Veteran's Administration Hospital. With a keen interest in science and technology issues as they affect African Americans, she sponsored legislation to "bridge the digital divide" to improve math and science preparation for African American youth and expand access to health care facilities and resources. In the 108th Congress she was chair of the Congressional Black Caucus and served as deputy Democratic Whip in the previous Congress.[20]

Shelia Jackson-Lee, elected from the Houston area, is a Yale University political science graduate, holds a University of Virginia law degree, served on the Houston City Council as associate Municipal Court judge, and practiced corporate and private law in the state. Her committee service has been on the House Judiciary Committee, including the Subcommittee on Crime and Investigation, and the Committee on Science with its Subcommittee on Space and Aeronautics. Founder of the Congressional Children's Caucus, she worked successfully to establish an Office of Special Population to gather statistics needed to demonstrate health needs of women, minorities, the elderly, and children. Also the ranking Democrat on the Subcommittee on Immigration and Claims, she has worked to overhaul the immigration laws of the nation. She emerged early as one of the most active and visible members in response to both national and international crisis situations and as an advocate of Historically Black Colleges and Universities. Significantly, the *Congressional Quarterly* selected her as one of the fifty most effective members of Congress.[21]

In addition to winning election to office, some African American women with Texas roots and affiliations have received high-level executive appointments. President Carter appointed more blacks and women to high-level positions than all of his predecessors combined—285 blacks to his staff, seventy-one females,[22] among them was Hortense Williams Dixon. A Texas Southern University professor with degrees from Prairie View, Minnesota, and Texas Tech, Dixon took a leave to become executive assistant to the mayor of the city of Houston in 1975. In 1979, she was the coordinator for Texas Southern University as host institution for a conference on women's equity issues sponsored by the U.S. Department of Education, bringing together women from across the nation to focus on critical issues in this area. She served as guest professor and lecturer at the University of West Virginia, Michigan State University, Bishop College, and numerous other institutions of higher learning. She was a board member of United Fund, the San Jacinto Girl Scouts, and the Houston Council on Human Relations and was also chairperson of the Houston Urban Coalition. She left higher education to join the Carter administration as manager of community development for the Tennessee Valley Authority.[23]

Other presidential appointees include Azie Morton, a Huston-Tillotson graduate, business executive, and a long-time worker in equal opportunity compliance review activity. Morton was a member of President Kennedy's Committee on Equal Employment Opportunity in 1961–63, was a special assistant to the Democratic National Committee chair under Robert Straus from 1972 to 1976, and was appointed by President Jimmy Carter as U.S. Treasurer, which resulted in her signature on the nation's currency.[24]

Gabrielle McDonald of Houston was appointed to the U.S. District Court in Houston in 1979 by President Carter, one of six black women he appointed to the Federal bench.[25] She later served on the International Court of Justice in The Hague, where she was Chief Justice of the International Criminal Tribune and the only American on the eleven-member judges bench. A Howard University Law School graduate, she also served as a law school professor.

When President Carter appointed Spelman College graduate and Texas native Marcelite Jordan Harris as a White House aide there was no way of predicting what was ahead in her outstanding career. She became the first and only black woman to earn the rank of general in the U.S. Air Force. Earlier she had been the first female wing commander of air training at Kessler Air Force Base in Mississippi, the training site for all branches of the military in highly technical fields. The city of Houston designated February 11, 1991, Marcelite J. Harris Day in tribute to her achievements.[26]

Another important appointee was Jewel Limar Prestage who became member and chair of the National Advisory Council on Women's Educational Programs, U.S. Department of Education, after appointment by President Carter and Senate confirmation. She was the first minority woman to chair that council. Prestage affiliated with Prairie View A&M University in 1989, after long tenures with universities in Louisiana and Iowa.[27]

Ambassador Cynthia Shepard Perry, professor of education at Texas Southern University, served as U.S. ambassador to Sierra Leone from 1986 to 1989 and U.S. ambassador to Burundi from 1990 to 1993, appointed by presidents Ronald Reagan and George Bush, respectively. Perry, who holds a B.A. in political science from Indiana State University and a doctorate from the University of Massachusetts at Amherst, also spent the period of 1982–86 as chief of education and human resources for the Africa Bureau of AID in its Washington office. She also worked for six years for the United Nations in Kenya and Ethiopia. Perry received honorary degrees from Chatham College, the University of Massachusetts, Indiana State University, and the University of Maryland. She is a "first" as a Texas African American woman appointed to ambassador rank by an American president.[28]

President Bill Clinton appointed numerous black women "firsts."[29] Gaynell Griffin Jones, a Waco native, was the first African American woman appointed as full U.S. Attorney in the American South. She was assigned to Houston, Texas, in 1993 and served until 1997. An undergraduate of Emerson College with a law degree from Boston College, Jones launched her career as a prosecutor in Louisiana and continued in the Houston district attorney's office.[30]

Another first was Vanessa Gilmore, appointed by Clinton to the Southern District, U.S. District Court, in Houston in 1994. Upon appointment she became the nation's youngest sitting member of the Federal bench, as she had been the youngest member of her freshman class at Hampton University. In 1981 she received a Juris Doctorate from the University of Houston Law Center. During her thirteen-year civil litigation law practice in Houston she was very active in civic and political affairs, attracting the attention of Governor Ann Richards. This led to her appointment by Richards to the Texas Department of Commerce Policy Board, of which she became the first African American chair in 1992. Appointment as chair of Texas for NAFTA in 1993 brought her into working relationships with diplomats and world leaders. Gilmore not only was the first African American woman from Texas to be appointed to the Federal bench, but she also was the first University of Houston graduate to be appointed.[31]

African American women came of age politically at the state level as well as nationally as Texas underwent changes that were historic in nature between 1974 and 2000. Democrat Dolph Briscoe ushered in the period with control by his party of the state governorship and both houses from 1973 to 1978. However, in 1979, Texas elected its first Republican governor since Reconstruction, as William Clements was sworn in. He was defeated by Democrat Mark White in 1983 but won again in 1987, serving until 1991. Democrat Ann Richards became only the second woman governor of Texas that year, and her tenure was marked by significant appointments of African American women to high-level positions. This pattern prompted Ruthe Winegarten, in 1995, to note, "Governor Ann Richards has appointed the most black women to staff boards and commissions of any Texas governor to date."[32] In 1994, Richards lost to George W. Bush. According to Thomas R. Dye, Bush appointed women to 37 percent and minorities to 22 percent of the posts he filled during five years in office, while Richards had used "about 45 percent women" and "about 35 percent minorities."[33]

Gubernatorial political appointments on the state level included Myra McDaniel, who was appointed secretary of state by Governor Mark White; he appointed Hazel Obey as his legislative liaison. Bill Clement appointed Naomi Cox Andrews and Carole A. Fleming to the Texas Southern University governing board. Ann Richards appointed Allison Leland to the Texas A&M University board of regents, Naomi Lede to the Texas Public Transportation Advisory Commission, Claudia Smart as regional coordinator of the Texas War on Drugs, Gaynelle Griffin Jones as a justice on the First Court of Appeals in Houston, and Winsome Jean as director of the governor's Office of Finance and Business Development. In addition, in selecting members of the first Texas Commission on Women Richards appointed six blacks among the twenty-nine total. Richards also named Zinetta Birney to the University of Houston governing board and Lori Moon to the Texas Southern University board.[34]

African American women began to seek and win seats in the Texas House of Representatives in the early 1970s. In fact, in 1973 the second black woman to serve in the Texas Legislature was elected to the House from Dallas. Eddie Bernice Johnson formed a winning coalition among African Americans, women's groups, veterans' groups, and her professional colleagues in nursing. Her priorities focused on criminal justice, consumer affairs, racial discrimination, and what have been labeled "traditional women's issues," like child care, maternity leave for teachers, and free breakfast for low-income schoolchildren.[35] She left the Texas House in 1977 but reemerged in the Texas Legislature as a state senator in 1986, where she again pushed these interests. After the 1990 census, the Texas Legislative Subcommittee on Congressional Redistricting, of which Johnson was a member, drew a majority black district in the Dallas area. She ran for and won that seat.

Representative Wilhelmina Delco, elected in 1973 from Travis County, the city of Austin, played a significant role as chair of the Higher Education Committee in 1980 in extending benefits of the Permanent University Fund (PUF) to include Prairie View A&M University. The PUF until that time supported the University of Texas and selected predominantly white institutions. A graduate of Fisk University, Delco was one of the first black elected officials in Texas after the passage of the 1965 Voting Rights Act. As a school board member in Austin, Delco was a participant in the "First Southwide Conference of Black Elected Officials" held in Atlanta, Georgia, in 1968. She soon became a participant in state and national activities and organizations of elected officials as a member/speaker/lecturer. Her Texas House peers chose her speaker pro tempore in 1991. She retired from the legislature in 1996.[36]

Senfronia Thompson is the state representative with the longest tenure in office among both women and African Americans. In 1987, she chaired the first standing committee to have a female majority, and for many years she chaired one of the busiest committees in the legislature—House Judicial Affairs. More than once she has been cited as one of the "top legislators" and has been in the forefront of every campaign against discrimination on the basis of race and gender over the last four decades. She holds a bachelor's degree in biology, a master's in education, and a law degree and a master's of law in international law. Among the laws she has authored or coauthored are Texas' first alimony law, laws prohibiting racial profiling, the James Byrd Jr. Hate Crimes Act, and the state Minimum Wage Act. She has gained many honors statewide and nationally for her outstanding work as a "legislator."[37]

The first African American woman to enter the Texas legislature as a successor to her husband was Lou Nell Sutton, elected at age sixty-six in 1976, from San Antonio. Her husband, C. J. Sutton, "the first Black person in the South" to win public office in the twentieth century with his 1948 election to the San Antonio Union Junior College District Board of Trustees, won a seat in the Texas House in 1972 and reelection in 1974. Ms. Sutton ran unopposed in a 1976 special election and replaced her husband on the powerful House Appropriations Committee. She retired from the House in 1989. Her accomplishments included the C. J. Sutton Building, the first state building outside of Austin; a mental health facility for San Antonio; funding for St. Philip's College;

equalizing tuition for higher education and special education; and compulsory liability insurance.[38]

In 1977, Lannell Cofer won a special election to replace Eddie Bernice Johnson and won full terms in 1978 and 1980. Educated at East Texas State University and Texas Southern University Law School, she was inspired by Barbara Jordan to study law. Cofer advocated redistricting to give more representation to minorities, allowing heirs to retain defaulted property, increasing funding for Prairie View and Texas Southern Universities, requiring sprinklers for nursing homes, and establishing the Martin Luther King holiday in Texas. She lost her seat in the 1982 Democratic primary.[39]

Karyne Conley was elected to the House of Representatives from Bexar County in 1988, to replace Lou Nell Sutton. Educated in Atlanta at Clark College, and with an M.P.A. from Northern Illinois University, she was a congressional aide to U.S. Representative Andrew Young (D. Georgia) and his public affairs officer when he was U.S. Ambassador to the United Nations. Her tenure involved advocacy for traditional women's issues in a somewhat nontraditional manner, as she regarded her role as that of "irritant in pushing to get local banks to provide loans to local entrepreneurs, minority contracts for state service, and a college fund for low income students." During her fourth term in 1996, Conley left the legislature.[40]

Two women from Dallas County, Yvonne Davis and Helen Giddings, won seats in the House in 1993. Davis holds an undergraduate degree from the University of Houston, is the owner of a small business, and serves on the Committee on Government Reform and the Committee on Juvenile Justice and Family Issues.[41] Giddings, who is from De Soto, Texas, is a former student at University of Texas at Arlington, is also an owner of a small business, and sits on the committees on Business and Industry, Higher Education, and House Administration. She has become a national leader among women lawmakers, serving as vice president of the National Order of Women Legislators in 1999 and president elect for 2000.[42]

Dawnna Dukes was elected from Travis County, the Austin area, in 1996. A Texas A&M University graduate, she travels as ambassador for the state of Texas and the United States and does research and writing about race and gender relations in Japan. Issues she addresses are environmental racism, historically underutilized business programs, and improving public and higher education. Her committee assignments include chair of Budget and Oversight for the Culture, Recreation, and Tourism Committee and membership on the Appropriations Committee.[43]

Ruth Jones McClendon, a graduate of Texas Southern University, with a master's from Webster University, was elected in 1996. She had been the first African American woman elected to the San Antonio city council in 1993, and had served as mayor pro tempore until August 1996. Her major legislative agenda included funding for a pediatric cancer center in San Antonio, harsher penalties for crimes against senior citizens, funding to modernize adult nursing homes, and special provisions to allow asthma inhalers in school for children who need them. She served on the Economic Development, Public Safety, Juvenile Justice and Family Issues, Public Health, and State Affairs committees. For seventeen years she worked in the juvenile justice system.[44]

Terry Hodge, elected in 1999—the last black woman to be elected to the Texas Legislature in the twentieth century—came from the Dallas area. After graduating from high school in Los Angeles, California, she migrated to Texas. She worked her way up from telephone operator to manager between 1966 and 1991. In the House she has been assigned to the committees on Criminal Jurisprudence, Defense Affairs, and State-Federal Relations.[45]

Across the nation and in Texas, blacks have been especially slow in gaining access to office at the county level. Each Texas county has four commissioners, each elected from a single member precinct; and one county judge, elected at large, who comprise the Commissioner's Court governing body. There are a total of 1,270 members of commissioner's courts throughout Texas—254 county judges and 1,016 elected county commissioners. According to the Joint Center for Political Studies, there were no African American county commissioners in the state of Texas in 1970 or 1979. By 1983, Texas had elected eight blacks to county commissions; however, it was not until 1988 that Dionne Bagsby became the first black woman to be elected a Texas county commissioner when she won the position in Tarrant County. No woman of any race and no minority person had served as county commissioner in Tarrant County prior to Bagsby's election. This was also Bagsby's first bid for public office. She was approached to run after an Anglo woman department chair was fired by the all male Commissioner's Court and fought back against what was widely regarded as the "unfair" basis for her firing. According to Bagsby, the public became more conscious not only of women's issues in the workplace but also of the work and power of the county government. Bagsby's "cross-over appeal," the ability to attract support from the district's 65 percent nonminority population; "high name recognition"; and respected ability as an educator were her major assets. In a telephone interview, she articulated a "10 point agenda" to "change the culture of her county" and to "get things done." In the end she asserted that "8 1/2 points of the 10 point agenda got done." A hometown newspaper suggests that her term of office was productive for her precinct and for the county at large.[46]

The only other black woman elected as county commissioner before 2000 was Iris Lawrence, chosen in Amarillo (Potter County) in 1999. Former gubernatorial appointee to the State Board of Pardons and Parole, Potter County Democratic chairperson, St. Augustine College graduate, delegate to the Democratic National Convention in 1994 and 2000, 2000–2004 Texas Democratic National Committeewoman, and motivational speaker, Lawrence is a member of the governing board of the Texas Organization of Black County Commissioners. She has been the recipient of many honors and awards for civic and community service.[47]

The early statistics on the election of blacks generally and of black women in particular to public office in Texas reveal that in 1970 there were twenty-nine total black elected officials, twenty-six local and three at the state level. Of these, four were women and all were local except state senator Barbara Jordan. By 1979, of the eighteen women officeholders, four were at the state level and the rest at the municipal and local levels. Although the number had more than doubled by 1983 to forty-two, only three were state level and none held countywide office; the rest were local. Through the year 2000 that pattern prevailed. Black women also became a part of the judicial branch of Texas government.

Assessment of black Texas women's presence in the judicial branch involves access to the more than 2,900 judicial positions in Texas. These judgeships include: nine on the state Supreme Court, nine on the Court of Criminal Appeals, eighty on the Court of Appeals, 409 on District Courts, 457 on county level courts, 1,226 on Municipal Courts, and 838 justices of the peace. The first black woman to serve as a judge in Texas was Charlyne Ola Farris, appointed as Wichita County Judge Pro-Tem in July 1954 in absence of the regular county judge "for 3 days, the first such appointment in the American South." According to Farris in a 1976 exchange, "it was news only because it marked a first in the South."[48] Black women judges known to have served at the county level or above in Texas between 1974 and 2000 are listed in the notes.[49] There are also a number of black women serving as Municipal Court judges and justices of the peace across the state. Federal District Court judges, Gabrielle MacDonald and Vanessa Gilmore, were discussed earlier in this chapter.

On the precollegiate level, black women's roles as classroom teachers is legendary, but there has been a historical dearth of black women at the leadership ranks in institutions of higher education, in the professional ranks, and in the leadership of professional and scientific learned societies. To some extent this pattern seems to be changing, and Texas women have been a part of that reversal. Their impact on higher education has taken essentially two directions. Women associated with Texas institutions had a major impact, and women with Texas "roots" acting outside of the state's borders also had an impact.

In the public sector of higher education, of the states' higher education institutions the state of Texas has identified "three (3) institutions of the first class." These are the University of Texas, Prairie View A&M University, and Texas A&M University. At these institutions no African American woman has ever served as president. Only at Prairie View have there been black women in the position of provost. The first was Flossie M. Byrd, a Florida native, Ph.D. in home economics from Cornell University, and former faculty member at Florida A&M University and Oregon State University. She served as president of the National Council of Administrations of Home Economics, president of the Association of Administrators of Home Economics, chair of the Southern Region of Home Economics Administrators, and was recipient of the Distinguished Service Award from the American Home Economics Association. At Prairie View she was dean of home economics and vice president.[50] The second woman provost at Prairie View was E. Johanne Thomas-Smith, a long-time member of the faculty and chair of the Department of English and an academic administrator under Provost Flossie Byrd.

Elaine Adams, vice president for student affairs and associate vice president for academic affairs with President Percy Pierre at Prairie View A&M University in the 1980s, was one of the highest-ranking women in an institution in the Texas A&M University system at the time. A graduate of Xavier University (Louisiana), with a Ph.D. from the University of Southern California, her post–Prairie View career included assistant commissioner for Equal Opportunity Planning at the Texas Higher Education Coordinating Board, president of Northeast College in the Houston Community College system, interim president of Central College in the Houston Community College system, and vice chancellor for educational development for the Houston Community College system.

The first African American woman appointed president of a major public institution of higher education in Texas was Marguerite Ross Barnett, at the University of Houston in 1990, after she served as president of the University of Missouri–St. Louis, and vice president for academic affairs at City University of New York. Although her tenure at Houston was abbreviated due to her death from cancer in 1992, she was especially celebrated for collaboration with the business community, fund-raising, determination to raise the level of all academic programs, and the ranking of the University of Houston among national universities. She was a political scientist with a doctorate from the University of Chicago.[51]

Carol D. Surles served as president of Texas Woman's University from 1994 until 1999. She earned a Ph.D. at the University of Michigan and had worked in university administration in Mississippi, Michigan, and California, and served on boards of directors at several businesses in Denton.

Texas Southern University in Houston selected its first black female president, Joan Horton, in 1993. In 1995, she left the position. Priscilla Slade became the university's second female president in 1999, after serving as a faculty member and dean in its College of Business. A Ph.D. in accounting from the University of Texas at Austin, Slade holds degrees from Mississippi State University and Jackson State University in Mississippi. In addition, she served on the Federal Reserve Board, the Board of Directors of the American Association of Collegiate Schools of Business, and on the Quality Review Oversight Board for the state of Texas.

Black Texas women have been successful in the state's community colleges as well. In the Houston Community College system there are currently five campuses, and the system has had two different African American women presidents, Elaine Adams and Margaret Ford. Adena Williams Loston served as president of San Jacinto

College South for five years. In San Antonio, Angie S. Runnels has served at the helm of St. Philip's College in the Alamo Community College system. Adena Loston, product of an HBCU, Alcorn State in Mississippi, has a master's degree and doctorate degree from Bowling Green State University with educational leadership study at Harvard. Prior to San Jacinto she was campus CEO with the Transmountain and Valle Verde campuses in El Paso County and dean of professional and vocational programs at Santa Monica College in California. She left San Jacinto for a position with NASA. Angie S. Runnels of St. Philip's, former interim president of North Lake College in Irving, Texas, was appointed in 1997. Her doctorate work was done at University of Texas at Austin.

The number of African American women faculty members affiliated with Texas universities who emerged as leaders at the national or regional levels in higher education in their respective fields continued to expand during the 1974–2000 period, as did their areas of specialization. Linda Williams-Willis, a Texas Woman's University Ph.D., became the first woman in the state of Texas to head Cooperative Extension when she was named at Prairie View in 1996; she has received many awards. Among them are the 1990 Early Career Service Award and the "1890 Model Program Award" in 1990. Cecille Harrison, professor of sociology at Texas Southern University, has become one of the leading scholar-activists in her discipline in the state and region. Holder of a Ph.D. in sociology from the University of Texas at Austin, she became the first African American female to be elected president of the Southwestern Sociological Association in 2000. Clifton Sparks became dean of the College of Education at Texas Woman's University in Denton, Texas, after serving as chair of the Department of Counselor Education and Personnel Service there from 1973 to 1982. Barbara Posey Jones, dean of the College of Business at Prairie View, in the 1990s was president of the National Economic Association and was on the board of directors of the American Association of Collegiate Schools of Business and served on its executive committee. At the University of Texas, Barbara P. White made history as the first African American dean of the School of Social Work and as president of the National Association of Social Workers.

As dean of the Prairie View School of Nursing, 1992–99, Dollie Johnson Braithwaite developed, produced financial support for, and implemented Prairie View's first master's degree program in nursing.

She also established its endowed Minority Health and Research Chair, was chair of the Texas Medical Center Council of Nurse Executives, was appointed by Governor Ann Richards to the Texas Council on Offenders with Mental Impairments, and served as Equal Opportunity officer for the U.S. Army Reserve unit in Houston. Nationally, she was a member of an elite mentoring body in African American nursing whose objective was to increase the number of senior scholars in academic leadership positions in the field, and pioneered with a national research group that took students to Africa to conduct research and establish linkages with African universities and individual scholars.

Ruth Murdock McRoy is a distinguished teaching professor, associate dean for research, Ruby Lee Piester Cultural Professor in Services to Children and Families in the University of Texas at Austin School of Social Work, and a researcher with the Hogg Foundation for Mental Health. Shelia Walker, an early African American woman on the faculty at University of Texas at Austin, was director of the Center for African and Afro-American Studies.

Clarice Pierson Lowe, a multitasking academician who spent nearly four decades on the Texas Southern University faculty, began her remarkable career as a seventeen-year-old magna cum laude B.A. degree recipient in English. With a library science degree, a master's in speech pathology and audiology from Northwestern University, and a Ph.D. in speech communication from the University of Wisconsin–Madison, she taught English and later speech, served as chair of the Speech Department, crafted the proposal for a new School of Communications, and became active in professional and scholarly organizations in English and Speech. At conferences in Africa, Asia, Europe, and South America, as well as across the United States, she presented her research and scholarly writings. Committed to learning "lifelong," she did further study and also served as consultant and lecturer. Her influence on her profession was widespread, as reflected in service to and office-holding in the National Communication Association, the International Communication Association, and the Speech Communication Association, as well as cofounding the National Association of Black Communication Educators.[52]

The higher education leadership record of Jewel Limar Prestage, political scientist, who became dean of the Benjamin Banneker Honors College at Prairie View in 1990, has included vice president of the

American Political Science Association as its first black female, president of the Southern Political Science Association with similar distinction, president of the Southwestern Social Science Association as the
first woman and first black, and first woman president of the National
Conference of Black Political Scientists. In 1993 she was elected president of the National Association of African American Honors Programs. The American Political Science Association and the Southern
Political Science Association presented her their top awards for contributions to "development of the profession," and the National Conference of Black Political Scientists has created and named an award
for her. Prestage received a Ph.D. from the University of Iowa at age
twenty-two and is the recipient of three honorary degrees.[53]

Notable among women outside of Texas with Texas roots are
Gloria Randle Scott and Ruth Simmons. Scott, born in Houston,
graduated salutatorian in her class at Jack Yates High School and, with
a full competitive scholarship, earned three degrees from Indiana University. Then came a stellar career that included teaching, beginning
at age twenty-three, at several institutions, ending with an executive
vice president position at Clark College in Atlanta, and, in 1987, president of Bennett, an all female college in North Carolina, where she
remained until 2001. Outside of academia, President Carter appointed
Scott to the National Advisory Committee on Historically Black Colleges and Universities and Black Higher Education, and she was the
national president of the Girl Scouts of the USA, 1975–78. Presidential
appointments related to women's issues included membership on the
International Women's Year Commission in 1976–78, chair of the National Defense Advisory Committee on Women in the Services in 1981,
and member of the National Research Committee on Girls, 1991–93.[54]

Ruth Simmons, born in Grapeland, was the twelfth and last child
of Texas sharecroppers who moved into Houston; she grew up in the
Fifth Ward area, a poor overwhelmingly black neighborhood that borders downtown Houston. Simmons graduated at the top of her high
school class, won a scholarship to Dillard University in New Orleans,
where she majored in French, and graduated summa cum laude in 1967.
In 1973, she earned a Ph.D. from Harvard in romance languages, and
in 1995 became the first African American president of Smith College
after extended tenure in higher education. The great-granddaughter of
slaves, there was no way she could recognize that "segregated Texas"
was her land of opportunity. In 2001, Simmons assumed the presidency

of Brown University, the first black woman to lead an Ivy League institution.[55] Simmons remains one of the most influential leaders in
American higher education.

Some black Texas women educators earned accolades and made
achievements in the field of medicine. Charleta Guillory, associate
professor of pediatrics, Baylor College of Medicine, with a specialty
in neonatology, is director of the Texas Children's Hospital neonatal-
prenatal public health program. She is a product of Louisiana State
University Medical School, the University of Colorado, and the Baylor
College of Medicine, site of her postdoctoral fellowship in neonatal-
prenatal medicine. She received national recognition in *The Best Doctors
in America*, and was chair of 1995–97 March of Dimes perennial needs
assessment. Her major research focused on decreasing infant mortality.
In addition, she is a frequent television commentator/consultant and is
a lecturer on health issues in a variety of venues.[56]

Judith Cravens earned both an M.D. and a Ph.D. and made
a historic impact on medical education as vice president for Minority Affairs and dean of the School of Allied Health at the University
of Texas Health Science Center–Houston in the mid-1980s. She was
able to mount a cooperative program in which faculty from the Center
interacted with students of Prairie View A&M University, including
students of the Benjamin Banneker Honors College, throughout the
1990s. Cravens was the first black woman to graduate from the Baylor
College of Medicine, in 1974.[57] Barbara Hayes became the first dean
of the Texas Southern College of Pharmacy in 2000 after Maryann
Galley had served as acting dean. The majority of black pharmacists in
Texas receive their education at Texas Southern.

Another African American female physician of special note who
has had a remarkable impact as educator, practitioner, and public servant is Karen Johnson. A faculty member of Pediatrics and Neonatology at the Baylor College of Medicine and popular television personality, Johnson received her B.S. from Xavier University–New Orleans,
her M.D. from Baylor, where she did postdoctoral, residency, and fellowship training as well. She is a medical correspondent for *Focus on
Health*, an educational series viewed by millions on the Houston CBS
affiliate TV channel.[58]

In the area of science and technology, Mae C. Jemison became
the first black female astronaut. An Alabaman by birth, she was raised
in Chicago, educated at Stanford University, and earned a medical

degree from Cornell University. Selection as an astronaut candidate brought her to Texas in 1987, and in 1992 she boarded the space shuttle *Endeavor* for a one-week mission "to study the effects of zero gravity on people and animals."[59] Joye Carter was the first black female medical examiner for Harris County. Her authorship of *I Speak for the Dead* was based on her experiences in that position.[60] The appointment of Jelynne LeBlanc Burley of San Antonio as special projects officer for the Office of Dome Development in 1990 represented a significant breakthrough for black women in Texas. Later Burley served as director of Facilities Planning and Construction, providing leadership and strategic direction to the consultants and the department, which managed major capital projects.[61]

Black Texas women explored other avenues by using their educational achievements. In 1999, Shirley DeLibero became the president and CEO of Houston's Metropolitan Transit Authority and became overseer of the city's modern light rail system. Against what seemed insurmountable odds, she developed a plan, acquired the necessary citizen support, and got the trains up and running. She became known as the "Queen of Transit" throughout the city.[62] Sylvia Brooks has an exceptional record of public service as president and CEO of the Houston area Urban League, once regarded as only "a branch office of a national entity that operated on the fringes of Houston's society." The League became "a major provider of leadership and social services for the community, controlled by African Americans" under Brooks's leadership, according to one newspaper editorial writer. Brooks is a 1950s Jack Yates High School graduate with a University of Southern California graduate degree.[63]

Maya Rockeymoore, whose hometown is San Antonio, is a nationally recognized researcher and consultant on social and economic security policy, and also a frequently featured spokesperson in the national media. Prior to becoming chief of staff to Congressman Charles Rangel (D. N.Y.), she earned a political science degree at Prairie View A&M University, where she was a part of the Benjamin Banneker Honors College. Rockeymoore earned her master's and doctorate from Purdue, with special study at the University of Leiden in the Netherlands. She is a principal adviser to the Congressional Black Caucus Foundation.

Naomi W. Lede is an educator, political activist, and professional public servant. Author of ten books and over thirty articles and reports, she spent most of her professional career at Texas Southern University as a tenured professor of transportation studies, chair of the Division of Transportation Studies, and founder/executive director of the Center for Transportation Training and Research. Under her leadership, Texas Southern became the major source of transportation professionals in the state and the nation. Upon retirement from Texas Southern, Lede joined Texas A&M University as a senior research scientist at the Texas Transportation Institute. She was the first black female appointed to the Houston Metro Transit Authority board.[64]

Texas has a strong tradition of civil rights leadership by black women. Principal among them during this period was Althea Simmons,[65] a Dallas lawyer, who was born in Shreveport, Louisiana, and earned a law degree from Howard University. Her work with the NAACP evolved from volunteer to professional as she served as chair of the Executive Committee of the Dallas branch and executive secretary of the Texas State Conference before completing stints as a professional in Los Angeles and Mississippi. In 1979, Simmons became the NAACP chief lobbyist in Washington, D.C., leading the nation in the direction of equal justice in education. She died in Washington in 1990, still in pursuit of NAACP goals. Algenita Scott-Davis, former president of the National Bar Association and 1974 Howard Law School graduate, played a pivotal role in efforts to secure district election of judges in Texas. She also has been a prominent leader in civic affairs in Houston and Harris County for two decades, especially relative to community development.

During the course of the past quarter-century, African American women in the Lone Star State have made tremendous strides, especially in the realms of politics and education. At the beginning of the twentieth century, black women did not have the vote, or hold political offices, though some were in other types of leadership positions, such as the Thurman WCTU. Very few held a college degree, let alone served as active leaders for African American educational efforts in both Texas and the nation. African American women in Texas were accorded legal access to equal educational opportunity after *Brown v. Board of Education* in 1954, and were legally franchised after passage of the Voting Rights Act of 1965. By the turn of the twenty-first century they achieved responsible leadership positions in many areas of life nationally and statewide. Perhaps none of these areas were more critical that those in higher education and in the political arena.

Today black women have the vote, and they have attained respected positions in politics and education. Their powerful influence
has helped them gain acceptance and responsibility in other avenues as
well; as chapter 7 of this volume depicts, they are key leaders and participants in many other avenues of Texas life. Their progress in a number of fields surpasses that of black males, and in education, surpasses
that of white women also (percentage-wise). Black female leadership
can be expected to increase in education and in politics, as in other
fields, well into the twenty-first century.

Notes

1. Barbara Sinclair Deckard, *The Women's Movement: Political, Socio-
Economic, and Psychological Issues,* 3rd ed. (New York: Harper and Row, 1983):
337–45.
2. See "Texas Culture," in *Texas Politics Today,* 4th ed., ed. William Earl
Maxwell and Ernest Crain et al. (St. Paul, Minn.: West Publishing, 1978),
2–8, and 5th ed.; and Terry Spurlock, "Political Culture, Political Socializa-
tion, and Regionalism, or, Bubba Don't Like Politics," in *Texas Politics Today,*
7th ed., ed. William Earl Maxwell and Ernest Crain et al. (St. Paul, Minn.:
West Publishing, 1995), 22–23, for perspectives on the changes in Texas political culture from 1970 to 1990.
3. Joyce Ladner, "The Black Women Today," *Ebony* (August 1997): 33–36,
38–40, 42.
4. U.S. Bureau of Census, 1970; *Texas Population, 2000.*
5. U.S. Bureau of Census, 1980, 1990; *Texas Population, 2000.*
6. U.S. Bureau of Census, 2000, *Texas Population 2000;* at http://
quickfacts.census.gov/qfd/, accessed April 30, 2007.
7. Steve H. Murdock, Md. Nazrul Hoque, Martha Michael, Steve
White, and Beverly Pecotte, *Texas Challenge: Population Change and the Future of Texas* (College Station: Texas A&M University Press, 1997): 109.
8. U.S. Bureau of Census, *Census of Population 1970 General and Social
and Economic Characteristics,* Summary of Final Report.
9. Bureau of Labor Statistics, *Geographic Profile of Employment and Unemployment Report, Annual Reports.*
10. Alwyn Barr, *Black Texans: A History of African Americans in Texas,
1528–1995,* 2nd ed. (Norman: University of Oklahoma Press, 1996), 236.
11. Available at http://www.census.gov/population/www/pofs-profile/
blackgroups.html.
12. Office of Institutional Research at Prairie View A&M University;
and Information at Texas Southern University.
13. Murdock et al., *The Texas Challenge,* 139.
14. Dhananjaya Arekere and Mitchell Rice, "A Note on the Improving

Status of Hispanics and African Americans in Texas," *RESI News and Notes* 1, no. 1 (College Station: Race and Ethnic Studies Institute, Texas A&M University, 2003), 3.

15. Information provided in letter from researcher at the Carter Center Library, Atlanta, Georgia. Primary source: Jimmy Carter Presidential Library. Pre-Presidential 1976 Campaign Materials, Box 205—"Delegate Selection Book for Missouri and Wisconsin."

16. Richard Scammon and Ben Wattenberg, *The Real Majority* (New York: Coward-McCann, 1992).

17. Ruthe Winegarten, *Black Texas Women: 150 Years of Trial and Triumph* (Austin: University of Texas Press, 1995), 286–87.

18. Statistics on black elected officials provided by the Joint Center for Political Studies/Joint Center for Political and Economic Studies, Washington, D.C., excerpt for 1970; Eleanor Farrar and Vernon E. Jordan, Metropolitan Applied Research Center.

19. Marianna Davis, ed., *Contributions of Black Women to America* (Columbia, S.C.: Kenday Press, 1982), 2: 236–37. See also "Barbara Jordan: Seeking the Power Points," *Newsweek* (November 4, 1974): 22; Craig Hines "A Voice for Justice Dies," *Houston Chronicle*, January 18, 1996; Merline Pitre, "Jordan, Barbara Charline," in *Black Women in America: An Historical Encyclopedia,* ed. Darlene Clark Hine et al. (Brooklyn, N.Y.: Carlson Publishing, 1993): 1: 658–59.

20. See Mary K. Garber, "Representative Eddie Bernard Johnson, Chair, Congressional Black Caucus," *Focus* (January 2001): 1; Donald Roach, "Legislating the Technical Mind," *Black Issues in Higher Education* 19 (November 13–August 15, 2002): 18–21. The focus in this article is Congresswoman Johnson and how to equip young Americans with skills to meet the nations technological and scientific needs.

21. Charles Dervarics, "Lawmaker Calls for More Training to Improve Student Visa Program," *Black Issues in Higher Education* 20, no. 6 (2003): 6.

22. See President Carter's Appointments of Blacks, Joint Center for Political and Economics Studies.

23. Hortense Dixon File, Hartman Collection, Texas Southern University Library.

24. Winegarten, *Black Texas Women: 150 Years of Trial and Triumph,* 263.

25. Ibid., 280; Marilyn Milby, "International War Crimes Judge," *Essence* 28 (April 1998): 62.

26. Linda Rochelle Lane, "Harris, Marcelite Jordon," in Hine et al., *Black Women in America,* 1: 538–39.

27. Ife Williams-Audah, "Prestage, Jewel Limar," in Hine et al., *Black Women in America,* 2: 940.

28. Cynthia Shepard Perry, *All Things Being Equal: One Woman's Journey* (New York: Stonecrest International Publishers, 1998).

29. Dewayne Wickham, *Bill Clinton and Black America* (New York: Ballantine Books, 2002).

30. Personal résumé.

31. Jessie Carney Smith, *Black Firsts*, 2nd ed. (Canton, Mich.: Visible Ink Press, 2003), 311; *Jet* (July 18, 1994): 20; *Who's Who among African Americans*, 14th ed., 476.

32. Winegarten, *Black Texas Women: 150 Years of Trial and Triumph*, 281.

33. Thomas R. Dye, L. Tucker Gibson Jr., and Clay Robinson, *Politics in America*, 4th ed. (Upper Saddle River, N.J.: Prentice Hall, 2001), 1824–25, 285.

34. Winegarten, *Black Texas Women: 150 Years of Trial and Triumph*, 278–82.

35. Marianne Guthers and Jewel L. Prestage, "Styles and Priorities of Marginality: Women State Legislators," in *Race, Sex, and Policy Problems*, ed. Marian Palley and Michael Preston (Lexington, Mass.: D. C. Heath, 1979), 221–35. See also biographical information provided in Nancy Baker Jones and Ruthe Winegarten, "Eddie Bernice Johnson," *Capitol Women: Texas Female Legislators, 1923–1999* (Austin: University of Texas Press, 2000), 169–73.

36. Jones and Winegarten, "Wilhelmina Ruth Fitzgerald Delco," in *Capitol Women*, 182–86.

37. Jones and Winegarten, "Senfronia Thompson," in *Capitol Women*, 176–79.

38. Jones and Winegarten, "Lou Nell Sutton," in *Capitol Women*, 187–88.

39. Jones and Winegarten, "Lanell Cofer," in *Capitol Women*, 191–92.

40. Jones and Winegarten, "Karyne Conley," in *Capitol Women*, 241–43.

41. Jones and Winegarten, "Yvonne Davis," in *Capitol Women*, 262.

42. Jones and Winegarten, "Helen Giddings," in *Capitol Women*, 263.

43. Jones and Winegarten, "Dawnna Dukes," in *Capitol Women*, 264.

44. Jones and Winegarten, "Ruth Jones McClendon," in *Capitol Women*, 267.

45. Jones and Winegarten, "Terri Hodge," in *Capitol Women*, 266.

46. Telephone interview, Jewel L. Prestage with County Commissioner Dionne Bagsby; Jeff Guinn, "In a League of Her Own . . . ," *Ft. Worth Star Telegram*, Tarrant Edition, August 21, 2005, G1; Darwin Campbell, "Commissioner Retired," *African American News and Issues: Austin Texas* (January 26, February 6, 2005): 1, 5.

47. Telephone interview with County Commissioner Iris Lawrence by Jewel L. Prestage, 2005.

48. Personal correspondence with Honorable Charlyne Ola Farris, November 8, 1976.

49. List of African American female judges developed from county Web sites of Bexar, Harris, Dallas, Tarrant, and Travis counties. Additional sources included Professor Marcia Johnson, Thurgood Marshall School of Law and print media. List: Gaynell Griffin Jones, 1st Court of Appeals, Harris County; Mary Ellen Hicks, District Court, Tarrant County; Faith Johnson, Criminal Juvenile Court, Dallas County; Carolyn Hobson, Civil Court, Harris County; Carolyn Wright, District Court, Dallas County; Brenda Green, Family Court, Dallas County; Carmen Kelsey, Juvenile District Court, Bexar County; Laura Livingston, Civil District Court, Travis

County; Cheryl Shannon, District Court, Dallas County; Belinda Hill, District Court, Harris County; Bonnie Fitch, Criminal Court, Harris County; and Brenda Kennedy, Court at law, Travis County.

50. Jewel L. Prestage, "Byrd, Flossie," in Hine et al., *Black Women in America,* 1: 211–12.

51. Ife Williams-Audah, "Barnett, Marguerite Ross" in Hine et al., *Black Women in America,* 1: 88–89.

52. Information provided by Office of Institutional Effectiveness, Texas Southern University.

53. See the following for information on the career of Prestage: Smith, *Black Firsts,* 177–78; Shelia Harmon Martin, "Jewel Limar Prestage: Political Science Trailblazer and the Mother of Black Political Science," *PS Political Science and Politics* 38, no. 1 (2005): 95–97; and Kay Cosby Ellis, "Firsts Part of Her Bag," *Dallas Morning News,* March 30, 1974, 1C.

54. Senella McFarlane, "Scott, Gloria Dean Randle," in Hine et al., *Black Women in America,* 2: 1018–19.

55. Michael Fletcher, "Ruth Simmons at the Pinnacle of Higher Education," *A Mind Is* 8, no. 1 (Spring 2001): 14–15, 16–18. See also "Ruth Simmons: Sister President and Remarks by Spelman College President Johnetta Cole on the Occasion of the Inauguration of Ruth Simmons," *Monthly Forum on Women in Higher Education* (December 1995): 28–29; Eric D. Duke, "Ruth Simmons," in *Black Women in America,* ed. Darlene Clark Hine, 2nd ed. (New York: Oxford University Press, 2005), 3: 117–20.

56. Guillory to Prestage, professional résumé provided by her office at Baylor College of Medicine.

57. Winegarten, *Black Texas Women: 150 Years of Trial and Triumph,* 267.

58. Karen Johnson professional information provided by her office at Baylor College of Medicine.

59. Smith, *Black Firsts,* 621–22; "Mae Carol Jemison," *African American News and Issues* 1, no. 1 (2003): 1, 6. Also "4 Women Join Hall of Fame," *Houston Chronicle,* September 11, 2002.

60. Joye M. Carter, *I Speak for the Dead* (Houston: Biblical Dogs, 2001); and her autobiography, *My Strength Comes from Within* (Houston: Biblical Dogs, 2000).

61. Personal résumé provided by office of assistant city manager, San Antonio, Texas.

62. For information on DeLibero's tenure, see R. Billingsley "On the Heels of a Rail Victory: DeLibero Calls It Quits," *Houston Defender* 73, no. 5 (2003): 1, 6; "Does Metro Want Citizens' Input or Approval?" *African American News and Issues* 8, no. 14 (May 7–May 13, 2003): 1, 7.

63. "Black Voting," *African American News and Issues* 6, no. 6 (2001): 1, 6.

64. Available at http//www.vita.edu/supa/content/new/34/50/. Additional sources provided by personal résumé, School of Public Affairs, Texas Southern University.

65. Kathleen Thompson, "Summer, Althea T. L.," in Hine et al., *Black Women in America,* 2: 1035.

BRUCE A. GLASRUD
and MERLINE PITRE

Black Women in Texas History

SELECTED BIBLIOGRAPHY

Allen, Ruth. "The Negro Woman." In *The Labor of Women in the Production of Cotton*, 174–208. Bureau of Research in the Social Sciences. Austin: University of Texas, 1931.

Armstead, Johnnie M. "Black Women and Texas History." In *Bricks without Straw: A Comprehensive History of African Americans in Texas*, edited by David A. Williams, 114–24. Austin: Eakin Press, 1997.

Ashbaugh, Carolyn. *Lucy Parsons, American Revolutionary*. Chicago: Kerr, 1976.

Atkinson, M. Jourdan. "Familialism in Texas: A Texan View." In *The Extended Family in Black Societies*, edited by Demitri B. Shimkin, Edith M. Shimkin, and Dennis A. Frate, 355–62. The Hague: Mouton Publishers, 1978.

Beil, Gail K. "Four Marshallites' Roles in the Passage of the Civil Rights Act of 1964." *Southwestern Historical Quarterly* 106 (July 2002): 1–14.

Blackwelder, Julia Kirk. *Styling Jim Crow: African American Beauty Training during Segregation*. College Station: Texas A&M University Press, 2003.

————. *Women of the Depression: Caste and Culture in San Antonio, 1929–1939*. College Station: Texas A&M University Press, 1984.

Blue, Carroll Parrott. *The Dawn at My Back: Memoir of a Black Texas Upbringing*. Austin: University of Texas Press, 2003.

Boswell, Angela. *Her Act and Deed: Women's Lives in a Rural Southern County, 1837–1873*. College Station: Texas A&M University Press, 2001.

Bradshaw, Benjamin Spencer. "Some Demographic Aspects of Marriage: A Comparative Study of Three Ethnic Groups." Master's thesis, University of Texas, 1960.

Brandenstein, Sherilyn. "Prominent Roles of Black Womanhood in *Sepia Record*, 1952–1954." Master's thesis, University of Texas at Austin, 1989.

————. "*Sepia Record* as a Forum for Negotiating Women's Roles." In *Women and Texas History: Selected Essays*, edited by Fane Downs and Nancy Baker Jones, 143–57. Austin: Texas State Historical Association, 1993.

Brewer, Rose M. "Black Women Workers: Yesterday and Today." In *Women in the Texas Workforce: Yesterday and Today*, edited by Richard Croxdale and Melissa Hields, 35–48. Austin: People's History in Texas, 1979.

Brooks, Christopher. "Coming Home: An Interview with Sippie Wallace." *Texas Humanist* (July/August 1985): 30–31.

Brown, Olive D., and Michael R. Heintze. "Mary Branch: Private College Educator." In *Black Leaders: Texans for Their Times*, edited by Alwyn Barr and Robert A. Calvert, 112–27. Austin: Texas State Historical Association, 1981.

Broyles, William. "The Making of Barbara Jordan." *Texas Monthly* 4 (October 1976): 33–47.

Bryant, Ira B., Jr. *Barbara Charline Jordan: From the Ghetto to the Capitol*. Houston: D. Armstrong, 1977.

Burka, Paul. "Major Barbara [Jordan]." *Texas Monthly* 24 (March 1996): 88–89, 110–11.

Burrow, Rachel Northington. "Juanita Craft." Master's thesis, Southern Methodist University, 1994.

Byrd, James W. "Aunt Dicy: Legendary Black Lady." In *Legendary Ladies of Texas*, edited by Francis Edward Abernethy, 123–31. Dallas: E-Heart Press, 1981.

Campbell, Randolph B. "'My Dear Husband': A Texas Slave's Love Letter, 1862." *Journal of Negro History* 65 (1980): 361–64.

———. "The Slave Family in Antebellum Texas." In *The American Family*, 1–28. Victoria, Tex.: Victoria College Press, 1988.

Carter, Joye M. *I Speak for the Dead*. Houston: Biblical Dogs, 2003.

———. *My Strength Comes from Within*. Houston: Biblical Dogs, 2000.

Cartwright, Marguerita. "Etta Moten: Glamorous Grandmother." *Negro History Bulletin* 18 (March 1955): 137–38.

Coffey, Jim. "Johanna July: A Horse-Breaking Woman." In *Black Cowboys of Texas*, edited by Sara R. Massey, 73–82. College Station: Texas A&M University Press, 2000.

Conner, Jeffie O. Allen. "A Study of Four Hundred and Sixty Negro Farm Families in Three Texas Counties." Master's thesis, Prairie View State Normal and Industrial College, 1944.

Craft, Juanita. *A Child, the Earth, and a Tree of Many Seasons: The Voice of Juanita Craft*. Dallas: Halifax Publishing, 1982.

Crawford, Ann Fears, and Crystal Sasse Ragsdale. "Congresswoman from Texas [Barbara Jordan]." In *Women in Texas: Their Lives, Their Experiences, Their Accomplishments*, 296–307. Burnet, Tex.: Eakin Press, 1982.

———. "Eddie B. Johnson." In *Women in Texas: Their Lives, Their Experiences, Their Accomplishments*, 309–19. Burnet, Tex.: Eakin Press, 1982.

Crawford, Audrey. "'To Protect, to feed, and to give momentum to every effort': African American Clubwomen in Houston, 1880–1910." *The Houston Review* 1, no. 1 (Fall 2003): 15–23.

Crouch, Barry A. "The 'Cords of Love': Legalizing Black Marital and Family Rights in Postwar Texas." *Journal of Negro History* 79 (1994): 334–51.

———. "Seeking Equality: Houston Black Women during Reconstruction." In *Black Dixie: Afro-Texan History and Culture in Houston,* edited by Howard Beeth and Cary D. Wintz, 54–73. College Station: Texas A&M University Press, 1992.

———, and Larry Madaras. "Reconstructing Black Families: Perspectives from the Texas Freedmen's Bureau Records." *Prologue* 18 (1986): 109–22.

Curlee, Kendall. "White, Mattie B. Haywood." In *The New Handbook of Texas,* edited by Ron Tyler, Douglas E. Barnett, Roy R. Barkley, Penelope C. Anderson, and Mark F. Odintz, vol. 6, 930. Austin: Texas State Historical Association, 1996.

Curtin, Mary Ellen. "Reaching for Power: Barbara C. Jordan and Liberals in the Texas Legislature, 1966–1972." *Southwestern Historical Quarterly* 108 (October 2004): 211–31.

Dailey, Maceo C., Jr., and Kristine Navarro, eds. *Wheresoever My People Chance to Dwell: Oral Interviews with African American Women of El Paso.* Baltimore: Inprint Editions, 2000.

Davis, Alecia. "Christia V. Adair: Servant of Humanity." *Texas Historian* 38 (September 1977): 1–7.

Decker, Stefanie. "Mama, Activist, and Friend: African-American Women in the Civil Rights Movement in Dallas, Texas, 1945–1998." Master's thesis, Oklahoma State University, 1998.

———. "Women in the Civil Rights Movement: Juanita Craft versus the Dallas Elite." *East Texas Historical Journal* 39, no. 1 (2001): 33–42.

de Graaf, Lawrence B. "Race, Sex, and Region: Black Women in the American West, 1850–1920." *Pacific Historical Review* 49 (1980): 285–313.

Ealy, Rachel Ann. "Dr. Paulene Hopkins: The History of a Community Leader." *Texas Historian* 53 (September 1992): 18–19.

Eckerman, Jo. "Artemesia Bowden: Dedicated Dreamer." *Texas Passages* 2 (Winter 1987): 1–2.

Emmons, Martha. *Deep like the Rivers: Stories of My Negro Friends.* Austin: Encino Press, 1969.

Evans, Eola Adeline. "Activity of Black Women in the Woman Suffrage Movement, 1900–1920." Master's thesis, Lamar University, 1987.

Faust, Drew Gilpin. "Trying to Do a Man's Business: Gender Violence and Slave Management in Civil War Texas." In *Southern Stories in Peace and War,* edited by Drew Gilpin Faust, 174–92. Columbia: University of Missouri Press, 1992.

Flandreau, Suzanne. "Victoria Spivey." In *Black Women in America: An Historical Encyclopedia,* edited by Darlene Clark Hine, Elsa Barkley Brown, and Rosalyn Terborg-Penn, vol. 2, 1098–99. Brooklyn, N.Y.: Carlson Publishing, 1993.

Franklin, J. E. *"Black Girl": From Genesis to Revelations.* Washington, D.C.: Howard University Press, 1973.

Franklin, Nobia Anita. *Madame N. A. Franklin's Improved System of Hair Culture,* 4th ed. Houston: Webster Printing, 1921.

Frear, Yvonne. "Battling to End Segregation in Dallas, Texas, 1945–1965:

Race, Gender, and Social Mobilization in a Local Civil Rights Movement." Ph.D. diss., Texas A&M University, 2007.

———. "Generation v. Generation: African Americans in Texas Remember
the Civil Rights Movement." In *Myth Meaning and Historical Meaning
in Texas,* edited by Greg Cantrell and Elizabeth Hayes Turner. College
Station: Texas A&M University Press, 2007.

———. "Juanita Craft." In *Black Women in America,* 2nd ed., edited by Darlene Clark Hine, 317–18. New York: Oxford University Press, 2005.

———. "Juanita Craft and the Struggle to End Segregation in Dallas, 1945–
1955." In *Major Problems in Texas History,* edited by Cary D. Wintz and
Sam W. Haynes, 429–36. Boston: Houghton Mifflin, 2002.

Freydberg, Elizabeth Hadley. "Bessie Coleman." In *Black Women in America:
An Historical Encyclopedia,* edited by Darlene Clark Hine, Elsa Barkley
Brown, and Rosalyn Terborg-Penn, vol. 1, 262–63. Brooklyn, N.Y.: Carl-
son Publishing, 1993.

———. *Bessie Coleman: The Brownskin Lady Bird.* New York: Garland, 1994.

Gaines, Jean Foley. "An Evaluative Analysis of Job Opportunities for Negro Students of Business Education in Houston, Texas." M.B.Ed. thesis,
University of Colorado, 1956.

Gilliam, Stefanie Lee. See Decker, Stefanie.

Glasrud, Bruce A. "Jim Crow's Emergence in Texas." *American Studies* 15
(1974): 47–60.

———. "Women." In *African Americans in the West: A Bibliography of Secondary Sources,* edited by Glasrud et al., 145–54. Alpine, Tex.: Sul Ross State
University Center for Big Bend Studies, 1998.

———, and Laurie Champion. "Women." In *Exploring the Afro-Texas Ex-
perience: A Bibliography of Secondary Sources about Black Texans,* edited by
Glasrud and Champion, 161–68. Alpine, Tex.: Sul Ross State University
Center for Big Bend Studies, 2000.

Gooch, Jane P. "Barbara C. Jordan: Her First Forty Years; A Rhetorical
Analysis." Master's thesis, Baylor University, 1977.

Goodall, N. H. "Arizona Juanita Dranes." In *Black Women in America: An
Historical Encyclopedia,* edited by Darlene Clark Hine, Elsa Barkley
Brown, and Rosalyn Terborg-Penn, vol. 1, 355–56. Brooklyn, N.Y.: Carl-
son Publishing, 1993.

Greenfield, Meg. "The New Lone Star of Texas [Barbara Jordan]." *Newsweek,*
March 3, 1975, 31.

Hales, Douglas. *A Southern Family in White and Black: The Cuneys of Texas.*
College Station: Texas A&M University Press, 2003.

Hall, Josie Briggs. *Hall's Moral and Mental Capsule for the Economic and Domestic Life of the Negro, as a Solution of the Race Problem.* Dallas: Rev. F. S.
Jenkins, 1905.

———. *A Scroll of Facts and Advice.* Mexia, Tex.: Houx's Printery, 1905.

Halsell, Grace. *In Their Shoes: A White Woman's Journey Living as a Black, Na-
vajo, and Mexican Illegal.* Fort Worth: Texas Christian University Press,
1996.

Hardman, Peggy. "The Anti-Tuberculosis Crusade and the Texas African American Community, 1900–1950." Ph.D. diss., Texas Tech University, 1997.

Harrigan, Stephen. "The Yellow Rose of Texas." *Texas Monthly* 12 (April 1984): 152.

Harris, Trudier. "'The Yellow Rose of Texas': A Different Cultural View." In *Juneteenth Texas: Essays in African-American Folklore,* edited by Francis Edward Abernethy, Patrick B. Mullen, and Alan B. Govenar, 315–33. Denton: University of North Texas Press, 1996.

Harrison, Daphne Duval. "Sippie Wallace." In *Black Women in America: An Historical Encyclopedia,* edited by Darlene Clark Hine, Elsa Barkley Brown, and Rosalyn Terborg-Penn, 1220–23. Brooklyn, N.Y.: Carlson Publishing, 1993.

Heintze, Michael R. "Branch, Mary Elizabeth." *The Handbook of Texas Online,* http://www.tsha.utexas.edu/handbook/online/.

Henson, Margaret. "She's the Real Thing." *Texas Highways* 33 (April 1986): 60–61.

Hines, Carrie P. *The Surmounters.* Amarillo, Tex.: Shepherd Printing, 1959.

Howard, Vicki. "The Courtship Letters of an African American Couple: Race, Gender, Class, and the Cult of True Womanhood." *Southwestern Historical Quarterly* 100 (July 1996): 65–80.

Hunter, J. Marvin. "Negress Died at Age of 125." *Frontier Times* 9 (1932): 200.

———. "Negress 106 Dies." *Frontier Times* 11 (1934): 524.

———. "Old Slave Mammy Becomes Wealthy." *Frontier Times* 5 (1928): 295.

Hutchinson, Janis. "The Age-Sex Structure of the Slave Population in Harris County, Texas: 1850 and 1860." *American Journal of Physical Anthropology* 74 (October 1987): 231–38.

Hyman, Rick, and Ronda Hyman. *My Texas Family: An Uncommon Journey to Prosperity (Featuring Photographs from 1912–1927).* Charleston, S.C.: Arcadia Publishing, 2000.

Ivy, Charlotte. "Forgotten Color: Black Families in Early El Paso." *Password* 35 (1990): 5–18.

Jackson, LaVonne Roberts. "Freedom and Family: The Freedmen's Bureau and African-American Women in Texas in the Reconstruction Era." Ph.D. diss., Howard University, 1996.

Jackson, Lela. "Rachel Whitfield (1814–1908)." In *Women in Early Texas,* edited by Evelyn M. Carrington, 288–93. Austin: Jenkins Publishing, 1975.

James, Allie Winifred. "The Homemaking Activities of a Selected Group of Negro Homemakers in East Texas." Master's thesis, Kansas State College, 1939.

Jones, Lillian B. (Horace). *Five Generations Hence.* Fort Worth: privately printed, 1916.

Jones, Nancy Baker. "Adair, Christia V. Daniels." *The Handbook of Texas Online,* http://www.tsha.utexas.edu/handbook/online/.

———. "Crawford, Roberta Dodd." *The Handbook of Texas Online,* http://www.tsha.utexas.edu/handbook/online/.

———. "Dupree, Anna Johnson." In *The New Handbook of Texas,* edited by Douglas E. Barnett, Roy R. Barkley, Penelope C. Anderson, and Mark F. Odintz, vol. 2, 732–33. Austin: Texas State Historical Association, 1996.

———, and Ruthe Winegarten. *Capitol Women: Texas Female Legislators, 1923–1999,* 176–79. Austin: University of Texas Press, 2000.

———. "Eddie Bernice Johnson." In *Capitol Women,* 169–73.

———. "Senfronia Paige Thompson." In *Capitol Women,* 176–79.

———. "Wilhelmina Ruth Fitzgerald Delco." In *Capitol Women,* 1182–86.

Jones, Yvette. "Seeds of Compassion." *Texas Historian* 37 (November 1976): 16–21.

Jordan, Barbara, and Shelby Hearon. *Barbara Jordan: A Self-Portrait.* Garden City, N.Y.: Doubleday, 1979.

Jordan, Julia K. Gibson, and Charlie Mae Brown Smith. *Beauty and the Best: Frederica Chase Dodd, the Story of a Life of Love and Dedication.* Dallas: Delta Sigma Theta Sorority, 1985.

Katz, William Loren. "Texas." In *Black Women of the Old West,* 48–50. New York: Atheneum Books, 1995.

Keir, Scott S. "Middle-Class Black Families in Austin, Texas: An Exploratory Analysis of Husbands and Wives." Ph.D. diss., University of Texas at Austin, 1987.

Kirk, Rita G. "Barbara Jordan: The Rise of a Black Woman Politician." Master's thesis, University of Arkansas, 1978.

Kossie-Chernyshev, Karen. "Constructing Good Success: The Church of God in Christ and Social Uplift in East Texas." *East Texas Historical Journal* 44 (Spring 2006): 49–55.

———. "Juneteenth: 'Freedom a Fantasy (?) . . . Why?': The Juneteenth Reflections of Lillian Bertha Horace (1886–1965)." *Houston Sun,* 2005.

———. "Lillian Bertha Horace (1865–1965). Forthcoming in *African American National Biography.* New York: Oxford University Press, 2008.

———. "To Write 'The' Book: Will It Ever Come True? The Publication Aspirations of Lillian Bertha Horace (1886–1965) and Mine." *Coordinating Council of Women in History Newsletter* (Winter 2005): 12.

Lanseley, Judith W. "Main House, Carriage House: African American Domestic Employees at Faddis House, Beaumont, Texas, 1900–1950." *Southwestern Historical Quarterly* 102 (July 1999): 17–51.

Lede, Naomi. *Precious Memories of a Black Socialite.* Houston: D. Armstrong, 1991.

Lewis, Linda. "Young, Gifted, and Black." In *No Apologies: Texas Radicals Celebrate the '60s,* edited by Daryl Janes, 62–71. Austin: Eakin Press, 1992.

Lucko, Paul M. "George, Zelma Watson." *The Handbook of Texas Online,* http://www.tsha.utexas.edu/handbook/online/.

———. "Hall, Josie Briggs." *The Handbook of Texas Online,* http://www.tsha.utexas.edu/handbook/online/.

Lundy, Anne. "Conversation with . . . Ernestine Jessie Covington Dent." *Black Perspective in Music* 12 (Fall 1984): 244–63.

Malone, Ann Patton. "Black Women." In *Women On the Texas Frontier: A Cross-Cultural Perspective*, 26–52, 63–78. El Paso: Texas Western Press, 1983.

Mathis, Annie Maie. "Negro Public Health Nursing in Texas." *Southern Workman* 56 (July 1927): 302–303.

McCroskey, Vista. "Barbara Jordan." In *Profiles in Power: Twentieth-Century Texans in Washington*, edited by Kenneth E. Hendrickson Jr., and Michael L. Collins, 175–95. Arlington Heights, Ill.: Harlan Davidson, 1993.

Miles, Merle Yvonne. "'Born and Bred' in Texas: Three Generations of Black Females: A Critique of Social Science Perceptions on the Black Female." Ph.D. diss., University of Texas at Austin, 1986.

Montgomery, Ellie Walls. *Juvenile Delinquency among Negroes in Houston, Texas.* Houston: Houston College for Negroes, 1936.

———. *Possibilities of Improving Negro Business through Better Business Methods.* Houston: Webster Printing, 1935.

———. *A Survey of Negro Youths Not in School—Houston, Texas.* Houston: Houston College for Negroes, 1936.

Moutoussamy-Ashe, Jeanne. "Elizabeth 'Tex' Williams." In *Viewfinders: Black Women Photographers*, 98–100. New York: Dodd, Mead, 1986.

Mullen, Harryette. *Tree Tall Woman: Poems by Harryette Romell Mullen.* Austin, Tex.: Red River Women's Press, 1978.

Nash, Sunny. *Bigmama Didn't Shop at Woolworth's.* College Station: Texas A&M University Press, 1996.

———. "A Mission Completed for Doll." In *State Lines*, edited by Ken Hammond, 40–44. College Station: Texas A&M University Press, 1993.

Neeley, Sarah LeVahn. "A Study of the Rehabilitation Program at Crockett State School for Girls." Master's project, Texas Southern University, 1958.

O'Connor, Louise S. "Henrietta Williams Foster, 'Aunt Rittie': A Cowgirl of the Texas Coastal Bend." In *Black Cowboys of Texas*, edited by Sara R. Massey, 67–72. College Station: Texas A&M University Press, 2000.

Owens, William A. "Seer of Corsicana." In *And Horns on the Toads*, edited by Mody C. Boatright, Wilson M. Hudson, and Allen Maxwell, 14–31. Dallas: Southern Methodist University Press, 1959.

Paley, Lillie M. "The Education and Responsibilities of Negro Home Demonstration Agents in Texas." Master's thesis, Kansas State College of Agriculture and Applied Science, 1941.

Parks, Carole A. "J. E. Franklin, Playwright." *Black World* 21 (April 1972): 49–50.

Parks, Katie. *Remember When? A History of African Americans in Lubbock, Texas.* Lubbock, Tex.: Friends of the Library/Southwest Collection, 1999.

Pemberton, Doris Hollis. "Josie Briggs Hall." In *Juneteenth at Comanche Crossing.* Austin: Eakin Press, 1983.

Pinsky, Robert. "On 'Eve Tempted By the Serpent' by Defendente Ferrari, and in Memory of Congresswoman Barbara Jordan of Texas." *Salmagundi* 113 (Winter 1997): 174–75.

Pitre, Merline. "Barbara Charline Jordan." In *Black Women in America: An Historical Encyclopedia,* edited by Darlene Clark Hine, Elsa Barkley Brown, and Rosalyn Terborg-Penn, vol. 1, 658–59. Brooklyn, N.Y.: Carlson Publishing, 1993.

———. "Black Houstonians and the 'Separate but Equal' Doctrine: Carter W. Wesley versus Lulu B. White." *The Houston Review* 12, no. 1 (1990): 23–36.

———. "Building and Selling the NAACP: Lulu B. White as an Organizer and Mobilizer." *East Texas Historical Journal* 39 (2001): 22–32.

———. "In Retrospect: Darlene Hine's *Black Victory.*" In Darlene Clark Hine, *Black Victory: The Rise and Fall of the White Primary in Texas,* 25–40. Rev. ed. Columbia: University of Missouri Press, 2003.

———. *In Struggle against Jim Crow: Lulu B. White and the NAACP, 1900–1957.* College Station: Texas A&M University Press, 1999.

———. "Lulu B. White." In *Black Women in America,* 2nd ed., edited by Darlene Clark Hine, vol. 3. New York: Oxford University Press, 2005.

———. "Lulu B. White and the Civil Rights Movement in Houston, Texas, 1939–1957." In *Invisible Texans: Women and Minorities in Texas History,* edited by Donald Willett and Stephen Curley, 192–203. Boston: McGraw Hill, 2005.

———. "Lulu B. White and the Integration of the University of Texas, 1945–1950." In *African American Women Confront the West, 1600–2000,* edited by Quintard Taylor and Shirley Ann Wilson Moore, 293–308. Norman: University of Oklahoma Press, 2003.

———. "Lulu B. White, the NAACP, and the Fight against Segregation in Houston." In *Major Problems in Texas History,* edited by Cary D. Wintz and Sam W. Haynes, 419–36. Boston: Houghton Mifflin, 2002.

———. "White, Lulu Belle Madison." In *The New Handbook of Texas,* edited by Ron Tyler, Douglas E. Barnett, Roy R. Barkley, Penelope C. Anderson, and Mark F. Odintz, vol. 6, 929. Austin: Texas State Historical Association, 1996.

Ponder, Janace Pope. "SEPIA." Master's thesis, North Texas State University, 1973.

Pratt, Susan Norma. "We Are Here: Activism among Black El Paso Women (1955–1965)." Master's thesis, University of Texas at El Paso, 2001.

Prestage, Jewel L. "Flossie M. Byrd." In *Black Women in America: An Historical Encyclopedia,* edited by Darlene Clark Hine, Elsa Barkley Brown, and Rosalyn Terborg-Penn, vol. 1, 211–12. Brooklyn, N.Y.: Carlson Publishing, 1993.

———. "In Quest of the African-American Political Woman." *Annals of the American Academy of Political and Social Sciences* (May 1991): 88–103.

Pruett, Bernadette. "Exodus, the Movement: People of African Descent and Their Migrations to Houston, 1914–1945." Ph.D. diss., University of Houston, 2003.

Pruett, Jakie L., and Everett B. Cole. *As We Lived: Stories by Black Story Tellers.* Burnet, Tex.: Eakin Press, 1982.

Rabe, Elizabeth R. "Slave Children of Texas: A Qualitative and Quantitative Analysis." *East Texas Historical Journal* 42, no. 1 (2004): 10–24.

Randle, James Patrick. "The Nouveau Black Middle Class of Houston: Social Arenas and Self- Identity." Master's thesis, University of Houston, 1994.

Reid, Debra Ann. "Farmers in the New South: Race, Gender, and Class in a Rural Southeast Texas County, 1850–1900." Master's thesis, Baylor University, 1996.

Reynolds, James Talmadge. "The Preretirement Educational Needs of Retired Black Women Who Were Domestic Workers in Dallas, Texas." Ph.D. diss., East Texas State University, 1981.

Reynolds, Lois Arnell. "Sustenance Position of Texas Negro Domestic Servants in the Texas Economy." Master's thesis, Prairie View State Normal and Industrial College, 1942.

Rich, Doris L. *Queen Bess: Daredevil Aviator.* Washington, D.C.: Smithsonian Institution Press, 1993.

Riley, Glenda. "African American Women in the West." In *A Place to Grow: Women in the American West,* 43–57, 262–266. Arlington Heights, Ill.: Harlan Davidson, 1992.

———. "African Daughters: Black Women in the West." *Montana: The Magazine of Western History* 38 (Spring 1988): 14–27.

Roberts, Velma, and Ruby Williams. "Welfare Is a Right." In *No Apologies: Texas Radicals Celebrate the '60s,* edited by Daryl Janes, 110–19. Austin: Eakin Press, 1992.

Robinson, Dorothy Redus. *The Bell Rings at Four: A Black Teacher's Chronicle of Change.* Austin: Madrona Press, 1978.

Rodenberger, Lou Halsell. "A Developing Tradition: African-American Writers." In *Texas Women Writers: A Tradition of Their Own,* edited by Sylvia Ann Grider and Lou Halsell Rodenberger, 247–52. College Station: Texas A&M University Press, 1997.

Rodriguez, Roberto. "Mamie McKnight: Promoting Education and Preserving Black Dallas History." *Black Issues in Higher Education* 10 (December 16, 1993): 24–25.

Rogers, B. Ann, and Linda Schott. "'My Mother Was a Mover': African American Seminole Women in Bracketville, Texas, 1914–1964." In *Writing the Range: Race, Class, and Culture in the Women's West,* edited by Elizabeth Jameson and Susan Armitage, 585–99. Norman: University of Oklahoma Press, 1997.

Rogers, Mary Beth. *Barbara Jordan: American Hero.* New York: Bantam Books, 1998.

Roses, Lorraine Elena, and Ruth Elizabeth Randolph. "Lauretta Holman Gooden." In *Harlem Renaissance and Beyond,* 126–27. Houston: G. K.

Hall, 1990. Also, "Maurine L. Jeffrey," ibid., 193–94; "Lillian Tucker Lewis," ibid., 221–22; "Birdelle Wycoff Ranson," ibid., 277–78; "Bernice Love Wiggins," ibid., 347–48; "Gwendolyn B. Bennett," ibid., 11–15.

Sanders, Charles L. "Barbara Jordan: Texan Is a New Power on Capitol Hill." *Ebony* 30 (February 1975): 136–42.

Scarborough, Dorothy. *On the Trail of Negro Folk-Songs.* Cambridge, Mass.: Harvard University Press, 1925.

Schaffer, Ruth C. "The Health and Social Functions of Black Midwives on the Texas Brazos Bottom, 1920–1985." *Rural Sociology* 56 (Spring 1991): 89–105.

Shackles, Chrystine I. *Reminiscences of Huston-Tillotson College.* Austin: N.p., 1973.

Shange, Ntozake. "Recipes from the Gypsy Cowgirl." *American Visions* 13 (February/March 1998): 33–35.

Shannon, Mary Gamble. "An Occupational Study of Negro Maids in Dallas." Master's thesis, Southern Methodist University, 1941.

Sharpless, Rebecca. *Fertile Ground, Narrow Choices: Women on Texas Cotton Farms, 1900–1940.* Chapel Hill: University of North Carolina Press, 1999.

Simond, Ada DeBlanc. "The Discovery of Being Black: A Recollection." *Southwestern Historical Quarterly* 76 (April 1973): 440–47.

———. *Looking Back: A Black Focus on Austin's Heritage.* Austin: Austin Independent School District, 1984.

Smallwood, James. "Black Freedwomen after Emancipation: The Texas Experience." *Prologue* 17 (Winter 1995): 303–17.

———. "Emancipation and the Black Family: A Case Study in Texas." *Social Science Quarterly* 57 (1977): 849–57.

Smith, Gloria Lawsha. "Bessie Coleman: From the Cotton Fields to the Airfields." In *KenteCloth: African American Voices in Texas,* edited by Sherry McGuire and John R. Posey, 160–67. Denton: Center for Texas Studies, University of North Texas, 1995.

Smith, Melinda. "Minority Women Attorneys Share Their Thoughts and Experiences." *Texas Bar Journal* 53 (October 1990): 1050–56.

Smith, Thomas H. "Blacks in Dallas: From Slavery to Freedom." *Heritage News* 10 (Spring 1985): 18–22.

———. "'Cast Down Your Bucket': A Black Experiment in Dallas." *Heritage News* 12 (Spring 1987): 13–18.

Snapp, Elizabeth, and Harry F. Snapp, eds. "African American Women." In *Read All about Her!: Texas Women's History: A Working Bibliography,* 9–11. Denton: Texas Woman's University Press, 1995.

Spurlin, Virginia Lee. "The Conners of Waco: Black Professionals in Twentieth-Century Texas." Ph.D. diss., Texas Tech University, 1991.

Standifer, Mary M. "Covington, Jennie Belle Murphy." *The Handbook of Texas Online,* http://www.tsha.utexas.edu/handbook/online/.

Stanley, William David. "Southern Black Women's Orientation toward Interracial Relations: Study of a Small Nonmetropolitan-Urban East Texas Town, 1970–1977." Master's thesis, Texas A&M University, 1982.

Steele, June M. "Edward Struggs and Mae Simmons: Two African American Educators and the Provisions for Black Schools in Lubbock, Texas, 1930–1970." *West Texas Historical Association Year Book* 77 (2001): 86–98.

Stewart, Ruth Ann. *Portia: The Life of Portia Washington Pittman, the Daughter of Booker T. Washington.* Garden City, N.Y.: Doubleday, 1977.

Tomkins-Walsh, Teresa. "Thelma Scott Bryant: Memories of a Century in Houston's Third Ward." *Houston Review* 1, no. 1 (Fall 2003): 48–58.

Trammell, Camilla Davis. *Seven Pines, Its Occupants and Their Letters, 1825–1872.* Houston: privately printed, 1986.

Turner, Martha Anne. *The Life and Times of June Long.* Waco, Tex.: Texian Press, 1969.

———. *The Yellow Rose of Texas: Her Saga and Her Song.* Austin: Shoal Creek Publishers, 1976.

———. *The Yellow Rose of Texas: The Story of a Song.* El Paso: Texas Western Press, 1971.

Verheyden, Cindy Bland. "They Danced until Dawn and Other Untold Texas Legends." In *Bricks without Straw: A Comprehensive History of African Americans in Texas,* edited by David A. Williams, 105–13. Austin: Eakin Press, 1997.

Werden, Frieda. "Bernice Love Wiggins." In *American Women Writers,* edited by Lina Mainiero, vol. 4, 414–15. New York: Ungar Publishing, 1982.

White, Clarence Cameron. "Maud Cuney Hare." *Journal of Negro History* 21 (1936): 239–40.

Wiggins, Bernice Love. *Tuneful Tales.* 1925. Reprint; edited by Maceo C. Dailey Jr. and Ruthe Winegarten. Lubbock: Texas Tech University Press, 2002.

Williams, Lorece. "[Untitled]." In *Growing Up in Texas: Recollections of Childhood,* 111–18. Austin: Encino Press, 1972.

Williams, Patricia R. "Literary Traditions in Works by African-American Playwrights." In *Texas Women Writers: A Tradition of Their Own,* edited by Sylvia Ann Grider and Lou Halsell Rodenberger, 253–55. College Station: Texas A&M University Press, 1997.

Williams-Andoh, Ife. "Jewel Limar Prestage." In *Black Women in America: An Historical Encyclopedia,* edited by Darlene Clark Hine, Elsa Barkley Brown, and Rosalyn Terborg- Penn, vol. 2, 940. Brooklyn, N.Y.: Carlson Publishing, 1993.

Winegarten, Ruthe. *Black Texas Women: 150 Years of Trial and Triumph.* Austin: University of Texas Press, 1994.

———. "Black Texas Women: 150 Years of Trial and Triumph." *Medallion* 29 (February 1992): 8–9.

———. *Black Texas Women: A Sourcebook: Documents, Biographies, Time Line.* Austin: University of Texas Press, 1996.

———. "Texas Association of Women's Clubs." *The Handbook of Texas Online,* http://www.tsha.utexas.edu/handbook/online/.

———. "Texas Slave Families." *Texas Humanist* 7 (March/April 1985): 29–30, 33.

———, ed. *I am Annie Mae; An Extraordinary Woman in Her Own Words: The Personal Story of a Black Texas Woman.* Austin: Rosegarden Press, 1983.

———, and Sharon Kahn. *Brave Black Women: From Slavery to the Space Shuttle.* Austin: University of Texas Press, 1996.

———, and Debra Winegarten. *Strong Family Ties: The Tiny Hawkins Story.* Austin: SocialSights Press, 1999.

Woodson, Carter G. "Maud Cuney-Hare." *Journal of Negro History* 21 (April 1936): 438–39.

Wooten, Mattie Lloyd. "Racial, National, and Nativity Trends in Texas, 1870–1930." *Southwestern Social Science Quarterly* 14 (June 1933): 62–69.

Xie, Jiangjiang. "The Black Community in Waco, Texas: A Study of Place, Family, and Work, 1880–1900." Master's thesis, Baylor University, 1988.

Yerwood, Ada Marie. "Certain Housing Conditions and Activities of Negro Girls Enrolled in Federally Aided Schools in Texas as One Index of Their Educational Needs." Master's thesis, Iowa State College, 1936.

CONTRIBUTORS

ANGELA BOSWELL, Professor of History at Henderson State University in Arkadelphia, Arkansas, is a specialist in the history of women in the southern United States. Boswell received her Ph.D. from Rice University; among her publications is *Her Act and Deed: Women's Lives in a Rural Southern County, 1837–1873*.

BARRY A. CROUCH, deceased Professor of History at Gallaudet University in Washington, D.C., received his Ph.D. from the University of New Mexico. A specialist in Reconstruction, among his publications are *The Freedmen's Bureau and Black Texans* and (with Donally E. Brice) *Cullen Montgomery Baker, Reconstruction Desperado*.

STEFANIE DECKER is completing her Ph.D. at Oklahoma State University and teaches U.S. history at Amarillo College. A specialist in southern women's history, Decker published "Women in the Civil Rights Movement: Juanita Craft versus the Dallas Elite."

BRUCE A. GLASRUD is Professor Emeritus of History at California State University, East Bay, and retired Dean, School of Arts and Sciences, at Sul Ross State University. He earned his Ph.D. from Texas Tech University. A specialist in peoples of color in the western United States, Glasrud focuses on the black experience in Texas. He has authored or coauthored nine books, including (with Laurie Champion) *The African American West: A Century of Short Stories*.

KENNETH W. HOWELL received his Ph.D. in history from Texas A&M University. He taught for twelve years in the Texas public school system before becoming an Assistant Professor of History at Prairie View A&M University. Howell has several publications that focus on Texas and southern history, including *Henderson County, Texas, 1846–1861: An Antebellum History;* "George Adams: A Cowboy All His Life," in *Black Cowboys of Texas;* and "When the Rabble Hiss, Well May Patriots Tremble": James Webb Throckmorton and the Secession Movement in Texas, 1845–1861," *Southwestern Historical Quarterly.* Currently, he has submitted a book manuscript on James Webb Throckmorton for publication.

FRANKLIN D. JONES is Professor of Political Science at Texas Southern University. Jones earned his Ph.D. in political science at Atlanta University. His teaching and research interests focus on African American Politics, Political Theory, and Public Polic y. Among his publications are two edited volumes, *Readings in American Political Issues*. During his tenure at Texas Southern he served as Chair, Department of Public Affairs, and Interim Senior Vice President and Provost of Academic Affairs.

MERLINE PITRE is Professor of History and Dean of the College of Liberal Arts and Behavioral Sciences at Texas Southern University. She received the Ph.D. degree from Temple University. Pitre has published numerous articles in scholarly and professional journals, her most noted works are *Through Many Dangers, Toils and Snares: The Black Leadership of Texas, 1868–1900*, and *In Struggle against Jim Crow: Lulu B. White and the NAACP, 1900–1957.*

JEWEL L. PRESTAGE formerly served as Professor of Political Science and Dean at Southern University, and more recently at Prairie View A&M University. With a Ph.D. from the University of Iowa, Prestage became the first African American woman to achieve a Ph.D. in political science. Prestage's publications include (with Marianne Githens) *A Portrait of Marginality: The Political Behavior of the American Woman.*

REBECCA SHARPLESS is Assistant Professor of History at Texas Christian University. From 1993 to 2006 she directed the Baylor University Institute for Oral History. In addition to oral history, Sharpless focuses on the history of women in the southern United States. Among her publications is *Fertile Ground, Narrow Choices: Women on Texas Cotton Farms, 1900–1940.*

JAMES M. SMALLWOOD is Professor Emeritus of History at Oklahoma State University. Smallwood received his Ph.D. from Texas Tech University. A specialist in blacks during Reconstruction, he is the author or editor of more than twenty books, including *Time of Hope, Time of Despair: Black Texans during Reconstruction; A Century of Achievement: Blacks in Cook County, Texas; The Struggle for Equality: Blacks in Texas;* and *Born in Dixie: The History of Smith County, Texas* (2 vols.).

INDEX